Paupers' Barcelona

Miles Turner subsists in Portland, Oregon, and leaves home as often as possible. He is the author of *Paupers' Paris* and *Paupers' New York*, also published by Pan Books.

Miles Turner

Paupers' Barcelona

Pan Original
Pan Books London, Sydney and Auckland

First published 1992 by
PAN BOOKS LIMITED
a division of Pan Macmillan Publishers Limited
Cavaye Place London SW10 9PG

9 8 7 6 5 4 3 2 1

ISBN 0 330 31425 4

Phototypeset by Parker Typesetting Service, Leicester

Printed and bound in Great Britain by Clays Limited, St Ives plc

Contents

Map vi

Introduction 1

Català (Language and looks) 4

Anem (Preliminaries) 7

Viatges (Getting there) 17

Arribada i partida (Arrivals and departures) 20

Rodalias (Getting around) 26

Al llit (Sleeping cheap) 42

Menjar bé (Eating well) 86

La nit (Nightlife) 132

Espectacles (Sights and sounds) 137

Botigues i magatzems (Shopping) 180

Barcelona pràctic (Staying afloat) 199

Urgèncias (Emergencies) 226

Appendices:

  A: The list of Pamela Carewe 231

  B: Knavish tricks 234

  C: Day trips and getaways 238

  D: Vocabulary 244

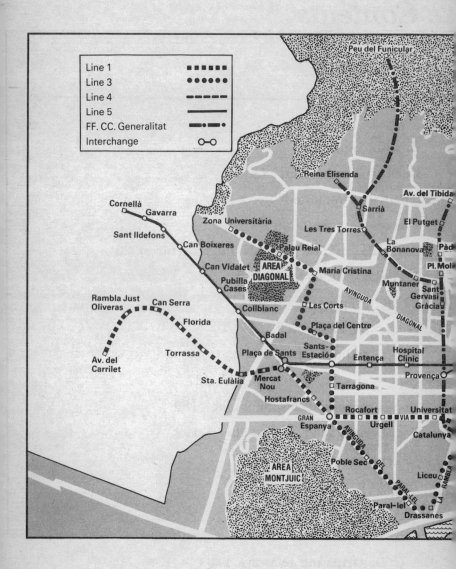

Line 1 ■ ■ ■ ■ ■
Line 3 ● ● ● ● ●
Line 4 ▬ ▬ ▬ ▬
Line 5 ▬▬▬▬▬
FF. CC. Generalitat ▬●▬●▬●
Interchange o─o

Peu del Funicular

Reina Elisenda

Cornellà
Gavarra
Av. del Tibida

Sant Ildefons
Zona Universitària
Sarrià
El Putget

Can Boixeres
Les Tres Torres
La Bonanova
Pàd

Palau Reial
Pl. Molí

Can Vidalet
AREA DIAGONAL
Maria Cristina
Muntaner
Sant Gervasi

Pubilla Cases
AVINGUDA
Gràcia

Collblanc
Les Corts
DIAGONAL

Rambla Just Oliveras
Can Serra

Florida
Plaça del Centre

Badal
Sants-Estació
Hospital Clínic

Av. del Carrilet
Torrassa
Plaça de Sants
Entença
Provença

Sta. Eulàlia
Mercat Nou
Tarragona

Hostafrancs
Rocafort
Universitat

GRAN
Espanya
AVINGUDA
Urgell
VIA
Catalunya

DEL
Liceu

AREA MONTJUIC
Poble Sec
PARAL-LEL
LA
RAMBLA

Paral-lel
Drassanes

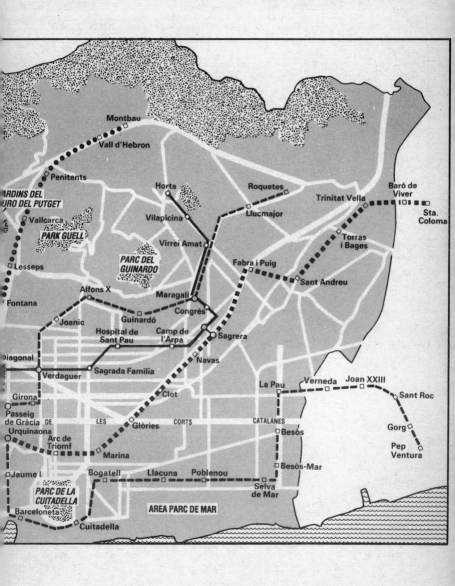

Introduction

Barcelona would be a quiet and conservative town if it weren't so full of contradictions. Its Catalan inhabitants love nothing better than their own unchanging neighbourhoods – but every fifty years or so they subject their quarters to swift and brutal renovation. They are happiest with home cooking – but thrive on everything from croissants to paella to pizza to fast food from McDonald's, all imports. They are cliquish and clannish, preferring the company of family and friends to the intrusion of outsiders, proclaiming their heritage in loudest Catalan at every opportunity – yet out of the blue they invite the entire non-Catalan world to the Olympics in 1992.

All these contradictions flavour the city: French *fin de siècle* architecture with an indigenous surrealistic twist; rustic cookery filtered through half a dozen foreign sensibilities; tumultuous politics and placid domesticity; a devotion to local saints that borders on the occult and waves of violent anticlericalism; passionate regionalism and cosmopolitan flair. What emerges is turbulent, idiosyncratic, paradoxical, *Barcelonés*.

The Olympic Games of 1992 are a case in point: a political ploy that has both enriched and disrupted the lives of every inhabitant. The bid to host the XXVth Olympiad was the means by which the city government – the Ajuntament – sought to enlist the support of Madrid and the Catalan provincial government – the Generalitat – in implementing crucial urban renewal, and in focusing world economic attention on this ambitious town. It was also a very hazardous venture, exacerbating tensions between conservative and progressive factions in the city, the state and the province, and inflaming the debate between Catalan separatists and those who would see Barcelona and Catalonia integrated with Spain. Ultimately, as a result of the Olympics, Barcelona will have new neighbourhoods, a new tourist industry, and probably (to the chagrin of Mayor Pasqual

Maragall, whose idea it was in the first place) a new city government.

During the few weeks before, during, and after the Games, Barcelona will be paradise for those who delight in chaos. It promises to be unmitigated hell for everyone else. Despite an airport reconstructed in record time, an instant slew of new hotels, an excellent Metro system and an abundance of taxis, the city cannot hope to accommodate the mob of fans expected to descend. Barcelona is a fragile creature at the best of times, verging on thrombosis at every rush hour, and several hundred thousand new faces will not improve the picture. We invite you to draw your own conclusions as to when to go.

Whether or not to go at all is an entirely different question. The city ensnares the traveller in its oddities, its whimsicality, its paradoxes: architecture that ranges from the playful to the pompous to the grotesque; museums devoted to the merest caprice; bright bombastic turn-of-the-century boulevards and dark labyrinths of medieval alleys; melancholy avenues lined with plane trees and riotous gardens stuffed with palms and bougainvillea; the rippling flow of spoken Castilian and the jagged articulation of Catalan, which sounds like eating carrots.

The people who built and populate this maze of contradictions reflect its contrariness. They are sophisticated citizens of the world, and passionate in their provincialism. They live in a metropolis of two million souls and treat it like a small town. They are incurable boulevardiers and miss their mothers' tables. They are the most serious workers of the peninsula and the most dedicated to the pursuit of frivolity and fun. And neither the city nor its inhabitants will let you rest until the paradoxes are resolved. For the curious traveller the question is not whether to go but when and how. Answers follow.

First, a few notes on the organization and conventions of this book. Generally we've listed hotels, restaurants, shops, galleries and museums by district: Eixample Dreta and Esquerra, Gràcia, Barri Gòtic, La Ribera, Poble Sec, and the rest. The districts are distinctive and their nomenclature is in common use (as Londoners would use Hampstead and Islington, or New Yorkers TriBeCa or the Village). You'll find broad definitions of the districts in the Getting around section on pages 26–41.

Although Castilian is in everyday use, the public language of Barcelona is Catalan, and since it appears on everything from maps to menus we've tried to employ it consistently throughout the book (and we delight in its idiosyncrasy). Lapses occur when the common usage is itself Castilian. You'll also find that Barcelonese use the 24-hour clock – military time – and we've followed suit, if only to accustom your eyes to this barbarism.

Not so many years ago Barcelona – and all of Spain – was a bargain-basement for the European traveller, but if you still count on cheap Iberian holidays it's time to brace yourself. The pall of the Franco decades has lifted and there is new life in the Spanish economy, more spring in the Spanish step. Spain is no longer isolated behind the Pyrenees, and the peseta is now actually worth something. In Barcelona, the Olympics and the reconstruction that has preceded them have supercharged the economy and you can expect prices – for tourists in particular – to go ballistic. The prices in this book were correct in the summer of 1991, but we expect radical mark-ups in the coming months, and hope for some settling by 1993 (after all, somebody has to pay for the new airport and all that massive urban renewal). In the weeks before, during and after the Games, hotels and restaurants will be packed, the Metro will be jammed and taxis nowhere to be found, and the cost of everything from bread to circuses will catapult: the ultimate test of the pauper's mettle. But while it's no longer possible to live high and spend little in Barcelona, with a little care and forethought – by avoiding the obvious and taking pleasure in the details – you can taste the best that the city has to offer without turning your pockets inside out.

This book is in large part the work of friends, relatives and accomplices: my travelling companions and moral supporters Martha Lomask, Bawn O'Beirne Ranelagh, and Ann Seibert; my generous hosts and mentors in Barcelona Charles Grant, Gail Murphy, Julie Resnick, and Teresa Taylor; and informants and researchers on every topic from *allioli* to the Zoo: Paquita Brotons, Salvador Brotons, Anna Durany, Jane Frey, Jane Hartline, Kathy Kurtz, Elaine Graves, Michael Kennedy, Elena Pavia, Earl Rees, Eloise Simons, Adri van Kooten. I thank them all, and apologize to my friends, colleagues and family (especially Ellen Hudetz, who qualifies as all three) for disappearing constantly and completely into Barcelona.

Català (Language and looks)

It might be news to you that there is no such language as Spanish. In fact Spain has four distinct languages. Castilian is the 'official' tongue, and the one most people mean when they use the word 'Spanish', but Galician, Basque and Catalan are at least as old and just as rich – just not so dominant. Ever since Philip II settled into the Escorial, just outside Madrid in Castile, the rest of the country has been in linguistic subjection to Castilian, and this has posed no end of problems for Catalonia.

If Catalonia weren't so blessed with water – the run-off of the Pyrenees – it would be just another luckless province for Madrid to kick around. But with water come agriculture and industry, and with these come money and power, and the inevitable tension between a Madrid rich in bureaucracy and a Barcelona rich in goods.

Natural resources account for some of Catalonia's wealth, but far more important is the character of the Catalans themselves. In business the watchwords are *murri* and *seny* – craftiness and common sense, with emphasis on the latter: the Catalan merchant is self-described as *tocant de peus a terra*, both feet on the ground at all times.

Along with the busy tax collectors of Castile, the riches of Catalonia have attracted swarms of workers from the rest of Spain, people who may settle in for generations but never quite lose the notion that they're temporary help, and who never quite lose their old linguistic affiliations.

As a result, the province is stratified as much by language as by rank: a governing class of Castilian-speaking Madrileño aristocrats at the top of the pyramid, a Catalan-speaking merchant class in the middle, and a sizeable layer of 'temporary' Castilian-speaking workers at the bottom.

First came the Habsburgs in the sixteenth century, then the

Bourbons in the eighteenth, and finally the Francoistas in the twentieth, all intent on subjecting a hard-headed prosperous race of Catalans to central Castilian authority. Both the Bourbons and the Fascists (in the name of order and uniformity, but equally as revenge upon a fractious population) imposed bans on the public use of Catalan, which resulted in generations of Catalans who could speak but not write their native tongue. When Franco died, not a moment too soon, in 1975, there was an instant resurgence of Catalan: the local governments mandated its use in schools and in public life, and Catalan became, if not the universal language of the province, at least politically correct.

The tensions remain: between the multitude of first- and second-generation Valencian and Andalucian immigrants who resent the obligation to learn an extra 'foreign' language; the pockets of crusty unregenerate Francoistas in the Pedralbes – the aristocratic foothills of Barcelona – who will mutter in Castilian to their graves; and the merchants and shopkeepers of the city who never cease to complain, in shrill Catalan, of their enslavement to the lisping bureaucrats of Madrid.

Centuries of obstinacy have done nothing to make a melting-pot of Barcelona, and the distinctive traits of the original inhabitants are undiluted. Catalans, men and women alike, tend to have round rather than long heads, broad cheekbones, well-defined noses, firm chins, wide high foreheads. (Compare these almost feline faces with the knife-edge features of El Greco's Castilian cardinals and you'll see what we mean.) Most striking are their strongly defined brow ridges, and the clearly marked brows which arch smoothly above beautifully set eyes. One ethnologist has remarked that this gives a look almost Etruscan: the thick natural arch that calls attention to eyes set very slightly slanting above wide cheekbones. It is a rather challenging look – which comes directly from the Catalan character.

Catalans, as more than one writer has noted, seldom if ever make direct eye contact with you, as do the more volatile French, the Italians, the Spaniards of the south. They gaze at you calmly but hardly seem to *see* you. They seem to be looking slightly beyond you, over your shoulder, and this gives them a misleading air of detachment, even disinterest.

Catalans on the Barcelona streets do not automatically give way as you come toward them, as Anglo-Saxon people tend to do: if there's a chatting group on the pavement, it is *you* who will move off the kerb and manoeuvre yourself around them. They are not discourteous: they simply haven't really grasped that you are there, in their city, on their street, in their living space.

Young Catalans, as is true almost everywhere in the Western world, are taller and slimmer than their parents. Middle-aged people may seem sturdy and strong-framed but never fat or slack-fleshed, and the elderly, while often minuscule, are straight-backed and walk tall.

It's tempting to speculate that the food on which the Catalans of Spain have thrived over the centuries has created these sturdy self-respecting people. Citizens as they are of the most prosperous industrial part of Spain, the Catalans have been working hard, eating well and living well for centuries: even the black years of the Civil War did not destroy this race of solid flesh built on solid bone.

Although in Barcelona you seldom see the flashing, brilliant-eyed beauties who light up the streets of Madrid, you quickly become attuned to the bone-deep beauty of this strange race, and to accept the almost impersonal gaze of Catalan eyes. We find them endlessly fascinating: inscrutable yes, ingratiating never, challenging one's imagination to see what lies behind the Catalan look.

Anem *(Preliminaries)*

Why?

The English-speaking world travels to Spain mostly to get warm, and on a couple of other impulses: romance and thrift. The second of these is becoming less of an inducement. Over the last decade or so the Spanish economy has picked itself up, become innovative and productive, and as the quality of goods and services has improved, prices have risen. It's still considerably cheaper to lodge and dine in Barcelona than in London or New York, but if price is your only concern you should probably head north and east to the fresh fields of Central Europe, as yet untrashed by barbarians seeking bargains. The Spanish are less tolerant of Britons in search of late nights and cheap alcohol than they have been in the past, and it shows in the prices they charge and in their not-quite-so-forgiving attitude toward mainstream tourists.

Which leaves Romance. Spain is a hot, hard country, isolated by sea and mountains, its internal discord shaped centuries ago by astounding windfall profits from the Americas, the total abjection of those who didn't get a slice, and religious exaggeration among all. Hence passion, rancour, pride, and temper uncooled by the easier winds of change that fan the rest of Europe. Northern travellers are helplessly attracted.

Although Catalonia has had its share – some might say more than its share – of Spain's sorrows, it holds itself aloof from the generality of Spain. It maintains a certain Northern distance in art, commerce, industry, culture, and most explicitly in language. One doesn't cross the Pyrenees into Spain but into someplace distinctly other, and the fountain of otherness is Barcelona.

The issue of language is most immediate and obvious. The first words you encounter as you step into the streets are slightly different: taxis are *lliure*, not *libre*. Streets are *carrers*, not *calles*, and avenues *avingudas*, not *avenidas*. A glance at the signage tells you that Catalan, which had been banned for decades under the Franco regime, is now the official language of the city and the province; a glance at the graffiti tells you that it is emphatically the tongue of choice for those who consider themselves Barcelona born and bred: not just embedded in the culture but politically correct. Since a sizeable percentage of the city's population are first- and second-generation Valencians and Andalucians who would rather speak Castilian than Catalan, the language question generates a certain amount of drama in Barcelona.

Less obvious at first glance, but more endearing, is the peculiarity of time in Barcelona. Every other doorway leads either into the late Middle Ages or the nineteenth-century Renaixença (and at times, with some of the Gothic revival buildings of the *fin de siècle* it might be hard to tell the difference). There is plenty of up-to-the-minute design in Barcelona, but what informs the senses above all is the architecture of other ages: not just another time, but another place.

If you haunt the museums and galleries of the city you'll find a staggering diversity of style and sensibility. The Belle Epoque painters Casas, Rusiñol and their contemporaries were indebted to Paris for their Impressionistic bent but retain an unmistakable singularity: qualities of light that appear only south of the Pyrenees. The two great modern painters of Barcelona, Miró and Tàpies, both perched on the edges of twentieth-century art, and were poles apart from each other and from everyone else on the scene. Picasso, an adoptive son, was arguably as much Barcelonese as anything else. And then there was Dalí.

The twin spirits of fantasy and contradiction come to a head in the Barcelonese kitchen. Catalan food is basically home cooking, simple in techniques and ingredients, more inclined to the mixed grills than to ineffable sauces – yet its cooks are drawn irresistibly to bizarre disjunctions such as beef and orange peel, chicken livers and raisins, pork and pomegranate, squid and chocolate, salt cod and honey, duck and pears.

What draws the traveller to Barcelona? Its oddities of cuisine and eccentricities of architecture, the capricious quality of its art and the iconoclasm of its inhabitants – in short, its otherness.

Who?

A glimpse of the giant tour buses that navigate the Diagonal, the Gran Via and the Laietana – virtually the only streets wide enough to accommodate them in Barcelona – should turn you off the idea of travelling in large groups. The only way to see anything is on foot, at your own pace, and the only way to swim in the culture, like a Maoist guerrilla, is on your own. If your Castilian is bad (and your Catalan worse) and you're travelling with a fluent speaker of either, you'll probably get everything you want but you'll rarely get the chance to open your mouth and interact with the locals. Our preference is to travel with family or friends and split off alone at every opportunity. This method permits one to spend hours in front of obscure paintings in the Museu d'Art Modern and no time at all in the Sagrada Familia (or vice versa). It allows the energetic to whip through everything in an hour and the indolent to spend all day in the same café, soaking up coffee and atmosphere. At night you can meet for dinner and your triumphs and disasters will give you something to talk about.

When?

In Barcelona, heat is an issue in late July and August, when it combines with high humidity to approximate conditions in New Orleans or a steam bath. The city is backed up against hills which trap the damp Mediterranean air and indigenous pollution, and the sun does the rest. Late spring and early autumn are idyllic seasons, warm and breezy, with occasional thunderstorms that clear the air and sweep the city clean. The rain falls in November, February and March, and it falls in torrents. December and January tend to be cool and clear, with an average temperature of 54°F (12°C).

What to take

When you travel will affect what you wear in Barcelona, and what you'll pack. In the depths of summer you can safely limit yourself to light cotton clothing – anything that can be lightly rolled up to fit in your luggage without suffering undue creases. Take washables in preference to dry-clean-onlies: it can take a week (and plenty of cash) to extract your clothes from the dry-cleaners, but only 24 hours (and plenty of cash) from the *lavanderia*.

Most Barcelonese dress very casually but with plenty of style. For any impoverished tourist with a modicum of taste, it's fairly easy to avoid a clash with native fashion: keep it simple, on the sombre side, and you won't feel out of place. You're less likely to be taken for a tourist (and in some neighbourhoods that means *literally taken*) if you don't flash the accoutrements of tourism: video cameras, Union Jack T-shirts, beach togs on city streets. Most travellers don't need this reminder, but we do remember coming across a couple of citizens fitted out in lederhosen, with sheath knives tucked into knee socks – which would have been fine in the Black Forest but didn't go down at all well in Venice. So leave the sporran at home.

For maximum flexibility and comfort, *dress in layers* – especially in spring and autumn, when the weather can switch in a minute from brisk to balmy and back again. A sweater or light jacket stuffed into a shoulder bag, just in case, can make all the difference. Remember that loose garments lend themselves better to layering than do tight ones.

Take nothing you haven't worn before, and nothing that you don't love. Barcelona is a walker's town (and a hilly one). Take nothing you can't walk or climb in.

Take a couple of pairs of durable, comfortable, well-broken-in shoes.

In spring or autumn, bring waterproof shoes if possible. Nothing will halt you faster in your tracks than wet feet. A light raincoat may come in handy; a packable collapsible umbrella is an absolute necessity. For chilly nights, a good lambswool scarf and light gloves. For sunny days, sunglasses.

A biggish plastic bag for your laundry (don't count on picking up anything sizeable or durable in Barcelona supermarkets). A featherweight bag that folds into your luggage and can function as an overnight bag, a carryall for knocking around town, or an extra grip for the extra odds and ends you'll carry home with you.

Glasses or contacts if you wear them: take an extra pair and/or a recent prescription. Drugs: an adequate supply, or a refillable prescription.

For picnics (hotel or otherwise): a cup and an immersion heater if you *must* have tea (see Electricity, page 203). A small plate, a sharp knife, a fork, a spoon.

A clip-on reading light (220 volts) if you're in the habit of reading yourself to sleep. Hotel lighting in the cheaper venues tends to be overhead.

If you find it galling to wait for your luggage to fall out of an airport carousel, you should be able to find a way to cram everything you need into a bag that fits in the compartment above your plane seat. For this, the maximum dimensions of soft luggage are about 23″ × 15″ × 12″. If you're travelling by train there's more leeway, but don't forget who has to haul all those bags between Sants Estació and wherever you plan to sleep.

For an exhaustive and we think brilliant list of what to take on your travels, see Appendix A: The list of Pamela Carewe, page 231.

Money questions

How much to take

For denominations and mechanics, see Money, page 214.

For us, it's a balancing act. We've found that no matter how frugal our intentions, we yield inevitably to a number of wicked impulses and inevitably cut back in areas of less moment. The going rate for better-than-basic accommodation (with a private bath, say) is survival on coffee for breakfast, the basic *menú del día* for lunch, and rudimentary *tapas* at night. A low threshold in clothes stores translates into temperance and fortitude in the matter of taxicabs, and no gifts for anyone.

How you spend your money is a highly personal issue and we hesitate to intrude. We'll just provide some maximums and minimums and let it go at that.

Transport to and from Barcelona

Maximum: British Airways scheduled flight,
no limitations.   £159

Minimum: Air Europa charter, designated
dates and times.   £99
See pages 17–19 for details.

Hotel per night

Maximum: A nice bourgeois hotel in the
Eixample, complete with shower and loo.   6000 ptas

Minimum: Just enough room to turn
around in; shared shower and loo; clean and
simple.   1000 ptas
See pages 42–85 for details.

Food per day

Maximum: *Xuxos* and *ensaïmadas* for breakfast, lunch à la carte, *tapas* for an early
evening snack, a celebratory dinner in Ped-
ralbes.   7000 ptas

Minimum: A *cortado* to wake you up, a modest lunch on the *menú del día*, and for dinner
a picnic put together in the Boqueria.

See pages 86–131 for details.   1400 ptas

Getting around

Maximum: Enough for a week of post-
dinner taxis and for quick rides to and from
the airport.   5000 ptas

Minimum: A T-2 Metro ticket stretched to
its limit.   400 ptas
See pages 26–41 for details.

The sights

Maximum: Full-price admission to the Picasso Museum, an afternoon at Tibidabo, and
plenty of coffee to keep up your momentum.   2000 ptas

Minimum: The architecture of Barcelona
viewed from ground-level, and plenty of
coffee to keep up your momentum.   400 ptas
See pages 137–179 for details.

The shops

Maximum: How much have you got?   ? ptas

Minimum: Don't even window-shop.   0 ptas
See pages 180–198 for details.

Necessities

Maximum: Enough to buy a good atlas of
the city, send your jacket to the dry cleaners,
and phone your aunt in Brighton.   2500 ptas

Minimum: An afternoon in the launderette
and a postcard to your office.   775 ptas
See pages 199–225 for details.

Emergencies

Maximum and minimum depend upon everything from what the
bus driver had for lunch to the position of the stars. If you're
accident-prone, carry extra cash for emergencies. If you live a
charmed life, or have plenty of insurance, take less. But always keep
some money in reserve.
See pages 226–230 for details.

The pound is currently (September 1991) worth 173 ptas.

How to carry money

Cash

You'll need some within five minutes of your arrival in Barcelona: enough to get you into town from the airport; enough to pick up a Metro *tarjeta*; enough to check in your luggage, make a phone call, have a quick cup of coffee before pressing on. You can change pounds to pesetas in the airport or at Sants Estació, but you'll save a bit on commissions if you equip yourself before you leave home, at a bank where you know you'll get a good rate.

Traveller's cheques

Your own bank may offer them as a free service (but avoid the lesser known brands which can be difficult to cash in some Barcelona banks or bureaux de change). Our personal preference is American Express because every other bank or agency in Barcelona seems to regard exchange transactions as windfall profits (see Money, page 215). Size of denominations depends on how often you want to sign your name and how reckless you become when you've cashed a big one.

Visa, Access, Mastercard, Diners Club and such

If you keep in mind that the exchange rate at which you are billed is calculated by the issuing company on the day they bill you, not the day you used your card, you'll avoid being surprised when you come home to your credit card statements. The advantage of credit cards (*tarjetas de crédito*) is that they exact no exchange commission. The drawback is that few establishments – including most of the hotels, shops and restaurants in this book – accept them. The exceptions to this small-town attitude toward plastic are the omnipresent *caixas* – the neighbourhood banking service centres that appear on almost every corner, complete with automatic tellers. A major credit card and a PIN (personal identification number) are all you need to draw against your account. The same goes for your American Express card, which works in the ATM at American Express on the Pg. de Gràcia.

Your Access card will get you a maximum of 50,000 ptas a day (or up to your credit limit); the minimum draw is 5000 ptas. Visa cards yield a maximum of £200 per day in an ATM, and up to the top of your line of credit in a bank. Other credit cards behave similarly.

For some practical advice on safe carriage of money, see Appendix B: Knavish tricks, page 234.

Booking hotels in advance

If you know more or less what you want, and where you want to be, and how much you want to pay (see Sleeping cheap, pages 42–85), it's *essential* to reserve in advance. The last thing you need as you stagger on to the platform at Sants is to spend half the morning on the phone. And booking in advance can save you money: if you arrive to find your first choices booked up, you're likely to fall into a place that you can't afford (or can't tolerate) out of sheer desperation.

Once you've picked a hotel or hostal, write to the management – preferably in Castilian, to avoid misunderstanding. Use, if you like, the form letter below. Specify dates of arrival and departure, number of people, and your requirements.

The Director
Hotel _____
Address _____
Barcelona postcode _____

Estimado Señor(es):

Dear sir,

A través de la presente, le agradacería me informara de la condiciones y las tarifas para una estancia de _____ noche(s). Llego (llegamos) el día _____ del _____ (mes) del 19_____. Salgo el día _____ de _____ (mes) del presente (de 19_____).

I would be grateful if you would let me know your terms and prices for a stay of _____ nights, beginning _____, 19_____, and ending _____.

Nos gustaría (me gustaría) reservar una_____ (habitación sencilla) (habitación doble con cama doble) (habitación con dos camas) (tres camas) (cama de niño o cuna) (con/sin inodoro/baño/ducha).

We would like to reserve (single room), (double room with double bed) (twin-bedded room) (three beds) (child's bed or baby bed), (with/without WC/bath/shower).

Llegará (llegarán) _____ persona(s), _____ adulto(s), _____ niño(s), _____ (bebé, bebés menores de dos años de edad).

There will be _____ person/persons in our party, _____ adult(s), _____ (child/children), _____ (baby/babies under two years of age).

Le agradezco de antemano su atención.

Atentamente . . .

With my thanks . . .

Use an International Reply Coupon

If you're reserving a room or just asking for information from any Barcelonese source (other than the municipal tourist agency), it's a courtesy to include both an IRC and a self-addressed airmail envelope with your correspondence. They also increase your chances of getting a reply. IRCs cost 57p in Britain and are available at post offices.

Viatges *(Getting there)*

How you get to Barcelona depends on your finances, how long you plan to stay, and what time of year (or time of day) your schedule allows. For our purposes, this is a matter of seeking out the best deals on air fares: we assume that if you're travelling by train your itinerary most likely includes other parts of Spain, or the South of France, or who knows where: far too iffy for discussion here. If you're driving, we leave you to your own devices. And if you're travelling by coach, with a load of other merrymakers, you can skip this chapter (and most of the rest of the book, unless you can manage to slip off by yourself).

During the run-up to the Olympics, doubtless every travel agent on earth will be offering special deals. As in every getaway plan, take some elementary precautions: deal only with airline agents who sport the initials ATOL with a number, and travel agents who belong to ABTA. Even if the airline vanishes into thin air, you have some protection.

As the winter and spring of 1991 showed all too clearly, air tour companies fell off the high wire as the winds of war and currency fluctuations blew hard on them. An unsuspected trap: those who had booked and paid for ordinary tickets on what was essentially a charter airline (Air Europe in this case) got caught and sometimes stranded when its parent group fell apart, even though they had not been part of a charter group with special fares. And even if their tickets had been charged on credit cards, which are supposed to protect purchases over £100, many passengers had difficulty and/or long waits to reclaim their money.

At certain times of the year – around Easter and Christmas, for example – you will find some agents offering charter flights for as little as £80 return. Good deals, if through an ATOL agent. But you must book as soon as you see the advertisement or spot a notice in a reputable agent's window.

This may be the place to warn you about the old 'bait-and-switch' game which is played in the less reputable parts of the travel world. This consists of advertising a remarkably cheap price, backing out of it ('Sorry, dear, it's been sold out for weeks'), and substituting a lesser deal. Our researcher spent the better part of a day going through the classified travel sections of *Time Out* and four London freesheets, calling a total of 21 agents, checking on the cheap advertised prices for Barcelona one-way and return flights which were advertised, respectively, at from £39 and £69. Not to her surprise, none was available. The lowest fare offered was £109 for a charter; agents quoted anywhere between £120 and £159 for a scheduled British Airways flight. The cheapest one-way fare available was £79 – slightly more than double the advertised one.

Moral: Check your travel insurance policy carefully to make sure it covers cancellation costs for any valid reason. And shop around for travel agents who are willing to work hard for you. Over the long haul, the more business you throw their way, the better deals they'll find for you.

This is a shortlist of London agents: all numbers are prefixed 071. 'Midweek' means Monday to Thursday; 'weekend' means Friday to Sunday. Some charter flights offer low prices for outward flights on Sundays, while all scheduled prices go up. Scheduled flights can be booked up to the last minute if there's room on the plane. If you can reserve at least two weeks in advance, and don't mind buying non-refundable tickets, you can generally beat the going rate for scheduled flights. Prices in this list are as of May 1991, and undoubtedly will go up in 1992.

VE Tours
439 7861
Scheduled flights: midweek £125, weekends £135, British Airways.

Latitude 40
581 3104/5/6, ext. 5.
Scheduled flights: midweek £115, weekends £135, British Airways.

Major Travel
485 7017
Scheduled flights: midweek £120, weekends £130, British Airways.

Pilot Flights
631 0167
Special two-week offer at the time of writing: £99 flying out on Sundays or Thursdays, or Thursday out/second Sunday back, £99. Both are charters from Gatwick on Dan Air or SpanAir.
Scheduled flights: midweek £135, weekends £159, British Airways.

Flyrite
497 0055
Charter flights: £125 from Gatwick by VIVA AIR, part of Iberia Airlines.

Transiberica
229 9631
Charter flights: £99 from Gatwick for two weeks, AirEuropa (Spanish airline).
Scheduled flights: midweek £129, weekends £149, British Airways.

Leisure
436 8080
Scheduled flights: midweek £129, weekends £149, British Airways.

Travel Arcade
734 5873
Charter: £109, SpanAir.
Scheduled flights: midweek £130, British Airways.

Intatours
436 3005
Charter flights: £129, SpanAir, Gatwick.

Travel Cuts
255 1944
Scheduled flights: midweek £130, British Airways.

Iberia International, the Spanish National airline, often has special promotional fares for two people travelling together: in the spring of 1991 several agents quoted £99 for a midweek flight, £109 for weekends, smartly undercutting charter prices.

British Airways operates from both Heathrow and Gatwick. SpanAir and AirEuropa are Spanish charter companies flying out of Gatwick.

Arribada i partida
(Arrivals and departures)

Unless you've been brave enough to tackle a 24-hour journey by bus from London, or a train journey, chances are you'll come to Catalonia by way of El Prat (Catalan for the meadow), the airport 12 km from the city. At this writing, the magnificent new airport is partly completed. The major international airlines – BA, Air France, KLM, TWA, Swissair, Lufthansa, etc – as well as Spain's own Iberia, Balcan and Aviaco arrive there and it's a treat. Flying out, you leave from the old airport building 50 m away, and it's another story – but by the time this book is published the new departure facilities may be complete, and taking off from Barcelona will be almost as glorious as landing there.

Not surprisingly for a city that basks in exalted design, Prat is a Taj Mahal among airports: marble everywhere, plenty of light and air, great graphics that lead you smoothly through formalities, and a swift train link into the city. It's set to cope not only with Olympic crowds but with the coming decades of 'ordinary' travel, which means package tourists to the Costa Brava, business travellers, and the many Spanish who come to Barcelona from all over the country.

Passport and customs formalities are quick and relatively unobtrusive. There's a well-informed Oficina de Turisme, open from Monday to Saturday 09:30–20:00, Sundays and holidays 09:30–15:00. Stop there to pick up elementary city and bus maps, hotel information, and to find out what's going on around town during your stay. If you're arriving late at night, do this chore here because the Tourist Office in Sants Estació in the city closes at 20:00. The Banco Exterior de España is open from 07:00 to 23:00 daily. Two automatic cash-dispensers (Caixa de Catalunya and Caixa de Pensions) operate 24 hours a day and work with all international bank cards and your PIN.

The **train** to Sants, the central Barcelona train station, costs 175 ptas and takes just 18 minutes. It leaves every half hour, 12 and 42 minutes after the hour, from 06:12 to 22:42. After that (or if you just can't face train travel into Barcelona at this stage in the game) take a taxi: it should cost no more than about 1800 ptas, plus a tip, to the heart of Barcelona.

Sants is NOT the last stop on this train route but the third (not counting the departure point from the airport). It's hard to read station names after dark, but you know you've reached Sants because it's obviously a big-city terminal with high ceilings and lots of tracks. Be ready to get off quickly as the train doesn't halt for long: it continues to Plaça d'Espanya, a combination Metro/suburban train/railway station with no amenities and impenetrable corridors.

There is an **Aerobus** from Prat to Pça. d'Espanya which costs only 75 ptas in the daytime, 90 ptas at night. Bus No. EA runs from 06:35 until 22:05, then Nitbus No. EN which runs until 02:30, about every half hour. We have never tried it, but if you're game and want to save 100 ptas, ask the Oficina de Turisme at the airport where to catch it and when it leaves. At Pça. d'Espanya, you can take Metro Line 1 or 3, or a taxi.

Sants Estació – the central railway terminus of Barcelona – is lively and roomy: tracks on the lower level, the main hall upstairs. The immediate neighbourhood offers no joy; now is the time to get where you're going.

The **Metro** entrance is tucked away on one side of the main hall of Sants and if you're travelling light and feeling energetic (riding the Metro usually involves a stiff walk through a labyrinth of corridors) it's an instant immersion into the subterranean life of the city. It helps to know exactly where you're going (see pages 28–30 for instructions). Buy the T-2 (Tay-Dos) 10-ride ticket and you've taken your first step to independent travel. Metro trains run until 23:00. They are clean, swift, and perfectly safe. The bus system is infinitely complex and better postponed for sightseeing.

If you're not up to strenuous transport, take a **taxi**. The cabs – uniformly black-and-yellow – are ranked in front of the station; there are always plenty of them, and you are strictly enjoined to take the first in line. A taxi is free for business if the green light on top is lit; it will probably also display a sign through the windscreen, reading either *Libre* or *Lliure* – your first indication of the Catalan/Castilian split in the Barcelonese personality.

A taxi ride from Sants to the central neighbourhoods of Barcelona – the Barri Gòtic or the Gràcia or the Eixample among others – will cost you between 500 and 700 ptas. There's a small surcharge – about 200 ptas at this writing – for pick-up at the station, and the tip should be no more than 10%. If you don't speak much Castilian, write out your destination – name of hotel and street address, with the name of the street first and the number next – and show it to the driver.

If you need to telephone from Sants, look for the glass-walled enclosure near the main exit. Wall-mounted phones in the station are apt to be a) not working, or b) occupied by relentlessly chatting teenagers. In the glass enclosure, the 'hostess' will give you a cabin number. Make your call, and when you leave she'll tell you the cost. Calls are charged at an economical base rate of 20 ptas rather than the obligatory 25 ptas demanded by the wall-phones elsewhere.

Leaving town

Trains from Sants to Prat: 05:42, 06:12, 06:42, 07:12, then 28, 42, 58 and 12 minutes after the hour until the last train at 22:12. Get your ticket (175 ptas) from the ticket windows or automatic machines in the ticket hall. The airport is the last stop on this train run of just 16 minutes.

The Aerobus (No. EA) from Plaça d'Espanya costs 75 ptas by day, 90 for the Nitbus No. EN; ask the tourist office for its current schedule.

Check-in times at the airport vary, depending on season and volume of travellers. If you're travelling with hand luggage only, you can probably check in later and with more ease than the heavy-laden. Be advised that security is much tighter on your way out of the country than on your way in: allow yourself time to submit to it.

A tip from an arm-weary traveller on British Airways in spring 1991: coming back from Barcelona, check your luggage through and carry on *only* your duty-free and really small carrier bags. When you fly into Terminal 1 at Heathrow, you'll have to schlep your stuff down a metal stairway to the tarmac (no nice gantries for you) into a bus – and then UP a wide curving stone staircase inside the terminal. No escalator, no lift, no porters, and you can bet that no one is going to offer to help you. Steerage all the way. So let the plane take the strain and collect your heavier luggage from the carousel.

Train information

SNCF (French Railways)

Gran Via 656
Barcelona 08010
Tel: 318 01 91

RENFE (Spanish Railways)

Sants Estació
Pça. Països Catalans s/n
Barcelona 08014
Tel: 490 02 02

From Sants:
Long-distance trains throughout Spain
International trains to Paris via Limoges
to Geneva via Grenoble
Trains to the French border at Cerbère and la Tour de Carol
Trains to the beaches south of Barcelona: Sitges and Tarragona
Trains to El Prat airport at approximately half hour intervals
between 05:42 and 22:12.

FFCC (Generalitat Rail System)

Tel: 205 15 15

From Pça. d'Espanya:
Trains to Montserrat, Igualada, and Manresa

From Pça. Catalunya:
Trains to Sabadell, Terrassa, the Autonomous University of Barcelona, and Sant Cugat

Airline offices in Barcelona

Air France
Pg. de Gràcia 63
Tel: 487 25 26

Alitalia
Av. Diagonal 403
Tel: 416 04 24

American Airlines
Av. Diagonal 605
Tel: 410 77 60

Avianca
Gran Via 634
Tel: 302 56 49

British Airways
Pg. de Gràcia 85
Tel: 487 21 12

Iberia
Pg. de Gràcia 30
Tel: 401 33 82

TWA
Pg. de Gràcia 55
Tel: 215 81 88

Sea transport

The International Sea Terminal – embarkation point for the
Balearics – is temporarily located on the Moll de Sant Bertran, at
the base of Montjuïc, while the Port Vell project on the Moll de
Barcelona is underway.

Ferries to Mallorca, Menorca and Ibiza are run by the Compaña Trasmediterránea, Via Laietana 2; tel: 412 25 24. Service is daily between Barcelona and Palma, four days a week to Ibiza, three days a week to Mahon. The fare is about 4800 ptas (reclining chair) or 12,500 ptas for a cabin, one way. Cars, about 12,000 ptas.

Rodalias *(Getting around)*

Barcelona is laid out with the same combination of the rational and the fantastic that characterizes its architecture. In the space of a few minutes you can be entangled in the medieval labyrinths of the Barri Gòtic and the Born, and emerge into the formal gardens of the Ciutadella. You can thread your way through the narrow alleys and bohemian squares of the Gràcia, bolt through express traffic on the Diagonal, and find yourself sauntering along the gridlines of the Eixample. If you don't want to get lost, it helps to have a map.

For elementary tourism, you can rely on the basic city maps published by the municipal Patronat de Turisme, and available, free, at the tourist office in Sants Estació. (When last checked the tourist office at the airport, run by the provincial government [the Generalitat], handed out only the sketchiest of maps, published by the department store El Corte Inglés: half map, half advertising, and next to useless.)

The official city map, published by the Ajuntament, is clear and easy to read, and folds up to pocket size – but it won't get you out of the inner precincts and it won't tell you how to find a restaurant or museum, or for that matter any address. For this you'll need something heftier: the compact, hardbound (and very elegant) *Barcelona Carrers i Plànols*, which is put together and published by the Ajuntament. It consists of about 200 large-scale sectional maps: clear, detailed, in colour. Using the index, you can find any carrer, plaça, avinguda, ronda, passeig, or travessera in seconds.

The maps are overprinted with coloured symbols that graphically locate things you don't know you need until you need them: postboxes, telephones, first-aid stations, pedestrian-only streets, hospitals, funiculars, parking places and meters, taxi stations, petrol stations (with special symbols for those open at night and on Sundays and holidays), Metro stops, bus numbers along the streets, and postal codes. Plus churches, libraries, schools, police stations and monuments. The end-papers have a good big colour-coded Metro map. All in Catalan (which helps, because all of the city's street signs have been converted from Castilian to Catalan).

Even if you're only in Barcelona for a week or two, invest in it: 750 ptas, and worth every peseta.

We've also used the even more comprehensive (but not so slick) *Guia Urbana de Barcelona*, edited and published by Josep Pamias Ruiz. This consists of an awkward table-sized map and two pocket-sized volumes: one with sectional maps and an index, and the other a mass of general information: addresses and phone numbers of public agencies, hotels, banks, libraries, bingo parlours; bus itineraries; a concordance of addresses and cross-streets; a grab-bag of occasionally useful information which you can safely leave in your room. Available in Castilian or Catalan in department stores and bookshops.

Orientation

If you're accustomed to orienting yourself by maps with north at the top, think again. Virtually every map of Barcelona is aligned sideways, with the Mediterranean at the bottom and Tibidabo, approximately to the west, at the top. This will play havoc with your sense of direction, but if you want to find your way around town you'll have to adjust to the whims of available maps.

The simplest way to orient yourself in Barcelona is by using landmarks – Tibidabo to the east, Montjuïc to the south, the Mediterranean to the west – and your infallible sense that if you're heading downhill, you're probably facing the harbour.

Transport

Barcelona's public transport system is intelligently planned, runs flawlessly, and provides some of the lowest fares in Western Europe (it's bound to be heavily subsidized). For both Metro and bus systems, the flat fares mean that you can travel really long distances for 40–45 ptas – about 25p at the last known exchange rate of 173 ptas/£1.

At rush hour, buses and Metro trains are just as crowded as in London or Paris, but trains run about every three to four minutes at peak times, and buses never seem to travel in packs as they do in less fortunate cities. Barcelonese, of course, gripe about their transport system as do all city-dwellers, but to the visitor it's a dream.

Both Metro and bus close down at 23:00 on weekdays (see below for more specific information about hours), but there's a Nitbus service which takes over, beginning about 23:00 or 23:30, running every 20–30 minutes, and covering both centre and outskirts of the city. If you don't feeling like waiting half an hour for the Nitbus, taxis are cheap, plentiful and *honest*. See pages 32–3.

The Metro

Single fare: 75 ptas
10-ride ticket, Metro only: 400 ptas (called Targeta 2, T-dos, or simply *una targeta*)
1-, 3-, and 5-day passes: 300, 850, 1200 ptas

Hours:
05:00–23:00 Monday–Thursday
05:00–01:00 Fridays, Saturdays and evenings before holidays
06:00–24:00 Sundays
06:00–23:00 holidays

Metro stations are marked above ground by a large M within a diamond-shaped outline.

 Estació Metro

The kiosk downstairs offers single or multi-trip tickets – magnetized pasteboard strips numbered 1–10 along one side – and when you buy one of these, the seller will nip off the first segment if you're boarding the Metro immediately. Thereafter, each time you ride, you push the ticket into the slot at one of the automatic gates. This nips off the next segment, illuminates a yellow flasher, and releases the gate. In you go.

Although there are system maps on the walls of every Metro station, and clear, colour-coded directional signs everywhere, you'll find it useful to carry your own Metro map: a *Xarxa de Metro*, available at the tourist offices and at the cashier's window in the stations; or use the Metro plan on the reverse of the free Tourist

Office city maps. The map says it all: four distinct Metro lines, a fifth under construction, plus the independent Generalitat line (see below). Though not as extensive as those of Paris, London or New York, all are well laid out and cover the city completely.

Each line has its own colour code, and is marked with its beginning and ending stops.

Line 1 (RED): Feixa Llarga/Sta. Coloma
Traverses the city from southern to northern outskirts. *Important stops*: Espanya, Catalunya, Urquinaona, Arc de Triomf

Line 3 (GREEN): Zona Universitària/Montbau
Begins in the south-west (Pedralbes), loops east through the centre of the city and west again to the hills below Tibidabo. *Important stops*: Palau Reial, Sants Estació, Espanya, Drassanes, Liceu, Catalunya, Passeig de Gràcia, Diagonal

Line 4 (YELLOW): Pep Ventura/Roquetes
Runs from the northern outskirts to Pg. de Gràcia in the centre of town, then back to the north-west edge. *Important stops*: Ciutadella, Barceloneta, Jaume I, Urquinaona, Pg. de Gràcia

Line 5 (BLUE) Cornellà/Horta
Traverses from the south-west outskirts through the Diagonal to Horta in the north-west. *Important stops*: Sants Estació, Diagonal, Sagrada Familia, Hospital de Sant Pau

Colour-coded graphics guide you along with a minimum of confusion. For an English visitor fresh from wrestling with the problem of changing from the Piccadilly line to a Wimbledon train at Earls Court station in London, it's almost a pleasure to navigate the system unerringly. Connections between lines (*correspondèncias*) and between Metro and rail systems (*enllaços*) are clearly marked and coded – though in the larger stations (Pg. de Gràcia and Espanya, for example) they may entail long walks underground. Fortunately the escalators all work.

The stations are mostly floored and walled with tile or marble, and decorated – in some of the longer *correspondèncias* – with murals by schoolchildren, along with inevitable graffiti. They are clean, well lit, and safe (with few exceptions; for more details on safety see page 234). And you are soothed by unobtrusive music: classical or vintage showtunes beguile the short waits between trains.

On the trains themselves, announcements (in Castilian, not Catalan) are clear and distinct. On most lines, illuminated panels at eye-level show you *where* the train has come from, *which station* you are approaching, and as the doors close and the train moves out, what the *next* station is. And elegantly, at each end of each car, flashing red chevrons tell you which side to go out. For a New Yorker, accustomed to squalor, terrorism, excruciating din, and no signage whatsoever, the Barcelona Metro is the essence of Paradise.

Ferrocarrils de la Generalitat

The Generalitat – the provincial government of Catalonia – runs its own little underground within the city, sharing stations at Catalunya, Pg. de Gràcia and Provença with the Metro, and splitting off on its own towards the west and south-west. The system is commonly known as the Generalitat or FFCC, and the destinations you'll most likely use are Av. de Tibidabo (at the Pça. John F. Kennedy, from which the Tramvia Blau departs for Tibidabo) and Sarrià, a rich little hamlet at the base of the hills. You can use your Metro *targetas* on the Generalitat, or buy single-fare tickets from coin-operated machines in its stations. The timetable is the same as that of the Metro.

Tramvia Blau

This is an inexpressibly cute little trolley that runs from the Pça. John F. Kennedy uphill to the funicular that takes you to the fairgrounds on top of Tibidabo. At the moment the hillside has been torn up to accommodate a new freeway, and the Tramvia has been replaced temporarily by a bus. Your *targeta* (T-uno) works on it.

Funiculars

There are three: from Pça. del Doctor Andreu (where the Tramvia Blau stops) to the funfair on Tibidabo; from c/ del Bosc to Pça. Valvidrera in the hills above Sarrià; and from the Metro station at Paral.lel to Av. de Miramar on Montjuïc. These single-carriage cable-cars are hauled up and down the hills at about a 45-degree angle, packed with parents, small children, and miscellaneous teenage fun-seekers. Very pleasant as long as you don't worry about frayed cables. For real thrills try:

Telefèric and Transbordador Aëri

The Telefèric runs from Av. de Miramar (the top of the funicular) on Montjuïc and takes you first to the Parc d'Atraccions and then to the Castell de Montjuïc, now the Military Museum. The Transbordador Aëri del Port runs from the Moll Nou, on the harbourside at the south-west corner of Barceloneta, to the Jardins de Miramar on Montjuïc, with an intermediate stop at the Moll de Barcelona, near the Columbus monument. These are gondolas of the ski-lift variety, suspended on cables over the hillside and the harbour. You will inevitably ride with someone who likes to make it swing from side to side. The views are unequalled, but definitely not for the acrophobic.

Buses

Single fare: 75 ptas
10-ride ticket (Targeta 1 or T-uno), Metro, bus and Tramvia Blau (see above): 450 ptas
Nitbus: 90 ptas

The bus system in Barcelona is a fairly complex proposition, but with a little study it can get you closer to your destination than the Metro. A map (available at tourist offices and Metro kiosks) is essential, and a magnifying glass wouldn't hurt. There are about seventy routes, divided into four species:

1. All buses marked with RED signs pass through Pça. Catalunya (and the nearby Pças. Universitat and Urquinaona): the centre of Barcelona. Apart from that they have nothing in common.

2. All buses marked with YELLOW signs are 'transversal', running more or less north and south on different lines of longitude.

3. All buses marked with GREEN signs are 'peripheral' or 'other', which means they zigzag all over town, avoiding the central plaças.

4. All buses marked with BLUE signs are nocturnal – the Nitbus – and pass through Pça. Catalunya. There are eight Nitbus routes, with varying beginning and ending times (approximately 23:00 to

03:30 or 04:30), and run at 20- or 30-minute intervals. A special Nitbus map is available for these.

You can buy a single fare – a tiny scrap of yellow paper – from the driver, but 10-trip *targetas* (T-unos) are available only at Metro stops and Metro offices. With a *targeta*, the procedure is to hop on board, slip past the driver and push your ticket smartly into the machine at the top of the aisle, downward, with its face toward you. If the ticket is used up or inserted backwards or not all the way in, a warning system alerts the driver and you must correct the error, ignominiously.

All stops are request stops unless the driver is signalled by travellers waiting at bus shelters. There are request buttons on the posts near the doors. Most of the Barcelona bus stops identify themselves fairly clearly, but it helps to have a good idea of where you're going and where you are at any given time. If you're travelling at night, with no visual clues, you can ask the driver to let you know when you reach your stop.

There are random checks for fare-dodgers on both buses and Metro, so don't lose your ticket or *targeta*, and don't count on the apparent casualness of the system for free rides. The fine is 1000 ptas, cash on the spot.

Taxis

Taxis are among Barcelona's most delightful contradictions: luxurious *and* cheap. They are also small, nippy, and always seem to be available when you need them, even on rainy nights in out-of-the-way places. They're unmistakable: bright yellow and black, and you can spot them in the dark by the green light on the roof, which indicates availability. There's also a sign in the window: *Lliure* or *Libre*, which will give you an idea of the driver's linguistic and cultural predilections.

Rates are 225 ptas for about 2000 m or 6 minutes of waiting time (or if stalled in traffic).

Supplements:

Tarife 1: an extra 55 ptas per km within Zone A (Barcelona and a few close-in outskirts), Monday to Saturday 06:00–22:00.

Tarife 2: an extra 75 ptas per km in Zone A, Monday to Saturday 22:00–06:00, and all day Sundays and holidays; and Monday to Saturday 06:00–22:00 in Zone B (suburbs).

Tarife 3: an extra 85 ptas per km in Zone B, Monday to Saturday

22:00–06:00, and all day Sundays and holidays.
Plus:
200 ptas for pick-up or delivery at the airport
55 ptas for pick-up at Sants railway station
75 ptas for carrying a suitcase or package larger than 55×35×35 cm.

A ride to the airport from central Barcelona should cost no more than about 1800 ptas, and if you're too burdened or harried to cope with the Metro–Sants–Airport connection, worth it. Otherwise, see Arrivals and departures, page 20.

You can ask the driver for a receipt which shows the route taken, the fare, and the taxi number (helpful if you need to trace objects left in the cab).

In the near future you'll be able to buy a 'Taxi Card,' a credit card on which you can charge your journeys. Ask the Tourist Office about this, or, if you speak Castilian or can enlist the help of a bilingual friend, phone 412 20 00.

Taxis by phone:

Barnataxi	357 77 55
Taxi Radio Movil	358 11 11
Tele Taxi	392 22 22
Radio Taxi	490 22 22
Coop. Radio Taxi Metropolitana	300 38 11

These numbers are only for those fluent in Castilian; your hotel or hostal will call them for you.

Getting out of town

Pça. d'Espanya is the jumping-off point for the great monastery mountain of Montserrat (see page 238 for information on that) and for other nearby towns. If Sants was your first stop on your way into town from the airport, you'll know that it's fairly simple to understand and navigate. Pça. d'Espanya is another story, the Generalitat railhead hidden *inside* the Metro station where Lines 1 and 3 intersect. Look for the Generalitat emblem. The Pça. d'Espanya itself is littered with the bleached bones of travellers who have attempted to find the station from above ground.

Estació
Ferrocarrils de la Generalitat

Information for Montserrat is clearly displayed on the walls, and you buy your ticket (*anar i tornar* – return trip) from the kiosk directly at the entrance to the train platforms. There are automatic ticket machines nearby, but at the moment of writing they accept only cash not plastic.

Going further

The main train station is Sants Estació, where you arrived from your plane. Metro Lines 3 and 5 go there directly; all other lines make 'correspondences' so it's quick and easy to reach.

International trains for major European cities leave from and come into Sants, as do trains for the resorts along the Costa Brava – although the Francia station, the old depot for Spanish National Railways and international trains, located just south of the Ciutadella Park, is now under heavy renovation and may be open again for business when this book is in your hands.

The ticket windows at Sants are efficiently served, and in 'low seasons' – winter, early spring, late autumn – queues are fairly short. Summer is another story. There are automatic ticket machines in the main concourse which take cash and plastic.

Information about local trains from Sants is posted on four-sided *qiosks* near the main exit from the station. Immediate information about trains arriving or departing is clearly shown on big boards above the ticket windows.

This is where you look, for example, to find the time of the next train to Prat Aeropuerto, and from which *via* (platform).

An International Train Information office is in this station, many languages spoken but no local train information dispensed. It can get very busy at midday, so if you need any information urgently go early, 09:00 for preference. Woe betide you if you get behind someone who wants to go to Verona by way of Avignon and wonders whether she can stop in Genoa on the way.

Districts and neighbourhoods

Ciutat Vella

The city is made up of distinct neighbourhoods: some planned, others haphazard; some unchanged over the centuries, others in constant and rapid evolution. Barcelona developed backwards from the sea: the Roman walls of first-century Barcino enclosed about 30 acres on Mont Tàber in the present Gothic quarter that butts up against the waterfront. Traces of the Roman city emerge in a scattering of ancient streets and buildings: eroded bits of wall in the Pça. Ramon Berenguer, and excavated ruins under the Museu Frederic Marés and the Museu d'Història de la Ciutat.

The boundaries of the city hardly expanded over seven centuries of Roman, Visigothic and Moorish rule, and not until the thirteenth century did the city truly flourish, with independence from the Franks, sovereignty over the rest of Catalonia, successful wars of conquest in the Mediterranean, and the establishment of a mercantile empire.

The exaggerated profits of the thirteenth century funded a spectacular building boom in the fourteenth. The churches of El Pi and Santa Maria del Mar, the Saló de Cent and the Saló del Tinell were begun, the shipyards at Drassanes were expanded, and the c/ Montcada was laid in a straight line through the north quarter of the city, presaging the relentless urban planning of the future.

Unfortunately for Barcelona, all this progress came to a halt at the end of the century with plague, famine, overexpansion of empire, civil warfare, economic collapse. And as a result, fortunately for us, the architecture of the old city has remained frozen at its peak, with no new waves of capital to improve it out of existence.

The seven districts of the Ciutat Vella – the *barris* – are divided by the broad (some only relatively broad) avenues that have been imposed upon them over the centuries (see map, pages vi–vii):

Barri Gòtic is a neologism for the primeval core of the city – actually a collection of four tiny districts which from Barcelona's second-century Roman beginnings have housed the government, the church, and until recently the nobility. Every building that isn't a church property seems to be a palace. Those of the city and provincial governments – the Ajuntament and the Generalitat – stand opposite each other (in more ways than one) across the Pça. Sant Jaume in the centre of the quarter. A few streets away are the Palau Reial Major (which housed the counts), the Palau del Lloctinent (the viceroys), the Palau del Bisbe (the bishops), and the Casa dels Canonges (the canons). Dominating the scene is the Cathedral.

Mercè, the quarter that fronts the harbourside and runs up the Ramblas as far as c/ de Ferran, contains two perfect neo-classical squares. One is the Pça. Reial, an airy rectangle surrounded by arcades, with palm trees, a fountain ('The Three Graces') and streetlamps by Gaudí in the centre. It's also home to a thriving drug trade and a permanent police outpost. And facing the Moll de la Fusta, one side open to the harbour, is the diminutive Pça. Duc de Medinaceli: a few palms surrounding a modest fountain, monument to a bygone admiral, and a glimpse of the sea. Nearby: the Basilica de la Mercè, perfectly proportioned, with its bronze Virgin poised to take off from the roof.

La Ribera, in the north-east corner (bottom right on most maps), lies between the Parc de la Ciutadella and the Via Laietana, and is a repository of charm. Here are located the great warehouses and palaces of the medieval merchant princes, and the twisting streets that bear the names of ancient guilds and craftsmen: Argenteria, Sombrerers, Cirera, Vidrieria, Cotoners. The north end of La Ribera is called El Born, a relaxed and tranquil quarter which has recently acquired a spate of contemporary galleries and at least one futurist bar. And at the top of the Pg. del Born is the basilica of Santa Maria del Mar, whose vaulted interior will take your breath away.

Sant Pere, Santa Catarina, Sant Agustí: the north-west corner of the Ciutat Vella, between the Via Laietana, c/ de la Princesa and the c/ de Trafalgar, a busy street full of textile wholesalers. The *barri* contains the exquisite Palau de la Música in one corner, the ancient palaces of the c/ Sant Pere més Baix, which cuts through the centre of the district, and a swarm of narrow streets and alleys running in all directions. It reeks of age.

Portal de l'Angel was the domain of the fourteenth-century aristocracy, and still bears traces of elegance, despite the hubbub of shops on the Av. Portal de l'Angel. The district lies between the Ramblas and the Via Laietana, and is bordered on north and south by the Pça. de Catalunya and the Av. de la Catedral. Pleasing prospects: the neo-classical Palau Castanyer in the Pça. Cucurulla, and the nearby *xocolateria* Fargas; the Font de la Maja in the Pça. Vila de Madrid; the eponymous Gothic church in the c/ Santa Anna, with its fifteenth-century cloister.

Raval de Ponent and **Raval de Sant Pau**, the districts just south of the Ramblas, have an unsavoury reputation: the alleys toward the harbour are known as the Barri Xinès, the behavioural sink of Barcelona, and they are not easy on the eye. But close by you'll find gems such as the gardens of the old Hospital de la Santa Creu, between the c/ del Carme and the c/ Hospital; the incredible Boqueria, Barcelona's lushest public market; Gaudí's more-than-slightly sinister Palau Güell; the ancient dockyards at Drassanes.
Poble Sec is bisected by the Av. Paral.lel, and the areas north and south of the avenue are the Barcelonese equivalents of Montmartre and Pigalle. The fleshpots and old-fashioned music halls (the Apolo, the Arnau, El Molino, the notorious Baghdad) are clustered at the seaward end of the Paral.lel, backed up against the Barri Xinès, while from the inland reaches of the avenue a jumble of domesticated streets and alleys leads upward into Montjuïc: tranquil, slightly shabby and run down. The Paral.lel itself runs parallel to nothing else in Barcelona. For 2 km or so it mimics exactly the parallel of latitude 44°44′; hence the name.

Barceloneta

The city has always seemed to suffer urban renewal as a result of civil calamity. The War of Spanish Succession, which ended Catalan independence in 1714, was the direct cause of the city's first application of a grid system to the urban landscape. After fourteen months of siege, the city surrendered to the Bourbon pretender Felipe V, whose army promptly razed the north side of La Ribera – what is now the Parc de la Ciutadella – and replaced it with a barracks. The evicted population was then resettled in new terraced housing in Barceloneta, designed by a military engineer for easy control of the area; and the long and not entirely miserable reign of the Bourbon monarchy began.

Barceloneta is the eastern extension of the town, a working-class *barri* from its beginnings, jutting out into the harbour slightly north of the Ciutat Vella. The neighbourhood has a miniature feeling about it: low buildings, many in pastel shades, slightly dilapidated, with awnings at eye-level. Until very recently the beachfront housed a string of wonderful rackety seafood restaurants whose tables extended on to the sand in summertime, but these have been reduced to a handful by municipal edict, while simultaneously the harbour edge of the neighbourhood has been turned upside down in a frenzy of excavation. The citizens are not pleased: gentrification is just around the corner.

Ramblas

Barcelona's urban renovations seem to spring up overnight, rather than evolving at their own pace. The Ramblas, the broad and shady promenade that runs from the harbour to the Pça. de Catalunya, are the most visible exception. The city's southern walls, built on a riverbed, were replaced with a raised walkway in the mid-eighteenth century, and a gradual accretion of plaças and palaces alongside the ancient convents attracted the presence of a leisured aristocracy. By the 1850s the Ramblas had become by default the place to see and be seen: nowhere else in town could one parade, by carriage or on foot, in anything but single file. The central walkway is still the city's prime location for a stroll or a chat, although now at various times it bustles with buskers, tourists, and cutpurses along with the general ruck. And many of the noble storefronts along its edges are in sad repair, exploited for mean purposes, anticipating another wave of urban renewal.

Eixample

Barcelona's next major overhaul, the building of the Eixample, was the result of a mixture of factors: mid-nineteenth-century over-crowding, disease, rapid industrialization and social unrest, which created a pressing need for expansion beyond the walls of the city; an enormous influx of colonial and industrial wealth, which funded it; and bungling on the part of the central bureaucracy in Madrid, which forced an unwelcome solution. A design competition for the *eixample* – the extension – of the city was held in 1859, with the clear popular favourite a plan by Antoni Rovira i Trias which would have integrated it with the old town. Madrid (which Barcelona holds responsible for all its ills since 1412) delayed a decision for ten years and finally, in 1869, when the need for expansion threatened havoc, imposed the wrong plan: a rigid grid designed by the engineer Ildefons Cerdà. In their haste to put up new housing, the builders dropped the parks and gardens that had enlivened Cerdà's original plan. The result was the rather dreary chequerboard that now occupies the area between the Diagonal and the Rondas that surround the old city.

The octagonal blocks of the Eixample, especially those close to the Pg. de Gràcia, were instantly snapped up by Barcelona's rich bourgeoisie, and the marriage of money and a taste for the exotic and the 'artistic' produced a flowering of Catalan architecture, the Moderniste movement. The Quadrat d'Or, a square of about 120 blocks of the Eixample between Pg. de Sant Joan and c/ Aribau, is peppered with the works of Domènech, Puig, Gaudí and a host of their lesser-known contemporaries and followers: designs that range from the subtlest stencilled tracery on plain stone fronts to full-blown fantasies of brick and tile, complete with undulating walls, twisted columns and distorted windows: houses that seem to live and breathe.

The Eixample has two distinct sides and temperaments: La Dreta, the right, lies north of c/ Balmes and contains the preponderance of Moderniste mansions and showy shops, the height of high bourgeois. L'Esquerra, on the left, south of Balmes, is merely bourgeois, the bare bones of Cerdà's master plan, undistracted by the imaginations of Domènech and Gaudí.

Ciutadella

The Universal Exhibition of 1888 was a spur-of-the-moment enterprise inaugurated by the city's mayor Rius i Taulet, a celebration of the city's economic boom. It was pitched in record time on the grounds of the old Citadel in La Ribera – the symbol of Castilian oppression – and included (among much else that was immediately dismantled) an Arc de Triomf at one end of the new Parc de la Ciutadella, Domènech's castellate café-restaurant (which wasn't completed on time and never opened, and now houses the Museu de Zoologia), the glass-and-iron Hivernacle and the wood-slatted Umbracle which house exotic plants and trees.

The setting for these imposing remnants of the exhibition is a serene and spacious park: lush plantings, formal avenues, a bombastic baroque-style fountain (La Cascada), a scattering of classical portrait statuary (on horseback and off), the Museu d'Art Modern, the Parlament de Catalunya (both housed in the old Arsenal buildings), and in the north-east corner, the Barcelona Zoo.

In the forty years between the Universal Exhibitions of 1888 and 1929, the outlines of the city became set. The Eixample closed the gaps between the city of Barcelona and the villages of Gràcia and Sarrià. The Via Laietana was driven through the heart of the Barri Gòtic, providing a direct route to the harbour and forcing a stuffy, tedious order on the ancient incoherent centre of the city. The Parc Güell was laid out, Gaudí's Sagrada Familia was begun, Domènech's sprawling Hospital de Sant Pau was completed, the gardens and exhibition halls of Montjuïc were installed, the funfair on Tibidabo was inaugurated. The city was primed for the heady Republican days that preceded the Civil War.

Gràcia

The nineteenth-century planner Antoni Rovira i Trias lost the design competition that resulted in the construction of the Eixample, but he was the popular favourite and still symbolizes Barcelona's uphill battle against Madrid. His bronze statue, life size, sits stoically on a stone bench in the Gràcia square that bears his name, and *his* plan for the Eixample is engraved in bronze at his feet. It bears an odd legend for a town that has endured so much urban planning: *Le tracé d'une ville est oeuvre du temps plutôt que d'architecte* (the outline of a city is the work of time rather than of the architect).

This is certainly true for the Gràcia, which was not much more than a village until the Eixample joined it to the city proper. It still manages to keep its distance: an enclave whose citizens affect never to set foot outside its bounds, where Catalan is spoken exclusively and with ardour, where the streets are narrow, the houses modest, the squares lively and congenial, the atmosphere one of entrenched bohemianism. Gràcia also abounds in restaurants, some of them old and trendy, others just old. The district is bordered more or less by the Diagonal, Gran Via de Gràcia, c/ de l'Escorial, and Travessera de Dalt. It contains a number of charming squares – the Pças. del Sol, Rius i Taulet, Diamant, Virreina, Rovira and del Nord – but few gems of architecture other than Gaudí's Casa Viçens on c/ de les Carolines: brick, tile, and plenty of Moorish influence.

These are just the most visible few of Barcelona's *barris*. There are plenty more to be discovered, scores of little Barcelonas where people live and work: Sant Antoni, Guinardó and Baix Guinardó, Prosperitat, Vall d'Hebron, Vallbona, Trinitat Nova, Turó de la

Peira, Torre Baró, Ramon Albó, Carmel, Roquetes, Bordeta, Font Castellana, Montbau, Horta, Guineueta . . . the list is endless, and all it takes to explore them is a modicum of curiosity, plenty of time and an unlimited supply of Metro tickets.

Al llit *(Sleeping cheap)*

Where to stay

Compared to the plethora of small private hotels and B & Bs in London, and the immensely long list of Paris hotels, Barcelona is relatively low in places to stay. However, the Spanish Tourist Office in London (57-58 St James's Street, London SW1A 1LD; tel: 071 499 1169) can supply you with a printed list of hotels from 4-star beauties to humble pensions. So can the Tourist Office at Sants Estació, and in the Palau de Virreina on the Ramblas in Barcelona itself.

An official hotel listing, in Barcelona or elsewhere, cannot tell you exactly what you'll get in terms of comfort. That's where our leg-work comes in: we've visited, and cast a cold eye on, more than a hundred fairly modest Barcelona hotels, hostals and pensions. Please do bear in mind that things can change, in hotels/hostals/pensions, from the time the place is inspected/slept in until the day you read this book. We fully expect – and you should bear in mind as you read this chapter – that prices will catapult during the 1992 Olympic year, and we can only hope that they will subside when it's over.

We set out with the 1990 printed list from the Spanish Tourist Office in London (the only one available during most of our research), plus the 1991 colour brochure from the Gremi in Barcelona, as well as a sheaf of valuable notes and recommendations from friends and friends of friends.

Some of our researchers found places to stay the hard way, wandering down streets that looked attractive, leaping off buses when passing a 'Hotel' or 'Hostal' sign. We found, not unexpectedly, immense variations in the standards of accommodation of places within the same category.

Some of the 1-star hostals were much better than we expected, certainly as good as some of the more modest hotels which were one category higher. In terms of lifts, pleasantly set out public rooms, bathrooms, decoration, even credit cards and telephones in rooms, they had a lot to offer. Others in the hostal category offered only minimal luxury but were perfectly acceptable – clean and neat, fresh-smelling and very inexpensive.

One of our researchers spent several nights in a hostal in the Gràcia district – the Greenwich Village of Barcelona – and found the rooms large and light, the bed comfortable, the communal bathroom newly tiled and equipped. When she asked for a bath towel, the receptionist gave her not one but three. Her room cost £10 a night.

Another stayed in a big, rather impersonal place where his room was only slightly larger than his single bed – but it had a telephone and, unbelievably, room service from a bar. The basin had a bright light over it and there was a shaver point. For that he was willing to pay £14 for a single room.

In some cases, the price charged for a room in a hotel (with basin only, no bath) would have bought a room with toilet, basin and shower in a delightful hostal; the drawback here: continuous noise from Vespas and cars in the daytime, making siestas impossible.

A hostal praised in an English newspaper in the spring of 1991 proved to be quite adequate – once you had edged up the grimy stairs, three flights of them, with backpackers roosting there. 'Fine for the young, fit, and skint,' our researcher noted; 'very central location on the Ramblas if that's where you want to be, very civil and helpful receptionist, good value at about £14 a night for double room (no bath).'

This book is not written to give a boost to Barcelona tourism. That will get along just fine without us. It does set out to tell you what you can expect to get, and to give even-handed, truthful appraisals. Naturally, the particular bias of the individual researcher enters into every report. One young man fled a good little place because it was noisy 18 hours a day; another had provided herself with earplugs, and liked it because the proprietors were kind, obliging and spoke Spanglais. A middle-aged friend cannot stay in any hotel where there's no reading light at the bedside. Most people don't mind paying cash; others want to know whether credit cards or Amex cheques can be used. These are personal idiosyncrasies, and we've tried to make accurate notes.

The glossy Spanish Tourist Board hotel booklet handed out in

Barcelona contained much useful information about each hostelry listed – credit cards, telephones, cable TV, house restaurants, room service, fax services. But for some reason it omits what to us is fairly essential – the presence or absence of a lift. By cross-checking sources, and by personal observation, we try to correct this omission.

The hotel booklet is illustrated with photographs of hotel and hostal façades, and of some 'typical' rooms – naturally, you are not going to find that big pretty room with the wide windows. We also felt that a few establishments we visited should not have appeared in this beautiful brochure, and indeed should never have been licensed for guests for even one night.

If you very much like or dislike the hotel, hostal or pension where you stay, do write to Gremi d'Hotels de Barcelona, Via Laietana 47, 08003 Barcelona; telephone: 301 62 40; fax: 301 42 92.

One of our researchers said, 'I would stay forever in Hostal XX if I could send home for money enough.' Another cried out (about a pension just off the Ramblas), 'How did this fleapit ever get a licence to operate!' We ourselves went to look at a pension mentioned in a 1991 book on Catalonia and couldn't bring ourselves to go beyond the first two steps in a rubbly hall. Another one in the same somewhat unpromising street proved to be a find: clean, well-equipped (and booked solidly from May to September).

Remember, modest Barcelona hotels do not supply soap or face flannels (washcloths). If there's no glass for your toothbrush, ask for one. Barcelona water is hard, so take a really creamy soap and shaving stuff, handcream, nailbrush, earplugs, a small squeeze-bottle of detergent for washing your smalls, and anything else necessary to your personal happiness under a strange roof.

We found no hostals or pensions with shaver points; a few hotels have them. Hotels may also have points in the room or bathroom for hairdriers or those nifty gadgets for boiling water in a cup for early morning tea. Hostals and pensions, in our experience, never.

Barcelona hotels

Note: Street addresses throughout are written in Spanish style, with the street name first, the street number next, then the five-number postal code. When writing to Barcelona, address your envelope like this:

Hostal Blank
c/ de Blank 100
08036 Barcelona
Spain

Classifications are established by the Barcelona Hotel Association
(the Gremi d'Hotels de Barcelona):
H: Hotels. Graded from the 5-star Avenida Palace type, down to
1-star establishments such as the Noya (page 60). Hotels must offer
rooms with bath/shower.

HS: Hostals. Graded from 3-star down to 1-star. They can be quite
luxurious and appropriately expensive, but will probably not offer
all Hotel services. Some of the starrier hostals have double and
single rooms with bath etc; the 1-star hostals may have some rooms
with private baths, but often rooms with basin only, plus of course
the obligatory communal baths and lavatories.

P: Pensions. Usually have only rooms with basins, although a few in
this classification do offer some rooms with private bath/shower.

CH: Guesthouse classification, which usually means a large flat
which has been divided into rooms. They have no private baths.

In some cases, if you are in a room in a hostal, pension or guesthouse without a private bath, you may be charged a small additional
sum every time you have a bath or shower. This is noted in our
information for specific places. Please note the word 'bathroom'
usually means shower stall, toilet, basin; seldom do they have the
luxury of a tub-cum-shower.

Credit cards: few hostals or pensions accept plastic. Where they do,
we've made mention of it. Hotels, on the other hands, will usually
take specified credit cards. Traveller's cheques, in our experience,
are politely refused by most inexpensive establishments. Eurocheques on the whole are not welcomed, and if accepted will carry a
surcharge to recompense the hostal for its bank charges. Personal
cheques on foreign banks are never accepted. (Well, maybe the Ritz
will take them, at 41,000 ptas a night for a double room.)

Bills, in our experience, are perfectly honest – although a travel
writer for the *Independent*, in a recent article on Barcelona,

mentions that when he queried items on his account at a fairly pricey hotel in the Ramblas, he was physically threatened.

Telephone bills: hostals and pensions, and modest hotels, usually charge you only 25 ptas per call, and you must ask the receptionist to let you use the telephone. Some, with a central switchboard and telephones in rooms, add a few pesetas as a service charge.

Note: Prices quoted do not include the 6 per cent IVA tax levied on all hotels, hostals and pensions.

Ciutat Vell: Barri Gòtic

California (H 1-star)

Raurich 14, 08002
Tel: 317 77 66
Metro: Liceu (L3)

Double luxury room with bath, TV, safe, 'music system,' VCR and TV, 6000 ptas
Double room with bath, 3500 ptas
Double room without bath, 3000 ptas
Single room without bath, 2500 ptas (No single rooms with bath)

This lovely little hotel is in the Barri Gòtic, just off the excellent shopping street c/ Ferran – in a neighbourhood crowded with good restaurants. The Cathedral is a few steps away, the stately Pça. Reial just around the corner.

At some unspecified time in the future it is closing for renovation which will include a lift. But the stairs are wide and shallow, easy to walk up. There are telephones in all the rooms, a switchboard that will take messages (preferably in Castilian). It has a bar, and breakfast can be served in your room – although with the plethora of coffee shops and snack bars within a few metres, this really isn't necessary.

The helpful receptionist spoke little English, but assured us that 'others' on the staff speak it better. We don't know what their renovation plans are, but hope they won't spoil the sweet character of the hotel as it was when visited. Book a month in advance in spring and autumn, two weeks ahead in winter, four to six weeks ahead for the summer. Visa, Amex cards and Eurocheques accepted.

Condal (HS 2-star)

Boqueria 23, 08002
Tel: 318 18 82
Metro: Liceu (L3)

Double room with bath, 3815 ptas
Single room with bath, 2705 ptas

This hostal is just off the main part of the Ramblas, and across the street from the historic Liceu theatre, where operas and concerts take place. You won't have any trouble finding it, as there are signs pointing to it, and to other hostals on the street, where it joins the Ramblas. The famous Mercat Sant Josep – the Boqueria – is an olive-stone's throw away. If you choose to stay in this neighbourhood, you must take into consideration the fact that it's lively and full of movement – which means noise – most hours of the day and night.

If this doesn't worry you, we would say that the Hostal Condal is a clean, bright, comfortable place to stay, and the rates aren't high for the neighbourhood.

There's a lift and a reasonably spacious reception room. When we were there we found no one who spoke English, although the agreeable man on duty that day spoke good French. We have been told that in 1992 most of the hotels in this popular area will be taking on staff who speak English, Italian and German.

We liked the attractive red chairs in the reception room, and thought it would be a restful place – despite its dimmish lights – to meet friends or lay out maps and guide books. All rooms here have private bathrooms, which means shower with toilet and basin, not a tub. And all are decorated in the same attractive way: red chairs, good floors, pleasing cream-coloured quilts on the beds, and what seemed to be adequate blankets.

All the rooms and bathrooms had a bright clean feeling, much pleasanter than some of the other places in the neighbourhood.

Each room has its own telephone, a small but useful amenity. When you go out for breakfast, stay away from the very touristy Ramblas places and plunge into some of the more attractive streets nearby. It's close to the good shopping street c/ de Ferran, the alluring little squares Pça. del Pi and Pça. Sant Josep Oriol, with what our writer friend Harriet Frank, Jr. calls Junqueries – shops and stalls with sub-antique rings and things, perfume bottles, fans, seals, chain purses. One day a week, other stalls appear with country honeys, soaps, herbs, dried flowers, chocolates, *turrón* ... Altogether an interesting neighbourhood in which to stay.

If you've read our sections on thievery in Barcelona (pages 227 and 234), you're already aware that all the Ramblas, from the Pça. de Catalunya down to the harbour, is pickpocket country: watch your valuables, don't carry more money than you can afford to lose, make sure your passport and traveller's cheques are safe in an inside zipped pocket. But don't spend your days walking around in a state of apprehension: Barcelona is to be enjoyed.

Dalí (H 2-star)

Boqueria 12, 08002
Tel: 318 55 80
Metro: Liceu (L3)

Double room with bath, 2900 ptas
Double room with bath for 3 people, 3900 ptas
Double room with basin, 2200 ptas
Double room with basin for 3 people, 3300 ptas
Single room with bath, 2000 ptas
Single room with basin, 1400 ptas

This is a real find, reports one of our friends who lived for many months in Barcelona and trekked around dozens of hotels, hostals, pensions and guesthouses for us. It's just off the Ramblas and near the Liceu theatre, on the edge of the Barri Gòtic. You walk up a clean marble staircase into a rather uninviting open reception area with white walls and conventional hostal-type brown furniture. Then you meet the very friendly and accommodating people. The rooms are medium-size with parquet floors, unusual in a city which is inclined to chilly marble and tile.

Windows look out on the street which is full of movement and bustle in the daytime but quiets down after dark. The Dalí is fairly large, 49 rooms, and many of the rooms have baths – which are new, spotless, well tiled and equipped. Some of the rooms have double beds plus an extra folding bed stored in a cupboard, which could be useful. This adds about 1000 ptas a day if three people occupy the room instead of two. We recommend it, but write well in advance of a projected stay. Centrally heated.

Inglés (H 1-star)

Boqueria 17, 08001
Tel: 317 37 70
Metro: Liceu (L3)

Double room with bath, 4920 ptas
Single room with bath, 2940 ptas

In the centre of the Ramblas, very close to the Liceu, the Boqueria, the pleasures of the Barri Gòtic and so forth. The Inglés is classified as a hotel because all its rooms have private baths, and it offers a certain number of useful extras such as a restaurant, room service, telephones in rooms, safes in which to stow your valuables.

Altogether we found it a conventional, comfortable, very convenient place to stay. Every floor of the Inglés had a sitting room with chairs and television – pleasant during the day, and one hopes that no one on your floor rolls in from dinner at midnight and decides to have a little look at late-night TV!

There's a lift, and a panelled lobby with some chairs. Everywhere was what we have come to think of as a very Spanish dim-lit ambience – a lot of beige-brown-gold colours – and rather romantic little electric-candle fittings on walls.

All the rooms are a 'realistic' size, not cramped, and have well-planned little bathrooms equipped with showers.

The general impression in the rooms was of low-key good taste, with high ceilings and good long curtains, but in one room someone had gone wild and added a jaguar-print blanket. In a large double room – the one photographed for the Gremi hotel guide – there were attractive gold-coloured spreads on the twin beds, and a dressing table. But the single reading light was a candle-bulb on the wall high above the two beds.

Cupboards were adequate, not large. There were no carpets but the floors were clean and well kept. We would advise that, if you want to escape noise from the street below, you ask for a room in the back of the hotel, or on the highest floor. Visa cards accepted.

Jardí (H 2-star)

Pça. Sant Josep Oriol 1, 08002
Tel: 301 59 00
Metro: Liceu (L3)

Double room with bath, 3500 ptas
Double room with basin, 3000 ptas
Single room with bath, 2750 ptas
Single room with basin, 1600 ptas

We love the pretty little squares on which the Jardí fronts – the Pça. del Pi and the Pça. Sant Josep Oriol. But we'd better declare here and now, they are both continuously brisk and noisy with street life that begins early and seems to stop only a few hours before it starts up again.

There are several street fairs here two or three days a week. Every day a lot of coming and going, chatting and whistling, and the occasional portable radio. A few underpowered but rackety motor bikes cut through on their way to nearby streets. The cafeterias in the square put their tables out early, and cups and glasses clatter back and forth all day and into the evening. We've put this up front to inform those who like to have a siesta in the afternoon after a late Barcelona lunch, or sleep in mornings after late Barcelona dinners.

The Jardí has charm, it's been 'discovered' over and over, and has appeared in several guide books and newspaper articles. The location is perfection, and if you looked it up on the Barcelona map, you'd assume it to be located in a quiet pedestrian enclave. If only it were!

The Jardí is a walk-up, and there are a lot of steps to climb. The reception room is stark and white, but there's a big room for sitting, well lit, with good windows, and a TV and tables and sofas. Everyone we met was charming, and various members of the staff speak both English and French. The rooms are pretty, with soft lighting and colour and real wood furniture, not mere hotel stuff. We liked the huge old wardrobes, and the pleasing blue bedspread in one room. You may want to take a few hangers of your own. The bathrooms are – well – adequate; the only ones we saw in any hotel or hostal in Barcelona which seemed almost unmodernized.

The communal bathroom, shared by five of the bedrooms, was modern enough, but at least one visitor (who didn't stay there) commented that the toilet seat was missing! This we hope was a temporary state of affairs.

The location couldn't be better, and if you don't mind street noises you could be very happy here. It's the centre of a network of beautiful little streets lined with expensive antique shops, good shopping for gifts and shoes right around the corner, the Cathedral and various museums nearby. Don't miss the extraordinary little Shoe Museum in the Pça. de Felip Neri, down a maze of entrancing alleyways. The Jardí is in the very midst of the Barri Gòtic, and you will enjoy the small antique/junk market stalls, and the honey, herb, soap and candle stalls for which these two tiny squares are noted.

Layetana (H 1-star)

Pça. Ramon Berenguer el Gran 2, 08002
Tel: 319 20 12
Metro: Urquinaona (L1, L4), Jaume I (L4)

Double room without bath, 2050 ptas in winter, 2350 in summer (15 June–15 September)
Single room without bath, 1200 ptas (winter), 1375 ptas (summer)

One of our serendipitous discoveries, seen from a passing No. 19 bus on the way to the Cathedral, and looked over the same day. It is in a building set well back from the rush of traffic in the busy Via Laietana, which divides the Barri Gòtic from the Born. The Layetana is in a well-kept building with a smoothly functioning lift; has a secure feeling, on an upper floor – no casual thief looking for carelessly stacked luggage is going to wander in.

The helpful young woman at the reception desk the day we were here speaks English well, and Italian; her parents speak French. There is an agreeable family feeling in this hostal. No rooms have private baths, but the communal bathrooms were well tiled, bright and extremely clean. Everything looks scrupulously maintained. A really big double room, with a basin and large wardrobes, looked comfortable, with armchair, writing desk and adequate lighting.

A bath or shower is charged at 200 ptas a time, by arrangement with the receptionist, but this isn't much of an addition to the low rates in this very good hostal.

It's only about a hundred metres from the Cathedral, and about five minutes' walk to the pleasures of c/ Montcada with its galleries, the Picasso Museum, and the pretty little square with the most beautiful church in Barcelona, Santa Maria del Mar.

Turn to the right from the Layetana, and you plunge into a maze of shopping streets like the c/ Ferran, and seductive little squares like the Pça. del Pi. A hundred yards down one of those winding streets and you are in the heart of the Ramblas, near the Liceu.

Paris (HS 2-star)

Cardenal Casañas 4, 08002
Tel: 301 37 85
Metro: Liceu (L3)

Double room with bath, 3300 ptas
Double room with basin, 2900 ptas
Single room with basin, 1500 ptas

How this one picked up a 2-star rating is a continuing mystery – especially when the elegant Oliva (page 68) has only one star ... Well, ours not to reason why. We would say that this is fairly minimal accommodation, located one flight up from the street, with the street door wide open in the daytime. In hostals where you ring for entrance and are buzzed in, there's much more of a feeling of safety and protection. In walk-up establishments, it could be possible for anyone standing around the lobby to pick up unguarded luggage and be off down the stairs – a Barcelona hazard noted in many English newspapers in 1991.

The reception room doubles as a place to sit, with a few chairs and a soft-drinks machine. The receptionist was watching TV when we arrived to look the place over. To our surprise, we were given a key and allowed to look – unaccompanied – at a room which was obviously occupied. Well, it's good to have such an honest face, but personally we wouldn't care to have anyone let into a room we were occupying in a hotel.

The Paris rooms are the opposite of luxurious – hotel-type furniture, walls needing paint. The windows have large wooden shutters which are probably to block out noise, but of course cut off light completely. One room that we saw had the smallest wardrobe ever – just a shallow cupboard behind a mirrored door. The bathrooms acceptable, small, not as modern as in many hostals we've seen.

Ciutat Vell: Mercè

Fontanella (H 1-star)

Via Laietana 11, 08003
Tel: 317 59 43
Metro: Urquinaona (L1, L4)

Double room with bathroom and bidet, 4200 ptas
Double room with basin, 2900 ptas
Single room with bath, 2300 ptas
Single room with basin, 1855 ptas

'My favourite of all the hostals in the central area,' says a friend who spotted this while strolling back from a good lunch at the Restaurant Neyras down the street. There are very nice public rooms with comfortable armchairs, everything clean and with good fresh paint. The owners and managers obviously take pride in the Fontanella. The clients seemed middle class, no backpackers, no stacks of luggage left in the reception room. The communal bathroom was large, well tiled and pleasant with a big tub and shower.

It's a perfect location, five minutes from the Ramblas, six or seven minutes from the c/ Montcada for the Picasso and Costume (Textil) museums, lovely craft shops and boutiques around the corner in the Barri Gòtic, many excellent restaurants and some good cheap ones nearby, and just a short street down to the Cathedral and its delightful surrounding lanes. The street is noisy in the daytime but quiet at night.

Book at LEAST a month in advance, as this is a hostal well known to travelling Spanish business people who know the value of a place like this, in the very heart of Barcelona.

Roma (HS 2-star)

Pça. Reial 11, 08002
Tel: 302 03 66
Metro: Liceu (L3)

Rooms here are priced according to the number of people occupying them.
Room with bath: four people, 4500 ptas

Three people, 4000 ptas
Two people, 3000 ptas
One person, 2000 ptas
Room with basin, no bath: four people, 3500 ptas
Three people, 3000 ptas
Two people, 2000 ptas
One person, 1700 ptas

Note: Prices will probably go up about 10 per cent for 1992. Write to the Roma for information.

This is a real find, very near the Ramblas, on a big square which is always full of activity and people. It could be noisy, as there is always something going on in the Pça. Reial, even on a rainy evening.

The Roma is perfect for students or for anyone who enjoys being in the thick of the action. The Roma has a lift, and it occupies several floors, with a great variety of rooms. Some are big enough for a group of three or four people, some have baths, some are really quite small but adequate. And despite the location, some are reasonably quiet.

The big rooms are priced, sensibly, for the number of occupants. All the rooms we saw had good simple furniture, well arranged, so there was a feeling of space. Each room had at least one table and a chair or two. The linen looked good, the bathrooms were good sized, modern, very clean.

The people at the front desk were friendly, and both English and French are spoken here. Although they don't serve breakfast, we had the impression that a large group booking in together could make some arrangement for *desayuno* in the hotel.

Two of the rooms we saw looked out over the trees of the beautiful square, and one even had a balcony. Everything is painted white in the hotel, and it's well lit – rather a rarity in Barcelona hostals and hotels. The rooms which do not overlook the square, we are told, have good natural light and do not feel closed-in.

There is no laundry service available at the Roma, but the receptionist will tell you where to find the nearest launderette.

The Pça. Reial is a paradoxical spot: one of the city's most beautiful squares, sunny and open, lined on all sides with stately early-nineteenth-century arcades, dotted with palm trees, and graced by a fountain and a pair of streetlamps by Gaudí. It is also a sort of Barcelona Needle Park, its dim corners infested with dopers and peddlers. The cops have made recent inroads but don't expect it to be squeaky clean.

Don't miss the extraordinary 'museum' in the square, full of stuffed coiled snakes, butterflies under glass, sinister black insects mounted in shadow-boxes, a crocodile at ankle-level. Beautiful chunky semi-precious stones would make great paperweights – plenty of things for sale, but not, alas, the gigantic bear.

Ciutat Vell: Raval de Sant Pau

España (Ḥ 2-star)

Sant Pau 9-11, 08001
Tel: 318 17 58
Metro: Liceu (L3)

Double room with bath, 6150 ptas
Single room with bath, 3610 ptas
Prices include continental breakfast

This hotel is very near the Ramblas, yet far enough away so that its constant hum of traffic is muted. Bear in mind that this end of the wide street is quite near the harbour, and verges on the raffish, especially when the fleet is in. The hotel itself is perfectly respectable – but across the street is an establishment that calls itself, with graphic simplicity, SEX SHOP. With a big illuminated sign.

The great attraction of the España is its Moderniste decor: though much of it has been renovated out of existence, you can still find remnants of Domènech i Montaner's interiors and an immense sculpted fireplace by Eusebi Arnau. The hotel restaurant, located behind the lobby, is dominated by a delightful (and much photographed) turn-of-the-century mural: art nouveau mermaids. Since breakfast is included in the price of a room, you can gaze on them to your heart's content.

Everything is in excellent taste, and we liked the staff who speak several languages and are used to dealing with foreigners. There's an efficient, rather impersonal air throughout, which has its own attractions.

The hallways are large, wide and brightly lit, which is a pleasure, and all the rooms attractively furnished. The bathrooms are quite large and charmingly tiled. Telephones in all rooms, room service, a bar, a snack bar, and major credit cards are accepted. The price of rooms is quite reasonable, given the location and what they offer. This is a hotel that deserves its 2-star rating.

Peninsular (HS 1-star)

Sant Pau 34-36, 0800l
Tel: 302 31 38
Metro: Liceu (L3)

Double room with bath, 4250 ptas
Double room with basin, 3260 ptas
Single room with bath, 2435 ptas
Single room with basin, 1910 ptas

This hostal is a Moderniste extravaganza on the edge of the Barri
Xinès, the worst possible neighbourhood in Barcelona – tricky
enough in the daytime, and definitely a no-go at night. It's huge: 80
rooms set around an elaborate skylighted inner court, spacious and
airy, with a scattering of café tables usually clotted with students.
Word has flashed around from one tendril of the grapevine to the
other, and this is one of the best-known places for the young to stay in
Barcelona.

There's a lift, and a hotel safe where you can stash your valuables.
The Peninsular is not intended for long-stay travellers – more for
birds of passage. The rooms range from small to monastically small,
and the furnishings, to put it kindly, are minimal. Rooms facing the
courtyard have windows but not much light, though they are quieter
than the streetside ones, which are lighter, brighter and a lot noisier.

The Peninsular is quite fun if you don't mind the constant coming
and going, with a lot of chatter filtering up through the courtyard,
and the constant traffic in the c/ de Sant Pau outside. Everything's
clean, though with a slight smell of disinfectant. The concierge is
friendly, helpful and understanding. He'd have to be, to run this
kind of circus.

Breakfast is available at an exorbitant 400 ptas. It's much better to
go out and find a friendly café, not on the Ramblas, for coffee and
great pastry at about 175 ptas.

From the Peninsular, turn left and you'll come to the Ramblas, the
Boqueriā, the Liceu opera house, and the Barri Gòtic. But turn right,
into the narrow streets of the Barri Xinès, overhung with dripping
laundry, and you'll find yourself on the turf of the city's small-time
grifters and grabbers. Women in dirty bedroom slippers make you
all too conscious that while you may think you're a travelling pauper,
they know better: you're just another rich foreigner.

Ramos (H 1-star)

Hospital 36 (Pça. de Sant Agustí)
Tel: 302 04 30
Metro: Liceu (L3)

Double room with bath, 4000 ptas
Single room without bath, 2500 ptas

This is a very good place at the 'good' end of a street which tails off into litter and tacky shops at the edge of the Barri Xinès. The little plaça is in complete upheaval as we write – as are a lot of streets in Barcelona – while new gas and water lines and paving are being put down. But across the way is the very pretty church of Sant Agustí, and there's meant to be a lot of tree-planting next year. A quite posh hotel, the Sant Agustí, is just across the square.

Although a walk-up, the Ramos is on the *entresol*, a short flight up from the street door. It's very clean and the general feeling was that of welcome and a helpful interest.

'Looking forward to 1992!' said the receptionist in Castilian (no English here). Then, looking sharply at the friend who was viewing the hostal, he said, 'Americana? Inglesa?' Then – 'Inglés NO! FUTBOL!' Great gestures of repulsion and shaking of hands in the air, a display of temperament unusual among the rather reserved Barcelonese. As the Ramos is quite near the Ramblas which gets the worst kind of tourists, as well as some of the nicest, they have probably suffered from big sports events.

The rooms while not luxurious are compact and comfortable, the (smallish) baths are well tiled and the fixtures good and well cared for. The communal bathroom is neat and so clean it looked as though it had been polished one minute before. AND they take Visa and MasterCard.

The roar of jackhammers and shouting of workmen made it impossible to imagine what the plaça is like in 'peacetime', but the Ramos receptionist assured us that it's always quiet at night; although like all small enclosed spaces in Barcelona, the ever-present buzz of motorbikes goes on from 08:00 to about 20:00 six days a week.

Segura (H 1-star)

Junta del Comerç 11, just off the c/ del Hospital
Tel: 302 51 74
Metro: Liceu (L3)

Double room with bath, 3100 ptas
Double room with basin, 2700 ptas
Single room with basin, 1750 ptas
(No single rooms with baths)

A very pleasant surprise, this, when one of our hotel/hostal reporters was wandering around the rather raffish c/ del Hospital, near the Ramblas. A largish hostal in a quiet street, with a respectable feeling even though at one end you find the unsavoury c/ de Sant Pau and the Barri Xinès (stay out).

The Segura is run by a totally delightful man, Señor Ruiz, with a lively sense of humour and a liking for making bilingual jokes. Many package tour companies use the Segura, but respectable ones: like many hotel-keepers in Barcelona, the patron has a horror of English football supporters.

The new paint, potted plants, wide halls, and the radiance of light everywhere are very attractive, as were the youngish people staying there who all looked well contented. Some rooms have small balconies or look out over a terrace in the rear of the building. The Segura is VERY booked up, so write to them a month ahead for a spring or autumn booking, six weeks ahead if you hope to get in in July or August. Credit cards: Visa, Amex, Diners Club.

Ciutat Vell: Raval de Ponent

Aneto (P)

Carme 38, 08001
Tel: 318 40 83
Metro: Liceu (L3)

Double room with bath, 4500 ptas
Double room with basin, 3000 ptas
Single room with basin, 1700 ptas
(No single rooms with baths)

This pension is a surprise, located as it is just off the Ramblas in a street that seems to be at the beginning of gentrification. Parts of it as you walk away from the Ramblas are very scruffy and almost sinister. There are many run-down-looking pensions in the c/ del Carme; one mentioned in a recent guide book had such filthy stairs that our hotel reporter couldn't bring herself to go in.

The Aneto, however, is an unexpected pleasure. Although classified as a pension, its standards were certainly as high as some hostals we saw. It has a lift! There are some rooms with private bath! The people at the reception desk were welcoming, spoke some English and helped to piece together our minimal Castilian. The rooms, while not large, are sensibly arranged, with adequate cupboards (enough hangers in those we saw for a travelling-light wardrobe), good bedspreads and several blankets on the beds. In one of the double rooms we saw, the tiny bathroom – with shower stall, not tub – was handsomely tiled, had good, new, long shower curtains and two new towels. A single room with basin only was compact but comfortable. It's far enough from the noise and increasing squalor of the Ramblas to feel comfortable. There are Vespas and motorbikes all day long in the c/ del Carme, but we are told it quiets down at night. Get ready for a surprise: the Aneto takes Visa and Amex cards!

Ciutat Vell: Portal de l'Angel

Campi (HS 1-star)

Canuda 4, 08002
Tel: 301 41 33, 301 35 45
Metro: Liceu (L3)

Double room with bath, 4000 ptas
Double room with basin, 3000 ptas
Single room with basin, 1500 ptas

The entrance to the Campi is not very inviting, the halls and stairs are somewhat shabby, it's a walk-up, and the hostal itself is on the second floor (to Americans, the third). But this slightly run-down feeling is forgotten when you walk into the pleasant reception room which is decorated with prints and posters. The agreeable young woman at the desk was helpful: a lot of smiling, no English, but more than willing to help work out what the person with the sketchy Castilian vocabulary was asking.

We liked the rooms – which are large, giving you room to move around, not just turn like a waltzing mouse as in some 1-star hostals. The wardrobes are big, the furniture good and solid. And the bathrooms we saw, with the double rooms, were really extraordinary – real bathrooms, not merely cupboard-size cubicles. All the plumbing fixtures looked quite new and of excellent quality.

The c/ Canuda runs off the noisy Ramblas, and during the day there's considerable racket from small cars and the ubiquitous Vespas. At night, it is considerably quieter, although there is a constant murmur of traffic from the surrounding area. If you want to be in the throbbing heart of Barcelona, this is a perfect location. It's close to the Boqueria, a few minutes' walk to the Cathedral, and all around there are interesting streets.

Wander down to the Pça. del Pi for the street market, have lunch in one of the dozens of restaurants from grand to intimate. And don't miss the *xocolateria* Xicra, in Pça. Josep Oriol, for a cup of *xocolate*, like a hot melted Bournville bar in a cup.

After visiting the Hostal Campi we read the card the friendly girl had given us. 'Recommended for priests and nuns, Catholic families and people.' Could you ask for a better guarantee of quiet fellow-guests?

Noya (H 1-star)

Rambla de Canaletes 133, 08002
Tel: 301 48 31
Metro: Pça. Catalunya (L1, L3)

Double room with basin, 1500 ptas
Single room with basin, 1300 ptas

The Noya was mentioned favourably in a London newspaper in the spring of 1991, so we asked a visiting friend to have a look. She walked by it three times, unable to believe that such an unprepossessing building could be the one mentioned. This is her report: 'I nearly gave up when I found that the Noya was one of two cheapos in this same rickety-looking building. The stairs are narrow and grimy, the walls finger-marked, and you have to edge past backpackers roosting on the steps. It's a three-floor walk-up and my hopes dropped with every step.

'However, once inside the door it's a different picture: it's warmly welcoming, and quite clean with a fresh atmosphere. Lots of smiles, no English spoken when we visited it but considerable willingness to help with the fractured Spanish we speak.'

The Noya rooms are clean, minimally furnished, with clean basins and a communal bathroom that looked well kept. Take along an extra towel if you stay there, as the ones furnished looked thinnish. There are no private baths. This is a hostal for the young, adaptable and broke.

The Rambla de Canaletes is one of the noisiest and busiest streets, and when you step outside it's a commercial atmosphere with tacky shops, revolting souvenirs, loitering people. Some good hotels are nearby, and if you don't mind crowds and a lot of street thievery, the famous Ramblas of birds, flowers and so on are within strolling distance. *Patron*: Arsenio Gil Pastor.

Eixample

Ciudad Condal (HS 1-star)

Mallorca 225, 08008
Tel: 215 10 40, 487 04 59
Metro: Diagonal (L3, L5), Pg. de Gràcia (L3, L4)

Double room with bath, 4500 ptas
Double room with bath and three beds, 6500 ptas
Single room with bath, 2700 ptas

There is no lift to the Ciudad Condal, which is on the first floor (second to Americans) of one of the handsome buildings with decorative balconies dating from the early years of this century. C/ Mallorca is a fine street overhung with the big trees which give Barcelona its friendly and welcoming feeling.

Since the location is so superb, we tried not to be put off by the ultra-clean white-on-white ambience of the Condal, or by the cool and far from forthcoming response from the receptionist at the (white) reception desk.

To get information was rather like prying at an unwilling oyster. You begin to wonder if the result is worth the effort. However, once we'd got past the desk, we found the rooms adequate and well groomed. They were all grouped closely around the reception/

sitting area which had a couch and a TV. The receptionist told us 'no one ever comes to sit down and look at the TV', and by that time we could perfectly understand why. However, this lounge is big enough to sit down in and wait for friends, or consult maps and plan your day.

The rooms in the front which overlook this beautiful street will get a little more traffic noise than the ones in the rear, but it's a quiet street and at night the traffic is minimal. The beautiful Mercat de la Concepció is within walking distance from here, away from the busy city-centre streets, and we advise a visit: flowers and plants are arranged out on the street front, and since the market itself is completely unknown to tourists, it is wonderful to wander around in. You can collect everything you need for a snack lunch – or buy half a kilo of olives or capers to take home – or drop in to have a *bocadillo* (huge thickly filled sandwich), or a tortilla in one of the café-bars.

The double room we saw at the Condal wasn't very large, and the linoleum floors, although shining clean, were a bit clinical; the furniture felt spindly, there was a night-table just big enough to write letters, and a chair. Single rooms were small, and the quieter ones were rather dark. Bathrooms were, as usual in these big fine buildings that have been broken up into hostals, fitted with great economy of space into remarkably small areas. But they were perfectly functional and the plumbing looked good.

Here's another of those hostals to which we'd advise you to take an extra towel or two, as the ones we saw were adequate but far from luxurious.

There are telephones in the rooms and Visa cards are accepted, and there's a snack bar in the hotel.

The location is fabulous: halfway between two major Metro stops, almost at the Pg. de Gràcia. Although quieter than many main streets, the c/ Mallorca has good bus transport to the Barri Gòtic and all its delicious little rambling side streets. There are good restaurants nearby.

Din (HS 2-star)

Valencia 191, 08011
Tel: 252 12 00
Metro: Pg. de Gràcia (L3, L4)

Double room with bath, 5000 ptas
Double room with basin, 4200 ptas
Single room with bath, 4000 ptas

This hostal is in a pretty tree-lined street which is busy but not excessively noisy. Even the ever-present motorbikes seem quieter here, perhaps because the big trees help blanket their buzzing. It's only a few streets away from the Hospital Clinic, and we had the impression that quite a number of the clients had come to be near relations or friends who were in the hospital – therefore they tended to be quiet, not raucous holidaymakers.

The Din is just around the corner from the Rambla de Catalunya and the Pg. de Gràcia, very near Gaudí's Casa Battló at the corner of Pg. de Gràcia and c/ Arago.

A small lift takes you to the fifth floor (directions in several languages to help you on your way), and the staff of the hostal speak four or five languages between them. The reception room is small and rather poky, so the really big rooms come as a good surprise.

What's unique is that even the rooms without big windows still seem light and cheerful. A number of rooms have large terraces or small balconies, which would be lovely in spring or summer. The hostal is spotless, the decor is pleasingly simple, with white walls and red bedspreads. And the bathrooms at the Din are immense, clean, modern: well tiled and tasteful. Communal baths are shared by not more than two rooms, a big plus.

The hostal offers a laundry service, but the manager was nice enough to suggest a less expensive launderette nearby, and even volunteered that clothes could be hung to dry in the bathroom, or on a terrace.

Telephones in all rooms, room service, a bar, breakfast available (450 ptas in 1991, probably more in 1992). The Din is a delight, even though they don't take credit cards.

Fani (P)

Valencia 278, 08007
Tel: 215 36 45, 215 30 44
Metro: Verdaguer (L4, L5) or Diagonal (L3, L5)
(about 10 minutes' walk from either one)

Double room with basin, 1500 ptas
Single room with basin, 1000 ptas per day or 20,000 ptas a month

This is rather an oddity, as it is listed in the glossy Gremi book under the Pension heading. But our hotel reporter (who grew to know every nuance of classification in her months of covering Barcelona accommodation) was given the impression that it was for women only.

It's very cheap and clean, she says, and she liked the fact that you can stay for an indefinite length of time, paying by the month. It's on two floors, and a walk-up if the rather unreliable lift isn't running. There are 27 rooms in all, about 8 with double beds. The single rooms are small, with a narrow bed and wardrobe – bring some hangers of your own, she advises, and while the towels looked adequate you may want to supply an extra one yourself.

There's a large lounge at the Fani, with couches, tables and a TV. A pay-phone is available, but no telephones in rooms. Saving the best for the last: a communal kitchen is available for light snacks or breakfast; you are trusted to keep it clean and not to leave food standing around. A perfect chance to try some of those luscious fruits, prepared snacks, olives, and bread from the beautiful covered markets which enrich every neighbourhood in Barcelona. It goes without saying that the Fani is very popular and often full, so do write weeks before you intend to stay there. The woman who runs it is friendly and informative, and some English and French are spoken, but you'd do well to take along a good Castilian-English phrasebook. Write to Paquita or Maite for reservations.

Felipe II (HS 1-star)

Mallorca 329, 08037
Tel: 258 77 58
Metro: Verdaguer (L4, L5)

Double room with bath, 3975 ptas
Double room with basin, 3200 ptas
Single room with bath, 3750 ptas
Single room with basin, 1900 ptas

The Felipe II (fondly called the Felipe Dos) is in the Eixample, the 'extension' area laid out early in the twentieth century as the city spread out from the ancient walled *barri* in the centre. The neigh-bourhood is quiet, spacious, with huge trees bordering every one of the fine wide streets. There's a lot of traffic, but the sound is muted, absorbed by huge buildings and thick trees.

The hostal is on two floors of a beautiful building. A lift takes you up – but there's an eccentric twist here: you can't use it to descend. When you step out on your floor, you are required to push a button which sends it down to the ground floor for the next arrival. *You* will be walking down.

The Felipe II is family run, by kind people who have been there for more than sixteen years. They take wonderful care of their guests and have many repeaters.

Rooms, as so often in these fine buildings now turned into hostals, are compact rather than spacious – although a few of the double rooms are really big. Furniture is neatly fitted in, rooms have small bedside/writing tables, small chests of drawers, good cupboard space. The bathrooms are a triumph of space-fitting: narrow, func-tional, everything you could need including a glass shelf for tooth-brushes etc. The fixtures are modern, the water is hot, the plumbing works.

Communal bathrooms are equipped with a shower over the tub; there are, as well, separate lavatories with toilet and basin on each floor. In the cold rainy spring of 1991 we were very glad of the three wool blankets and a heavy bedcover. The light over the bed was adequate for reading a few pages before falling asleep.

The security at the Felipe II is very good: you ring the bell at street level, give your name, and are buzzed in. If you expect a visitor, give his or her name to the patron, who speaks French and some English, and he'll admit your guest – but no unexpected strangers get in.

There are no telephones in the rooms, but guests may use the one in the reception room and calls are added to your bill when you leave.

Except for the minor inconvenience of the one-way lift, there's little to criticize about the Felipe Dos and much to like. As can be imagined, they get heavily booked in summer, a month's notice is not too much. In low season (early spring, autumn, winter) a room can often be secured by a telephone call a few days or a week in advance.

Maria (CH)

Consell de Cent 470, 08013
Tel: 231 41 10, 231 86 54
Metro: Verdaguer (L4, L5)

Double room, 1700 ptas
Single room, 900 ptas
No rooms have private bathrooms

A good value guesthouse at really rock-bottom prices, if you're prepared to be somewhat away from the centre of Barcelona in an area which has not much to offer in the way of shops or markets or street life. The CH classification is below the pension level; that is, it resembles a large flat that has been converted into guest accommodation. 'Maria' is really a person, and she does speak English. She runs a no-frills guesthouse for someone fairly undemanding who just wants a place to sleep. It's usually full – even in winter – so if you are content with minimal accommodation, write several weeks in advance. The reception room is tiny with a few armchairs crowded together, but you probably won't be spending any time there so it hardly matters. Paint and plaster have seen better days, but the communal bathrooms are clean.

Bus services into the centre of Barcelona are excellent: Nos. 6, 19 (to the Barri Gòtic and environs), 50; and two Nitbuses (see pages 31–2).

Mediterraneo (HS 2-star)

Rambla de Catalunya 106, 08008
Tel: 215 09 00
Metro: Diagonal (L3, L5)

Double room with complete bathroom (including bathtub), 4500 ptas
Double room with toilet, basin and shower, 4000 ptas
Double room with basin, 4000 ptas
Single room with shower, 3500 ptas
Single room with basin, from 2000 ptas

We discovered this very good hostal when going up the delightful Rambla de Catalunya on a bus; the location is wonderful and the transportation exceptional with the Diagonal Metro almost on the doorstep. The elegant Pg. de Gràcia with its alluring shops is only one street away, and there's much to find on the Diagonal which intersects it here. A wealth of banks just down the street, and best of all, the obliging American Express office with its very low commission for changing money is close by (see Money, page 214).

The Mediterraneo has a lift, and there are telephones in the rooms and a laundry and pressing service. It's old-fashioned but comfortable. The paintwork could do with freshening up, but we liked what we saw of the rooms. A charming and friendly young man let us look around in a leisurely fashion. Some English is spoken. The street doors are open in the daytime but locked at night; the hostal felt safe. Obviously no street-thief was going to bother to take the lift up, ring the (locked) hostal door and say 'This is your friendly local luggage thief, let me in.'

Neutral (HS 2-star)

Rambla de Catalunya 42, 08007
Tel: 318 73 70, 318 73 78
Metro: Pg. de Gràcia (L3, L4)

Double room with bath, 3900 ptas (complete bath with tub and shower)
Double room with shower, toilet and basin, 3000 ptas
Single room with bath, 3800 ptas

This hostal is in a wonderful location, very near the Pg. de Gràcia Metro stop, and within a minute or two of all the delights of this area – yet not too near the noisier Ramblas which begin below the Pça. de Catalunya. It's a walk-up, but only one flight of stairs, and all on one floor. The lobby is dimly lit, but the furnishing is modern and attractive, and there's a place to sit, not always the case in hostals. The staff speak English and some French, and are friendly and willing to put up with any attempts at Castilian.

There are telephones in each room – a real convenience. While no laundry service is provided, the receptionist kindly told our hotel scout where to find a launderette a few streets away. Breakfast (coffee and pastries) is available at a cost of 318 ptas, but as you probably have gathered by now, we advise you to find a neighbourhood café where you can observe the local residents, read your paper, and spend about half as much.

The rooms at the Neutral have high ceilings, with interesting mouldings and medallions, obviously left over from the building's previous life. There's a clean and well-kept air everywhere. The furnishings are fairly standard, lights in rooms rather dim and not for prolonged reading or writing. All in all, you'll probably choose to stay at the Neutral for its fine location and nearness to everything the city offers, and for its reasonable rates.

Note: The Gremi official hotel book shows the Neutral as providing both double and single rooms with basin, no bath, but unless our notes are faulty, we have the impression that all rooms have baths – which usually means shower/toilet/basin, but in one case with an actual tub.

Oliva (HS 1-star)

Pg. de Gràcia 32, 08007
Tel: 317 50 87, 317 52 99
Metro: Pg. de Gràcia (L3, L4)

Double room with bath, 4400 ptas
Double room with basin, 3330 ptas
Single room with basin, 1750 ptas

'This is my favourite!' exclaimed our hotel scout, who was understandably becoming a little jaded after snooping in and out of dozens of possible hotels/hostals/pensions. Her enthusiasm was confirmed by a London friend who was able to get a booking in this delightful hostal at very short notice in March 1991. It's an unbelievably good location, on the top floor of a handsome building, with a pretty lift which actually has a bench and looking-glass.

You enter the building and find yourself in a sort of atrium. The lift takes you to a remarkably attractive reception area, well lit. Little English is spoken, but good French. The charming woman who runs the Oliva is very protective of her guests' privacy – it took some wheedling to allow us to see a room which was just in the process of being vacated.

The overall feeling of light, glossy cleanliness and great charm makes you wonder why this is a 1-star and not a 2-star hostal. Possibly it's because they haven't as many rooms with private baths as some other attractive hostals we've seen?

Linen is crisp, huge wardrobes have a country feeling, furniture is massive and comfortable, rooms are really big. To get one of the rooms with a complete bath, you must choose to stay in the back of the hostal, not as sunny as the front but quieter. There's no public sitting room, and no phones in rooms, but those are minor drawbacks.

Incidentally, the double rooms are so big that they can be 'family' rooms with extra beds or cots for children, which is a real money-saver.

Obviously, since the Oliva is so delightful, it's popular. Usually one must reserve two–three weeks in advance in spring and autumn, a good month ahead for summer. *Patron*: Claustro Cases Oliva.

Palacios (HS 2-star)

Gran Via 629 bis, 08010
Tel: 307 37 92
Metro: Pg. de Gràcia (L3, L4)

Double room with bath, 3500 ptas
Double room with basin, 3200 ptas
Single room with bath, 2500 ptas
Single room with basin, 2300 ptas

Here's an odd one: a 2-star hostal which at first glance looks like a garage! After you're buzzed in, you find you are among cars parked on the ground floor. You wonder if you're in the wrong place. This block of the Gran Via (it does have a full and rather pompous name, but is always spoken of and written with just those two words), has few of the pretty and interesting shops which you may have seen as you approached it. In fact, this stretch of the street is quite sterile and seems to offer little, but it's very close to the beautiful Pg. de Gràcia which provides you with all the window-shopping anyone could want.

There's a lift to take you to the door of the hostal which, like so many of this classification, is located on the upper floors of a commercial building. The interior of the Hostal Palacios is dim; but if you look further you find a sitting room with sofas and chairs and a TV, all part of the reception area. The rooms overlooking the Gran Via have more daylight, but could be noisy, as traffic never seems to stop until late at night. The quieter rooms, in the rear of the building, are not very light, if that matters to you. Furnishing is uninspired but comfortable enough, and wardrobe space adequate.

We were courteously received, but found that no one speaks more than a few words of English, so arm yourself with a good Castilian/English phrasebook if you choose to stay here. There are no private phones in rooms – you must ask the receptionist to let you phone. Although we are told there is a pay-phone in the hotel we didn't see it. Laundry service is available on request. The rates are very reasonable, considering the location – and they take Visa cards.

Windsor (HS 2-star)

Rambla de Catalunya 84, 08008
Tel: 215 11 98
Metro: Pg. de Gràcia (L3, L4)

Double room with bath, 4900 ptas
Double room with basin, 4000 ptas
Single room with bath, 2800 ptas
Single room with basin, 2200 ptas

This is a fabulous location, and the rates are very moderate for this well-equipped and hospitable hostal. There's a lift to the second floor where you are greeted in a small reception room with a marble counter-top, and some pretty and elegant touches. A good feature is a small sitting room with TV, comfortable chairs, and carpeted floors which make for a quiet atmosphere.

Several languages are spoken, including fair English, and everyone we saw was easy to talk to and smiled rather a lot.

The Hostal Windsor has a variety of rooms to choose from: with or without bath, some more spacious than others. There are no telephones in rooms. One room, at the back of the hotel, was notably quiet and had a small terrace. Two of the front rooms we saw were large and very pleasant. We have to say that one of the front rooms with its own bathroom had the smallest shower stall we've ever seen. And if you were in one smallish front room without a private bath, you'd be practically in the main reception area as you crossed to the communal bath.

Everything was beautifully clean, cosy, with soft lights and muted colours which were restful to the eye. We had the impression that three people could occupy a double room, with an extra bed, without the price being pushed up – but check this if you are travelling in a group or *en famille*.

The Pg. de Gràcia is perfect for shopping; there are many good restaurants not far away; the Metro is nearby; you can drop in to the delicious little Museu del Perfum down the street; banks are thick on the ground; and it's perfect strolling-and-looking terrain – you're a brisk walk (or a couple of Metro stops) from the street life of the Ramblas and the Boqueria. You're in a ritzy part of the city when you step out from the Windsor to start your Barcelona day. Book weeks in advance and specify the front rooms if light is important to you.

Gràcia

Bonavista (HS 1-star)

Bonavista 21, 08012
Tel: 237 37 57
Metro: Diagonal (L3, L5)

Double room with bath, 2548 ptas
Double room with basin, 1981 ptas
Single room with basin, 1415 ptas

The c/ Bonavista is a two-way street and therefore slightly wider and noisier than most streets in the villagey Gràcia area. This charming hostal has no lift: you walk up one flight to a big entrance hall with marble floors and pretty furnishings. It's quite small, only 9 rooms, and there's a very cosy domestic feeling here.

'A good place to settle in and get to know the Gràcia,' was the reaction of a friend who stayed there for four days of her two-week stay in Barcelona. She moved on to a larger, more expensive, less atmospheric hostal only because the Bonavista couldn't let her stay longer. They tend to get quite booked up, as a number of French and German travellers know about it.

The rates are low for what it offers, the rooms comfortable even if not large. No single rooms have baths, but if you are travelling alone it's really worth paying the double-room rate in order to have the advantages of privacy, convenience, a shower-tray over which to hang your drip-dry shirts or tights.

The patronne whom we met was sweet and friendly, and some attempt is made at speaking English. Book about a month in advance, especially in the summer.

Cartuja (HS 2-star)

Tordera 43, 08012
Tel: 213 33 12
Metro: Joanic (L4)

Double room (very large) with bath, 5000 ptas
Double room with basin, 4000 ptas
Single room with bath, 3500 ptas
Single room with basin, 2500 ptas

This 2-star hostal is in our favourite Gràcia neighbourhood, where the streets are narrow and fascinating. You have only to step out of the door of the Cartuja to find little shops, snack bars, restaurants, small squares full of kids and dogs. Real life, in fact.

The Cartuja has no lift but it's an easy walk up: the reception room is a short flight up from the street. The abbreviation PARL which you see as you enter means 'Principal' – the main floor. Other rooms are on other floors. The welcome is friendly and interested, but neither English nor French was spoken, so get out your Catalan dictionary or Castilian phrasebook and be prepared to improvise with a lot of hand-waving if you get stuck. *Patronne*: Dolores Culi Fornells.

This is a hostal for sleeping in, not for sitting around, as they don't have a sitting room with chairs or TV for their guests – but who cares when the Gràcia is just outside the door? The rooms, when we were there, could have done with some repainting, but like all hostals of the 2-star class, the Cartuja is well cared for.

Lighting in this hostal is low, and really not more than adequate. Our advice to those who want to read a newspaper or write a letter is: find a comfortable, bright, local cafeteria and settle in with coffee, pastry, reading material, guide book, and writing paper before you set off to conquer the city.

Valls (HS 1-star)

Laforja 82, 08021
Tel: 209 69 97
Metro: Fontana (L3)

Double room with bath, 4488 ptas
Double room with basin, 4114 ptas
Single room with basin, 2150 ptas
Prices include breakfast

The Hostal Valls has only 9 rooms, and they tend to be booked up months in advance. When we looked it over, we quite understood why. The Valls is clean, simple, wonderfully friendly, it has a lift, there's a small dining room where you breakfast, and a sitting room overlooking the quiet street. It really IS quiet, situated in this staid and residential neighbourhood.

Many of the Valls' clients have obviously stayed here before. Some, we gathered, had come here to be near family members or friends mewed up in one of the two or three well-known clinics and hospitals nearby.

The concierge is friendly and speaks some English, some French, good Italian. The Valls has a 'family' feeling which we found most attractive. Possibly this is enhanced by the fact that they are not seeking to attract transient guests in and out in a couple of nights.

Reserve a room at the Valls well in advance, if you want to stay in a quiet, friendly and welcoming atmosphere. The nearest Metro is not very near, about 10 minutes' stroll away, but bus services are good, and the neighbourhood itself is interesting, a world away from the better-known parts of Barcelona.

Poble Sec

Abrevadero (HS 2-star)

Vila i Vilà 79, 08004
Tel: 241 22 05, 241 22 06
Metro: Paral.lel (L3)

Double room with bath, 4800 ptas
Double room with basin, 3500 ptas

Single room with bath, 3200 ptas
Single room with basin, 1800 ptas

We like the Poble Sec neighbourhood for its wide, tree-shaded streets, and its feeling of being a community. *Poble* in Catalan means, among other things, 'village,' and Poble Sec has a pleasant air of remoteness from the bustle of Barcelona's busier streets. That's why we were pleased to find a good 2-star hostal in such attractive surroundings. We liked, too, the warm-looking red blankets on a sunny cool autumn day, the simple furniture and the fact that rooms had writing-tables and ample wardrobe space.

The man at the reception desk was extremely agreeable and spoke good French and English. Even the rooms overlooking the beautiful street seemed quiet (and this on a busy day). The Abrevadero is very near the Parc Montjuïc, the sports centre of this sports-minded city – you could trot over there to jog, ride a bike, or participate in any of the many activities which go on all the time. For more about this fascinating park, see page 155.

We liked everything about the Abrevadero, including the telephones in the rooms, the cheerful bar with *tapas*, the restaurant – which we didn't try but will one day. Among other amenities, they'll park cars and if you are carrying anything precious you might want to know that there are individual strong-boxes available. AND they take Visa and Amex cards.

Note: According to the Gremi hotel guide for 1991, only some rooms, singles and doubles, are available with basin – but when we visited, we got the impression that all were so equipped. The Abrevadero is slightly more expensive than many of the hostals of the same classification, but for what it has to offer and for its prime neighbourhood, we consider it a find.

Metro Line 3, which serves the Paral.lel stop, is one of the great ones – Sants Estació only two stops away, Liceu and Urquinaona Metro stations very quickly reached, to take you to the Ramblas, the Barri Gòtic, and the Born area.

Barcelona (HS 1-star)

Roser 40, 08004
Tel: 242 50 75
Metro: Paral.lel (L3)

Double room with basin, 2200 ptas
Double room with three beds, 3300 ptas
Single room with basin, 1100 ptas

The c/ Roser hasn't as much charm as the nearby street where the Hostal Abrevadero is located, but nevertheless it's in the same charming villagey atmosphere of Poble Sec. Staying here, you're very close to the amazing great park of Montjuïc – the c/ Roser leads directly into it. A terrific place for people who like to exercise, our hotel scout was thinking – just as a whole bike team, with its bikes, came walking in! There's a municipal swimming pool in Montjuïc almost at the end of c/ Roser, wonderful gardens and walks. And the Olympic Stadium is in Montjuïc too.

The staff at the Barcelona are very friendly and forthcoming and were anxious to show every part of the hotel; they obviously had nothing to hide. They didn't speak English, just a little French, but it's probable that as Olympic year is just over the horizon, they'll take on more multilingual staff.

The Barcelona needs new paint and polish, the furniture is nondescript, rooms equipped with the minimum of what you'd need – a bed, a table, a chair, a washbasin. No rooms have private baths but the communal bathrooms are perfectly all right. When asked if laundry service was available, they pointed out the shirts and whatnot hanging on lines out the windows – in other words, they didn't care at all if their clients did their own laundry. It reminded us of hotels in Paris in the 1970s which were popular with students and backpackers, and you saw tights and shirts hanging everywhere to dry.

The Hostal Barcelona is very inexpensive and very good value – especially considering the area in which it's located. The Paral.lel Metro is almost on the doorstep, it's a short walk down to the harbour and the Columbus monument and the fascinating Maritime Museum; a reproduction of the Santa Maria is moored off the Moll Bosch i Alsina. The Liceu Metro station, for the Ramblas, is only two stops away on Line 3, and Sants Estació two stops the other way, very convenient for getting to and from the airport.

Coronado (H 1-star)

Nou de la Rambla 134, 84004
Tel: 242 34 48
Metro: Paral.lel (L3)

Double room with bathroom (tub and shower), 5618 ptas
Double room with bathroom (shower only), 4770 ptas
Single room with bathroom (shower only), 3180 ptas
Breakfast, 400 ptas

One of our more expensive choices, this hotel is in one of our favourite parts of Barcelona, Poble Sec, and only a few minutes from Montjuïc where a thousand things will be going on during the Olympic year. While the street is not one of Poble Sec's prettiest, the neighbourhood is full of interest. Since the Coronado is a hotel not a hostal, it has a lift and all its rooms have bathrooms, either with shower or tub and shower. In addition, every room has a TV and a telephone, and room service for drinks and snacks is available. There's laundry service and a bar.

The Coronado seems to be owned by the same company that operates the Alhambra and Abrevadero: it lacks the homelike welcome of many hostals we have visited, but it is well decorated and efficiently run. The reception room is spacious and well lit, with rugs, comfortable chairs, flowers and plants, a TV, and a table and chairs where snacks from the bar can be served. Breakfast, as is usual in hotels, is expensive. You'll probably find more pleasure in coffee and an *ensaïmada* in one of the many cafés nearby.

A double room with complete bath was of medium size, well arranged, with twin beds, a dressing table with a looking-glass, good chairs, an ample wardrobe. The bathrooms were new and spotless. English is spoken, Visa and Amex cards accepted. All in all good value, and in one of Barcelona's less-touristed areas.

Llopart (CH)

Concordia 44, 08004
Tel: 241 38 74
Metro: Poble Sec (L3)

Double room with basin, 2700 ptas
Single room with basin, 1700 ptas

Poble Sec is really a village, and the Llopart is a villagey hotel. It's almost primitive, you feel that it's a struggle for the owners to keep its 25 rooms going. While it's tidy enough, everything is quite minimal. Towels are about the size of a big bandanna, so either take along one of your own, or go straight to El Corte Inglés and buy one. For a shower, you must ask the manager, Sra Rosa Valls Martí, for the key. An American who looked at this guesthouse for us described it as 'funky' – interpret that as you will.

The Llopart has a restaurant downstairs, and a bar. No tourists have really discovered Poble Sec, although in 1992 it will become better known because it's at the foot of Montjuïc where a lot of Olympic events are going on. Even so, it will never be as well known as the area around the Ramblas. If you stay in this part of town you have a chance to eat where the locals do, experiment with *tapas*, get to know the people behind the bar in a good little cafeteria where you can drink coffee and eat luscious flaky pastries half the morning.

There are some excellent restaurants nearby (see page 115), and here you can eat well on the money you've saved by staying at the Llopart.

Elsewhere

Ballestero (HS 1-star)

Manuel Sancho 2, 08016
Tel: 349 50 53
Metro: Fabre i Puig (L1)

Double room with bath, 3390 ptas
Double room with shower and basin, 2900 ptas
Single room with bath, 2700 ptas
Single room with shower and basin, 2200 ptas

This hostal is in a very suburban part of Barcelona, on Metro Line 1 – a good 15-minute ride from the centre of the city, and about half an hour on one of several buses.

We have to say here and now that the managers of the hotel do not like English people – certain English, that is – as three drunken Brits wrecked one of their rooms to the point where it had to be completely rebuilt. This room was being reconstructed when our faithful hotel hound visited the Ballestero.

It's a walk-up but only one flight, on a busy street. The reception room looks more like a ticket office, as the man at the desk is behind a small glass sliding pane. The rooms themselves are quite adequate, with spotless modern bathrooms. Some rooms have balconies on the street, but for a quiet stay here we'd ask for a room on the back.

It's fairly inexpensive, and if you want to see how real people in Barcelona live, this could be a good choice – but otherwise we'd choose a more central hostal. No English or French spoken when we visited.

El Putxet (HS 2-star)

Ballester 13, 08023
Tel: 212 03 50, 212 01 01
Metro: Pça. de Lesseps (L3)

Double room with bath, 3595 ptas
Double room with basin, 3020 ptas
Single room with bath, 2170 ptas
Single room with basin, 1690 ptas

The Putxet is away from the centre of the city in a residential neighbourhood, yet accessible by very good public transport, and it's on a pretty, small street near the large bustling Av. General Mitre. There is no lift, and the hostal is on several floors; it appeals to the young and fit, of whom we saw a number when we were there. There's an attractive and homelike atmosphere.

The pleasant young man at the desk spoke English and French. We liked the rooms, simple and spare, with large wardrobes. A double room we saw had a really wide bed – queen-size, not the usual rather skimpy double-size. And the bathrooms were also good-sized, with pretty tiles and good lighting. There are telephones in the rooms.

Rooms on the back of the hotel are smaller, not as bright as the big-windowed ones facing the street. But the front ones do get a certain amount of traffic noise from the nearby Av. General Mitre.

A reasonably large sitting room on the second floor had chairs and couches and was well kept, with no brimming ashtrays or magazines thrown around.

Although there is no laundry service in the hotel, there's a *lavanderia* fairly nearby. If there are two of you, we'd suggest that you treat yourself to the inexpensive luxury of a bathroom – especially good at El Putxet – and take care of minor laundry projects yourself.

Good cafés, as always in Barcelona, are all around. Visa cards accepted.

Sans (H 1-star)

Antoní de Capmany 82, 08014
Tel: 331 37 00
Metro: Mercat Nou (L5)

Double room with bath, 3774 ptas
Double room without bath, 2500 ptas
Single room with bath, 2500 ptas
Single room without bath, 1651 ptas

You have to be willing to accept that the street is wide, noisy, and apt to be busy with traffic and lorries all hours of the night. But it's convenient for the Sants Estació. It has a commercial feeling, and we found the staff brusque, nearly unpleasant. It's a big 1-star hotel, with 76 rooms, on several floors. An English newspaper in 1990 gave it a moderately good report for cleanliness and convenience: from the nearest Metro stop, Mercat Nou, you can get quickly into central Barcelona, and Sants Metro and main train station are within easy reach for even more convenience. It has a lift, room service, telephones in all the rooms, and accepts Visa cards.

Travesera (HS 2-star)

Trav. de Dalt 121-123, 08026
Tel: 213 24 54
Metro: Alfons X (L4)

Double room with bath, 4400 ptas
Single room with bath, 2750 ptas

This 2-star hostal is situated in an agreeable residential neighbour-hood, out of the hustle and bustle of central Barcelona. Some rooms could be rather noisy, overlooking a wide, heavily trafficked street which cuts cross the 'top' end of the city from south to north. Side rooms in the Travesera will be quieter than the front rooms. It's clean and modern, with 23 rooms, everything quite new-looking.

Our hotel scout commented 'The Travesera reminds me of a small Spanish Holiday Inn, and I liked the efficient air of it.'

All rooms here have private baths, and they are very well designed and comfortable, with good linen, towels, bedspreads. Each room has a telephone, and there's laundry service available. If you want modern convenience and glossy cleanliness, you couldn't do better. Since the Travesera is well out of the centre of the city, you may miss having the glories of life in Barcelona at your doorstep – but you'll also dispense with the tumult. *Patron*: Manuel Ballo Catara.

Amilcar (H 1-star)

Amilcar 118, 08032
Tel: 255 30 42
Metro: Virrei Ammat (L5)

All rooms have private bathrooms
Double, 3113 ptas
Single, 1887 ptas

The Amilcar is in a very quiet part of Barcelona, ideal for those who want to be away from the wasp-swarm of Vespas and don't mind the rather suburban feeling which could be a thousand miles from the busy city. In fact, in Olympic Year '92, it could be a real haven of peace! It's not far from the rambling Parc del Guinardó, and the Metro stop is convenient for whizzing you into the centre of town. The tree-lined streets and pleasant residential neighbourhood are in 'real' as distinct from 'tourist' Barcelona.

If you stay in a neighbourhood like this for more than a day or two, the coffee bar people and news vendor recognize you and smile at you, though they seem to wonder what you are doing in their quarter.

The ambience at the Amilcar is friendly, and the general feeling is that of inexpensive luxury – perhaps because all rooms have private baths with showers.

But we have to say that, while the Amilcar is shown in the Gremi 1991 brochure with a photograph of a pretty room with tiled fireplace, handsome table and chairs, this proves to be a private living-space not available to residents. It is not typical of any other rooms. The room rates are reasonable for the amenities offered, but do remember that you will be somewhat off the map.

Bed and Breakfast

In 1992, many Barcelonese families are willing to offer their spare bedrooms, with breakfast, to visitors. While this is meant mainly to relieve the pressure on the city hotels during the period of the Olympics, it is probable that such facilities will be on offer before and after the Games. It's worth enquiring, as obviously it's a wonderful way to make acquaintance with Catalan families.

This list of organizations – set up to handle Bed and Breakfast accommodation in private homes – was given to us by the central Tourist Office in Barcelona. Write well in advance of your proposed stay. (If you must telephone, try to have a bilingual friend standing by to help you out. Some of these organizations have English or French-speaking staff – but don't count on it.)

Alobarna
Copernic 37, 1-er, 08021
Tel: 414 66 79; Fax: 414 66 55

Barcelona Bed and Breakfast '92
Sant Elíes 29, 6e., 08006
Tel: 202 20 53

Barnahome
Estació 10, 08880 Cubelles
Tel: 895 25 84; Fax: 895 33 75

Olimpic Advisors
Santalao 135, 08021
Tel: 414 40 00; Fax: 414 40 99

Search
Diagonal 401, Atc, 08008
Tel: 415 38 33; Fax: 415 48 24

Urbe '92 (B & B)
1 Consell de Cent 118, 08015
Tel: 426 26 77; Fax: 426 38 13

Welcome Barna
Dr Augusti Pi i Suner 12, Entl., 08034
Tel: 205 74 89, 205 52 56

For longer stays – studying, researching, or merely taking a long holiday in Barcelona – it is possible to rent furnished rooms in private homes, with or without breakfast by arrangement, through these organizations:

Barcelona Allotjament (B & B)
Pelai 12, Pral, 08001
Tel: 301 47 00, ext. 56

Habit Servei (B & B)
Muntanyer 206, entlo. 1-a, 08036
Tel: 209 50 45; Fax: 414 54 25

International Student Agency (B & B)
Trav. de Gràcia 8, Atc., 08021
Tel: 200 89 25

We ourselves have not seen any of the B & B rooms which will be on offer in 1992; none were available to be visited while our research was being done. We think it's a great idea, perhaps the only way you will ever get to know a Spanish or Catalan family. But we do suggest that when booking through any of these agencies, you ask them to be specific about what you will get, and – this is important – what part of the city it is in.

Get a good map of the city from the Spanish Tourist Office in London and check the location: you may not want to find yourself out at the end of a Metro line in Horta, for example, or in a flat in the more raffish end of town near the harbour. Ask the approximate size of the room, whether it has a bath, shower, basin, toilet: if you arrive to discover that you've been allocated the maid's room – and from the size of the bed she was a tiny little thing – with the only bath one floor away in the master bedroom, it will be too late to find alternative accommodation.

In any B & B arrangement, ask all the questions: Can you receive telephone calls or messages? Do you have a key to the front door AND your room? Are you expected to make your own bed? Can you use the washing machine if there is one? Do they provide only coffee and pastry for breakfast? Will the owners of the flat be there, or is it managed by someone else? Cash? Credit cards? Traveller's cheques? In our limited experience of Barcelona flats and houses, the bathrooms and lavatories are usually beautiful and present no plumbing problems; a lot of cleaning, polishing and brushing up goes on all the time. There will be no books in English, possibly some in French (but we've given you the name of a great bookshop [page 186] which sells second-hand English and American books, many paperbacks, very cheaply so you won't go mad for lack of bedtime reading).

Most people who will be offering B & B arrangements in 1992 will probably be middle class or even upper middle class, hence some English is to be expected, and probably good French. So you'll at least be able to ask what time you should appear for breakfast, possibly be invited to watch TV (in Castilian or Catalan), even allowed to make a cup of tea. But don't presume on your status as a guest. Spain is full of rather formal people. Let them offer.

Home exchange

Our family has made a number of highly successful exchanges of flats and houses over the years, in Paris and in the United States. It's wonderful: you stay in considerable comfort, with plenty of room to spread out, often with a garden or terrace, TV, stereo, sometimes with a car or bikes thrown in. No money changes hands. In return, the foreign family stays in your house or flat, feeds your animals, waters your plants, sees that windows and doors are locked at night, and so forth. Often, long-lasting friendships and return invitations come out of these exchanges.

All of our exchanges, except those done privately with friends, have been through Intervac, 9 Siddals Lane, Allestree, Derby. Tel: 0332 558931. There are other home exchange schemes, but as this is the only one we know personally – and it's been going for more than 30 years – we list it alone. Intervac will also list exchanges for young people and students for periods varying from one week to a whole college term.

It costs about £35 a year to list your name in Intervac directories, which come out in February, April and May. You provide information on what you are offering, where you want to go and when, how many people in your party, and so forth. It's the cheapest way we know to have an unusual holiday.

In 1990, our parents were offered five possible exchanges which included a villa just outside Barcelona, a studio flat with occasional use of a beach house in a Costa Brava resort, a 3-bedroom flat complete with weekly cleaning, washing machine and car – in exchange for their London flat with garden, car and two cats to be cared for.

In the Olympic year, many Barcelonese families, understandably, will want to be anywhere but in their home city, and they may want to come to peaceful England. Get your listing in early and try your luck. The best and most centrally located flats, of course, go quickly, so make your arrangements as soon as you can.

When you receive a reply from a potential exchanger, write fully in English (or Castilian if you can manage it); but rather than risk misunderstandings because of an amateur translation, stick to English. Many Catalans and Spanish read English or can find someone to translate accurately.

Exchanges and home hospitality for young people and students can also be arranged through Intervac.

Other home exchange schemes are probably very useful too, but we can write only about what we know. Subscribers are all professional people, and by the time you've exchanged half a dozen letters and phone calls you will all know each other quite well.

Youth Hostels

They're called *albergs* in Catalan, and there are only five in Barcelona. Places *must* be booked as early as possible, especially in 1992.

Verge de Montserrat
Pça. Mare de Déu del Coll 41–51, 08023
Metro: Vallçarca (L3)
Tel: 213 86 33
Hours: 07:30–24:00. Youth hostel card required.

Hostal de Joves
Pça. Pujades 29, 08018
Metro: Arc de Triomf (L1) or Bogatell (L4)
Tel: 300 31 04
Hours: 07:00–10:00, 15:00–24:00

Pere Tarrés
Numància 149-151, 08029
Metro: Les Corts, Maria Cristina (L3)
Tel: 410 23 09
Hours: 08:00–10:00, 16:00–21:00

Kabul
Pça. Reial 17, 08002
Metro: Drassanes (L3)
Tel: 318 51 90
Hours: 24 hours a day

Albergue Studio
Ptge. Duquessa d'Orleans 58, 08034
Metro: Reina Elisenda (FFCC)
Tel: 205 09 61
Open July, August, September only.
Hours: 24 hours a day. Youth Hostel card required.

Menjar bé (*Eating well*)

Catalan food

'Catalan food is like the Catalans,' writes Juanita Raventos i Cadaf-ach from San Felíu; 'straightforward, strong, sometimes rude and hearty, unsubtle, without pretence – full of character!' The cuisine may be distinctively Catalan but its sources are diverse: the Phoeniceans, Greeks, Romans, Visigoths, Moors, the French from the Roussillon across the Pyrenees, the Italians whose ships plied back and forth from Barcelona to the Ligurian coast in the seventeenth century.

With the Romans came olives and grapes – oil presses, wine presses, pigs driven across mountains and plains, lentils, white beans, wheat and the wild yeasts that leaven the bread. Garlic may have crossed in galleys with the Roman troops: as early as the first century mention is made of a sauce of pounded garlic, oil, and the lees of wine – a direct ancestor of *allioli*.

Oranges, rice, almonds, saffron, sugar, figs, delicate pastry thin as rice paper: Spain owes these to the Moors. Aubergines (*albergínies* in Catalan, *berenjena* in Castilian) most probably came up across the Mediterranean from Turkey.

The coast of Catalonia has always been blessed with fish and shellfish, from the miniature red mullet, baby octopus, fresh sardines and tuna, to huge shrimp very nearly the size of crayfish but sweeter and richer, not forgetting the greatly prized sea monster, the monkfish engagingly called *rap* in Catalan.

Some Catalan dishes translate fairly easily into Anglo-Saxon kitchens. *Pa amb tomàquet* – the all-hours-of-the-day Barcelona standby – can be made at home if you have access to good crusty French bread, home-grown tomatoes of the lumpy flavoursome Marmande type, or very good tinned Italian plum tomatoes. *Allioli* takes a strong arm, a mortar and pestle, extra virgin olive oil, and fine fresh garlic, and really has to be made by hand, not in a machine. Others present more difficulty: *botifarra*, the mildly spiced pork sausage of the region, is available in a few Spanish delicatessens in London but non-existent elsewhere.

Crema catalana is a kissing cousin to crème brulée, but with a very Catalonian flick of cinnamon. *Sarsuela* – the great seafood and chicken dish of Catalonia – is yours if you can lay hands on Arborio round rice, free-range chicken, really good spiced sausages, fresh prawns, rockfish, squid (available now in good supermarkets) and more of those richly flavoured Italian plum tomatoes that come in tins.

Romesco, one of the 'foundation' sauces of Catalan cuisine, is made in Spain with dried sweet-and-pungent *ancho* peppers – but a very good facsimile, according to Juanita Raventos, can be made with a combination of ripe sweet red peppers, one or two ferociously hot dried pimentos, the ripest tomatoes you can find. Scrambled eggs with wild mushrooms would be made with morels or ceps (*bolets*) in Barcelona; a very good version created by a Spanish chef working in London is made with oyster mushrooms and a few dried morels soaked in sherry, and finished off with coarsely shredded fresh Parmesan.

The classic source book is *Catalan Cuisine*, by Colman Andrews (paperback edition, Headline Books, £7.95). It's most seductive reading – a book to make you want to try everything from *Cargols Estil Porreres* (snails as done in Mallorca) to *Bledes amb Panses i Pinyons* (Swiss chard with raisins and pine nuts). Catalan food is not exquisite and alluring to the eye, far from it, but it's uniquely satisfying – as complex and challenging as the Catalans themselves.

Hand-to-mouth in Barcelona

The awful truth is that if you want to scale the heights of Catalan cuisine you'll need to line your pockets before you set out, or stay at home and master the art in your own kitchen. You'll find the traditional exotica of the region – duck with pears, quail in pomegranate sauce – only in cookery books and occasionally in unaffordable upper-crust restaurants, along with nouvelle cuisine variations on simpler Catalan fare. What you'll find in low- to mid-range restaurants is often very good but almost always very simple: grilled lamb and rabbit and pork *a la brasa*, rudimentary salads, ultra-fresh seafood unpretentiously prepared, filling rice and pasta dishes, pleasant variations on a theme of sausages and lentils, minimalist vegetables, basic sauces, plain desserts. Occasionally a mysterious combination of flavours will leap out at you: prunes in an indefinable marinade of alcohol and spices, or fried potatoes in a startling garlic sauce; but also you can find yourself in front of a familiar plate of thin grilled pork loin and matchstick potatoes, or a perfectly good *crema catalana*, and a terrible sense of *déjà vu*. For occasions such as this, a few suggestions:

When the opportunity presents itself, choose the unusual or the unknown. Take *anguilas* or *anchoas* (eels or anchovies) over 'easy' dishes of chicken and pork. Experiment with the infinite varieties of country sausage: *botifarra*, *fuet*, *sobrassada*, *llonganissa*. Look for dishes cooked in sauces – *sofregit*, *picada*, *samfaina* – rather than grilled or roasted plain. And a number of the region's simpler specialties do show up on the menus of unpretentious restaurants: *espinacs a la catalana*, *pa amb tomàquet*, *arroz negro* and *fideuà*, *mel i mató* and *recuit*; and *allioli*, the ubiquitous garlic mayonnaise, can transport mundane grilled rabbit or chicken to astral planes.

Take advantage of Catalonia's incredible sweet tooth. Pastries, puddings, fruit melanges and ice cream dishes can redeem the blandest lunch. The Menorqueña company, for instance, which provides desserts for restaurants that don't make their own, has taken a simple idea and made it sublime: a whole piece of fruit (apple or lemon or orange, even coconut) sliced open and scooped out, the insides combined with perfect vanilla ice cream and then loaded back into the shell and frozen. The neighbourhood bakeries can provide you with a staggering variety of pastry: fat *xuxos* like tubular cream-filled doughnuts; *panellets*, the marzipan cookies that commemorate Tot Sants, All Saints' Day; a range of *cocas* – crisp almond-topped pastries, including *coca cabell d'angel*, topped with sweet threads of candied squash; *ensaïmadas*, *trufos*, *biscoxe*, *galletas* of all kinds.

Go easy on *tapas*: they're meant as a snack, not a meal, and filling up on them can be tempting but expensive; enough of those little dishes of tripe and tortillas at 300 or 400 ptas each can amount to the cost of a proper meal. And be choosy about what and when you order: an *ensalada russa* – pasta, red peppers and peas bound together in oil and vinegar – that has spent the day on a sunny café counter can turn your liver inside out.

Unless you're feeling very rich or very finicky, ask for the *menú del día* at lunch. The choices will be relatively limited: several salads or soup or pasta, up to four simple entrées, bread, wine or water and dessert, but you can easily spend double the price if you order à la carte. The *menú* is rarely an option at dinner, so your best chance to skimp is at lunch. And if heavy late-night meals don't appeal to you, it's perfectly acceptable to order a series of starters for dinner, or split a *plat principal* (the main course) with your companion.

Coffee is a staple in Barcelona. At any hour of the day or night you can order a *café con leche*, espresso with steamed milk; *cortado*, a short version of the same, served in a small glass; a simple *café*, which is a single espresso, or a *café doble*, a double. Or you can raise the octane by asking for a *carajillo*, espresso spiked with *anís* or cognac. No matter how you want your coffee, you can expect it to arrive lukewarm. There seems to be no remedy for this.

Unless you've been called by God to work your way through the wine lists of the world, you can survive perfectly well on the house wines of Barcelona restaurants: the *tintos*, *blancos* and *rosés de casa* (or simply *uno tinto, si us plau*). Quite often you'll be brought the whole bottle, but you'll only be charged for what you drink. And what you drink will frequently be very good.

The eating day in Barcelona begins early and ends late. Breakfast (a *café con leche* and a *croixant* or *xuxo*) occurs as early as you like at your local café; a mid-morning snack of *tapas* or a *bocadillo* follows; lunch is between 13:00 and 16:00; a *merienda*, or afternoon snack around 17:00 tides you over till dinner; and dinner itself occurs between 21:00 and midnight. Restaurants and cafés keep hours to accommodate these demands; exceptions are noted in the reviews that follow.

To give the prospective traveller an inkling of what to expect in Barcelona, and to remind those who've just returned of its pleasures, we've included a number of regional recipes at the end of this chapter of restaurant reviews.

Barcelona Restaurants

La Ribera/El Born

Nou Celler

Princesa 16 or Barra de Ferro 3
Tel: 319 90 24
Metro: Jaume I (L4)

This very pleasant restaurant has two entrances and hence two
addresses: from Princesa you traverse the bar into the restaurant;
from Barra de Ferro you enter directly into the dining room. What
was warehouse space centuries ago is now split into two levels: white
walls, tiled floor, ancient dark wood, classical music played quietly,
and pleasant but not rapid service. The à la carte menu is printed in
six languages, which presages hordes of tourists – but all we've
come across in several visits are a few tables of rather genteel
French business people. The *menú del día* is 1200 ptas, and the food
is simple Catalan: an excellent pâté with black pepper; *mandonguiles*
(meatballs) in a good brown roux; *ous farçits* (stuffed eggs, slightly
devilled); *amanida catalana* (cold cuts, tomatoes, beetroot, onion,
lettuce); *conill amb allioli*, served with fries, hard to eat with any
delicacy but an irresistible combination of roasted rabbit and garlic.
Postres (desserts) include *music*, a little plate of nuts, raisins, and
dried figs served with Grand Marnier; *pastis de la casa* – choice of
almond, chocolate, or tarte Santiago; a big slice of light orange cake
with almonds; plus many others. Dinner à la carte including bread,
wine and coffee comes to about 3400 ptas. Closed all day on Saturdays and holidays at night.

Costa Brava

Via Laietana 32–4
Metro: Jaume I (L4)

A rather businesslike place in a fascinating neighbourhood, a network of narrow winding streets on the edge of the Born. For just
600 ptas, the *menú del día* (lunchtime only) offered a thick and
flavoursome peasant soup, *entremeses* (six kinds of good sausages

sliced thin), salad or *arroz a la Cubana* (an ingenious combination of rice, ham, fried eggs and deep-fried bananas); then grilled fish, hamburger (over-seasoned but tasty) with a fried egg and wonderful chips, or grilled liver; followed by *flan*, fruit (an orange or an apple) or rather horrible synthetic-tasting packaged ice cream. A quarter-litre of red wine or mineral water and bread is included. For an early lunch you can expect rather an empty café and somewhat inattentive service, but things get better as business picks up. Coffee here is *hot*, which is unusual in Barcelona, and very good, which is normal.

Taberna Santa Maria

Abaixadores 10
Tel: 315 36 52
Metro: Jaume I (L4)

The clientele is workers and shoppers in the Born neighbourhood, and the room is beautiful, with high arched brick ceilings, seasonal decorations of wheat or sheaves of flowers, copper pots, farm implements. A good lunch for 700 ptas included a big plate of *entremeses* (thin slices of cheese, sausage, ham, cucumber, tomato wedges and thinly sliced onion), or paella or chicken soup; then chicken *en samfaina*, a sort of ratatouille sauce, or grilled steak, or *callos* – slivers of tripe in a delicious spicy thin sauce. To follow the *callos*, the smiling waiter suggested fruit salad, and he was right: cool refreshing sliced fresh fruit in orange juice. The bread was crisp and the wine came in a big pitcher – at least a third of a litre. It's closed Sundays and holidays, and prices at night are à la carte, of course, and could be moderately high. But it's our current favourite of all the places in this attractive neighbourhood for a weekday or Saturday lunch.

Picasso Museum Café

Montcada 15–19
Metro: Jaume I (L4)

The very smart glass-walled café is near the entrance to the museum but not inside, so you don't have to pay the 400 ptas museum entrance fee. It's self-service, and the menu at 1500 ptas is short but offers good choices. One day recently, they were serving a first course of cannelloni or a choice of salads, including thinly sliced Catalan sausages with tomatoes; then grilled chicken breasts with herbs, *calamares romana* (deep-fried squid) and escalope milanese. *Postres* were *flan* or ice cream, nothing very imaginative but good quality. Bread and beverage included in the menu price: wine or mineral water. Open during museum hours, 10:00–19:00; closed Mondays.

Senyor Parellada

Argenteria 37
Tel: 315 40 10
Metro: Jaume I (L4)

This beautiful restaurant is an updated version of the old Barcelona favourite Set Portes, run by younger members of the same family. The room is old, slightly warehousey with a big skylight, elegantly decorated in soft yellow and grey, subtly lit. It is frequented by an eclectic mix of people: students, young families with children, art dealers, museum people, people who work in the fascinating Born area in which the restaurant is located.

The food is exceptional: try the gratinéed onion soup, completely unlike the French kind – it's creamy, rich and in the bowl is the surprise of a poached egg. Fish and meat are beautifully cooked: we had *magret ametlles* (breast of duck with potatoes) in a luscious sauce. You might choose from several versions of *canalons* (the Barcelona version of Italian cannelloni). *Postres* are, as usual in good Catalan restaurants, worth indulging in – even if you eat with monastic simplicity the next day; we limited ourselves (if you can call it restraint) to a simple orange ice cream, but were tempted by a cherry clafouti. A meal à la carte can cost as little as 1300 ptas if you're careful, but to be more realistic, count on spending 2000–2500 ptas. Open 13:00–16:00, 21:00–24:00. Closed Sundays and holidays. Visa, Amex, Mastercard accepted.

Barri Gòtic

Can Culleretes

Quintana 5, just off c/ Ferran
Tel: 317 30 22
Metro: Liceu (L3)

This is the oldest restaurant in Barcelona, and family run, which makes an enormous difference in ambience and service. It offers no menu, but an English acquaintance who dined there with her husband praised the green beans with mountain ham and olive oil, 500 ptas; *espinacs a la catalana* (spinach with raisins and pine nuts), also 500 ptas; *conill amb allioli* (rabbit in the luscious rich Catalan version of garlic mayonnaise), 750 ptas. A chocolate tart called *pastis de mus de xocolata* was 'indescribably good', 450 ptas. The room is quite beautiful and the crowd animated, well dressed. This couple considered that they had fed very well for about 1800 ptas each, including mineral water but not wine – which came only in high-priced bottles. They loved the atmosphere and the attentive service. Open from l3:15 to 16:00, and from 21:00 to 23:00, closed Sunday nights and Mondays – a very good place to go for Sunday lunch, close to the Ramblas and the Cathedral. Visa accepted.

Mercè

La Parilla (Grill Room)

Escudellers 8
Tel: 302 40 10
Metro: Liceu or Drassanes (L3)

A delightful old Moderniste restaurant in the Ciutat Vella: tiled walls, an open grill, a few curios on the walls, with very good but semi-expensive food. We had lunch à la carte: salads, *canalons*, a classic dish of *botifarra* and *mongetes* (white beans), half a partridge with potatoes; plus bread, water, wine and coffee: a total of about 3500 ptas for two.

Cardoner

Ample 46
Tel: 315 22 60
Metro: Jaume I or Barceloneta (L4)

A big bustling restaurant, light and spacious, full of old regulars
and families, especially for Sunday lunch, all treated like their own
family by two overworked but cheerful waitresses (who therefore
tend to leave obvious tourists in the lurch). A huge menu of traditional fare, and a three-page wine list which you can safely ignore in
favour of the house *tinto* or *blanco*. For some reason they seem to
stock a variety of brands of bottled water. There is no *menú del día*,
but the à la carte prices are down-to-earth and the food is good.
We've had grilled *sèpia* (cuttlefish) at 650 ptas; a tortilla of asparagus
at 475; a rare entrecôte of lamb, 1050; *botifarra amb rovellons*
(sausage with four kinds of mushrooms). Open 13:00–16:30 and
21:00–24:00; closed Wednesdays.

Agut

Gignàs 16
Tel: 315 17 09
Metro: Jaume I or Barceloneta (L4)

Agut is comfortable and cosy, well established, well known for good
food and moderate prices, and hasn't suffered from overexposure.
The rooms have high rustic beams and aged panelling, an odd
assortment of paintings of Barcelona and the harbour, the Ramblas
and its personages; old-fashioned parcel racks hang above some of
the tables. When we were there a little group of French visitors were
happily setting to, always a good sign. The service is quick, amiable
and attentive. And the food is great: traditional Catalan cuisine
prepared with enough extra attention to detail to bring it out of the
ordinary. Among the starters, *llentillas estoffadas* (a thick lentil soup
with several kinds of sausage), or smoked eel on thick slabs of toast
with an underlayer of tomato. Then a fricassee of chicken thighs
with prawns, perfectly sauced, or a plate of mussels in lemon and
garlic. And for *postres* an enormous *crema catalana* or *mel i mató*: the
fresh ricotta-like cheese of the country drizzled with honey. With
wine, water, bread and coffee, dinner for two came to 3800 ptas:

more than a pittance, but excellent value in Barcelona. Closed Sunday nights and Mondays.

Pitarra

Avinyó 56
Tel: 301 16 47
Metro: Liceu (3)

Pitarra was the pen name of Frederico Soler i Hubert, the first modern poet to write in Catalan – an early intellectual hero in Barcelona. The *rebotiza* above this restaurant was his studio. But that's only incidental to its charm: scrupulous service, lively client-ele, pleasant rooms, excellent food and equally excellent prices make up the rest. An enormous display of seasonal fruits and vegetables greets you at the door. The *menú del día* is only 750 ptas, and can include *fideus a la cassola* (a casserole of classic short Catalan noodles), *sopa de pescado*, *truita a la catalana* (an omelette with white beans and *botifarra*), *entremesas variadas* (egg, tomato, rice salad, and four kinds of sausage), *verduras* of the day (we had potatoes with white beans and *botifarra* – good), *ternera* (veal) *à la jardinière*, *merluz a la romana* (deep fried hake), *mandonguilles guisades* (a delectable meatball stew), escalope milanese *con pebrols farçits* (with stuffed green peppers), plus bread, wine or water, and excellent desserts *a la casa*: a huge *crema catalana* or a terrific *flan*, for example. The waiters are young, well trained and professional, and the patron takes an interest in his customers: for the most part a newspaper crowd and very animated. The *menú del día* doesn't arrive auto-matically with the à la carte list – you must ask for it – but it's well worth the effort. Closed Sundays.

Portal de l'Angel

Neyras

Julia Portet 1
Via Laietana 41, corner of Doctor Joaquim Pou
Tel: 302 46 47
Metro: Urquinaona (L1 or L4)

This is a very pretty place whose à la carte prices go swiftly out of reach. But they have two *menús del día* at lunchtime, of which we can report that the 850 ptas one had few but good choices. Wonderful fish soup, a delicious steak, and a big helping of *crema catalana*: bread is included but drink is extra, and we had the impression that wine was available only in bottles not carafes. By 13:30 the place was very crowded, so go earlyish. A *menú* at 1350 ptas offered wild mushrooms with tuna or fresh *taglialini* for a first course, then lamb chops, grilled fish and chicken, followed by a choice of sorbets or seasonal fruit. Again, drink was extra. Other possibilities, both extraordinary and out of our price range: *pastis fred de porros i llagostí* (a cold pie of leeks and shrimp). *Sopa de peix* (a fish soup) *amb formatge fresc. Rodanxa de salmó fresc amb mongetes* (white beans) *i salsa de fines herbes. Cuixes d'ànec banyades amb vi de Madeira* (*anec* is duck). *Rodanxes de rap* (monkfish) *amb ceps. Besquit d'avellana amb xocolata calenta.* Closed Sundays.

Raval de Sant Pau

La Morera

San Agustín 1, corner of Hospital
Tel: 318 75 55
Metro: Liceu (L3)

A pair of pleasant, light and airy rooms with a bar up front. We wandered in here for lunch because it's an offshoot of Taverna Can Margarit (page 115), which is one of the joys of Barcelona. The *menú del día*, at 750 ptas, offered some out-of-the-ordinary choices: for a salad, *arroz reina*, a rice-and-tuna concoction; then *orada* (sea bream) in a good red sauce, braised rabbit (a welcome change from the ubiquitous grilled variety), and a lemon and caramel *púding* for dessert. Closed Sundays and holidays.

Ramblas

Amaya

Rambla Santa Mónica 24
Tel: 302 10 37
Metro: Drassanes or Liceu (L3)

This is one of the restaurants that specializes in *cuina del mercat* – that is, whatever is fresh and good in the local market that morning – and its incredibly long menu changes almost every day. As the 'local' for the Amaya is the Boqueria, you know that their choice of game, meat, fruit and vegetables will be very good. The cooking is Basque, which makes an interesting change from Catalan food. It's possible to order half-portions, which allows a group of people to sample the big variety of dishes on offer: salads, *lentejas* or tortillas, *callos de ternera*. Don't be put off by the painted ladies who hang out in front of the place. Amaya is perfectly respectable, extremely popular, very well known. It's amusing to see worthy Catalan families brushing past the prostitutes without a glance. The lunch menu is 1350 ptas plus 6 per cent IVA; à la carte it can easily climb to 3500 ptas. But as portions are large and you'll probably be sharing, this isn't as expensive as it sounds. Open every day, from 13:00 to 00:30 the following morning, without interruption.

Xaloc

Les Sitges 6
Tel: 302 74 69
Metro: Pça. de Catalunya (L1 or L3)

A good *menú del día* is served for 800 ptas in this friendly restaurant off the very busy and very noisy Rambla Canaletes. The waiters are pleasant and the service good, which isn't always true in restaurants around the Ramblas. The satisfactory service may be because the Xaloc doesn't really attract tourists, but draws its clientele from the locals who happen to work in this very touristy area.

Xaloc offers Catalan cooking, and the menu changes often, as the owners decide in the morning while buying in the *mercat* what they will serve that day. We found gazpacho on the à la carte menu for 350 ptas; *esquixada* (a codfish salad) for 800 ptas; *bacallá amb salsa d'alls tendres* (codfish with green garlic sauce) at 1000 ptas; and an entrecôte of veal for 1200. There are cheaper restaurants in the c/ Sitges and in the c/ Tallers at the top of the street, some offering a *menú del día* for as little as 500 ptas – three courses with drink and bread, for about £3 – but in our experience places like this are offering little more than fuel food, the same every day, and quite dull. So Xaloc at a slightly higher price is a real buy.

The desserts here are excellent and offer more variety than the usual *flan*/apple/ice cream choices available on most lunchtime menus. Xaloc is popular with professional people, and with know-ledgeable shoppers who avoid the more obvious places in the Ram-blas. Women who have been buying their fruit and vegetables, fish and fowl in the Boqueria down the street often come here for lunch and to recuperate. An English girl studying in Barcelona reports that she found herself eye-to-eye, so to speak, with a plucked duck on top of a neighbouring carrier bag. Closed Saturday nights and Sundays.

La Taca d'Oli

Pintor Fortuny 25
Tel: 302 45 84
Metro: Pça. de Catalunya (L1 or L3)

Just around the corner from Xaloc, this restaurant looks from the street like any ordinary bar. But press on, says the friend who recommended it: inside there's an enormous room that can seat 140 people and often seems to be at full stretch. At lunchtime, there are many regulars from the offices in the area who obviously think the 800 ptas menu is great value. The Catalan cuisine at the Taca d'Oli indicates that they serve plenty of grills – meat, fish, rabbit, chicken – and that as usual in sweet-loving Catalonia, the desserts are exceptional. A la carte, the bill will probably come to about 1200 – 1500 ptas, which is still reasonable for the quality.

La Palmera

Jerusalem 30
Tel: 301 42 91
Metro: Liceu (L3)

Just behind the Boqueria, this is a good place to fall into for lunch when your feet are giving out and your appetite is sharpened by all that seductive food on display in the great *mercat*. The Palmera won't give you any surprises or very distinguished food, but you can have a *menú del día* at lunch AND at dinner for just 700 ptas. It's really good value, including as it does wine or water, and bread, as part of the three-course meal.

A friend who lunched there said that when eating in this kind of restaurant, she doesn't order one of the banal desserts but takes an apple or an orange if offered, then goes out and blows 200 ptas or so on a really *luxe* piece of pastry from a nearby shop, and eats it from her hand, crumbs scattering all over the street.

Keep it in mind for a day when you're economizing, perhaps after a 400 pta visit to the Picasso Museum. Closed Sundays and holidays.

Eixample

Can Soteras/Restaurante Diagonal

Diagonal 327
Tel: 257 49 39
Metro: Verdaguer (L4 or L5)

At various times this old-fashioned restaurant has endured hysterical bouts of redecoration, beginning with immense gilt friezes on a *mar i muntanya* theme – fish, fowl, and art deco Aphrodites – and ending with hideous 1960-ish light fixtures above the bar. The ground-floor dining room is deceptively small: the room is higher than it is wide, but there's an upstairs loft with extra seating and a downstairs banquet hall: we've seen plenty of well-dressed middle-aged, middle-class Barcelonese trooping cheerfully downstairs, and have never seen them return. Bridge clubs? Masonic lodges?

The service is *ancien régime*, the waiters amiable but never over-familiar, and all appear to have been here since the days of Primo de Rivera, napkin on sleeve, two serving spoons in one adroit hand. The food is unbeatable: *arroz negro* (a twenty-minute wait, which guarantees that it is made on the spot, not dished out of a day-old pot), *ensalada variada* (more *variada* than usual), *copa especial* – an extravaganza of ice cream, cake, fruit and whipped cream. And bread in the shape of snails.

Madrid-Barcelona

Aragó 282
Tel: 215 70 26
Metro: Pg. de Gràcia (L3 or L4)

If you wandered into this big old restaurant in its off-hours – the middle of the afternoon – you'd guess that it had seen better days and dismiss it as a has-been. The exterior is frumpy, anything but imposing; the long, cluttered bar is ancient steel; the walls might once have been white; everything is slightly frayed around the edges; even the waiters seem to have seen better days. But try to get in at lunchtime and you'll find it transformed by a horde of animated, excited eaters: an Eixample business crowd with high standards and long lunch hours. Lunch à la carte can run as high as 2500 ptas, but the quality is undeniable. The simple pleasures – grilled beefsteak or calves' liver with matchstick potatoes – are tender and cooked to perfection; but for transcendent food try *fideuà*, a Valencian paella made with short stems of pasta instead of rice, with shrimp and *rap* (monkfish) in a sauce of tomatoes and saffron: out of this world. Other specialities: *cervells a la romana, canalons de la casa, callos* (tripe) *a la madrilenya*. For dessert: *poma al forn amb gelat* (baked apple with ice cream). The kitchen juts into the dining room – a common phenomenon among old Barcelona restaurants – and you can see mounds of steamed spinach lined up for *espinacs a la catalana*, a pointed invitation to order it. Closed Saturday nights, Sundays, holidays. Amex, Visa, Mastercard accepted.

Tot Bo

Provença 373
Tel: 257 97 63
Metro: Verdaguer (L4 or L5)

The lunch menu at 600 ptas offered chickpea soup, *sopa de pescado, ensalada de arroz*, followed by pork fillets fried in batter and served with French fries, or *jambon asado, filetes de merluza*, or *bistec patatas*. Dessert was *flan*, fresh fruit (apple or orange), yogurt, *crema catalana*, coffee 70 ptas extra. A good filling lunch in a neighbourhood café that seats maybe 24 people: cheerful, prompt service.

El Gran Colmado

Consell de Cent 318
Tel: 318 85 77
Metro: Pg. de Gràcia (L3 or L4)

El Gran Colmado hasn't made up its mind whether it's a restaurant or a grocery. In either case it's elegant and inviting: a fine place for gazing, possibly to buy some small exquisite bit of food, certainly to have a meal. It's like Fauchon in Paris, but more accessible and less intimidating. Here you can buy 100 grams of tissue-thin *jamon serrano* (mountain ham), a handful of dried mushrooms, one black truffle, a bottle of wine for 600 ptas (or 6000), and such exotica as Jackson's of Piccadilly tea.

At the back of the shop you see half a dozen beautifully set tables with fine glasses and linen napkins. Here everything is à la carte, superb, expensive – meant for the well-to-do business people of the area, or shoppers at Loewe's luxurious leather shop down the street. In the centre, there's a long table set for about twenty people, and here you can have a wonderful lunch for 1400 ptas. The service is just as attentive as if you were the gentry at the individual tables. You have to put up with paper napkins, the plates and glasses are less luxurious, but everything is perfectly cooked.

Choices are few but distinguished: such as a creamy seafood soup with paprika, roast chicken, grilled rabbit in a fine sauce, deep-fried *lluc* (hake, whole, biting its own tail), an ice cream tart or chocolate-covered pears with mint for dessert. The price includes wine or mineral water, and good crusty bread. Major credit cards accepted for purchases in the shop part, but not for meals. Hours: 13:30–16:00, 21:00–24:00; closed Sundays and holidays.

Saler

Consell de Cent 314
Tel: 318 18 27
Metro: Pg. de Gràcia (L3 or L4)

The Saler is a seafood restaurant with a *menú del día* at lunch for 800 ptas. As you can imagine, it is very well known to those who work in the area and so tends to get crowded quite soon after its opening time. Get there at 13:00 and you'll find a table; wait until 13:45 and you are out of luck. There are two floors, and service is quite brisk without being overobtrusive. Those who eat here all seem to have happy and satisfied looks on their faces. Among the possibilities: a salad El Saler at 800 ptas; *crema de marisc* (a creamy seafood soup) at 625 ptas; braised asparagus at 725; *parillada de pescado* (fish

barbecue) for 2300; *mariscada* (a seafood extravaganza) 6850 ptas
for two; or *solomillo* (sirloin) at 1875.

As everywhere along the Mediterranean, those who love seafood
are finding that it gets harder every year to find fish that tastes as
though it has just been drawn from the sea and not the deep-freeze.
Most of the little fish restaurants in the run-down area along the
seafront, Barceloneta, have been washed away by the tide of urban
renewal, general upgrading of the area, and now the last ones are
clinging by their claws as the Olympic Village rises overhead. So a
restaurant like Saler is a find. Open 13:00–16:00 and 20:30–24:00;
closed Sundays. Visa and Mastercard accepted.

Gràcia

Cerveceria Lesseps

Menéndez Pelayo, at Pça. de Lesseps
Metro: Lesseps (L3)

This is a dropping-in place for *tapas*, sandwiches (*bocadillos*), and
snacks served all day long, from coffee-time in the morning until
late at night. In good weather, from April well into the autumn if
it's not raining, there are chairs and tables set outside. In our
experience, the waiters are kindly and will let you sit comfortably
with coffee or a glass of wine and snacks for as long as you like: a
great place for the fatigued and footsore. Sandwiches between 200
and 300 ptas, *tapas* 200–400 ptas; no *menú del día*. If you find, as
many visitors to Barcelona do, that you're sharp-set well before the
normal lunching hour of 13:00+, or beginning to starve at an
unfashionably early hour like 19:00, this is one place to make for.
Have a satisfying plate of four or five kinds of *tapas*, a beer or two,
and this will keep you happy until 22:00 or so when the more
patient Barcelonese begin to emerge for a real dinner.

For a plate of *tapas* and a beer, you'll spend about 600 or 700 ptas.
Tapas include such things as batter-fried aubergine, shrimp in a
spicy sauce, rice dishes, chicken wings, endless olive varieties, salads,
various pasta dishes such as cannelloni. A Barcelona-wise friend
advises having a couple of salad dishes first, then going back for hot
snacks which are microwaved on a plate for you in seconds.

The Cerveceria is a hang-out for people in the Gràcia, and for
students who meet their friends here, for young housewives waiting

to collect their children from school, for teenagers who come in for a drink and a snack after classes. Open 08:00–24:00; closed Saturdays (and probably Sundays in winter).

Flash-Flash, Truiteria

La Granada de Penedès 25
Tel: 237 09 90
Metro: Diagonal (L3 or L5)

Flash-Flash offers a plethora of omelettes (*truitas* in Catalan, *tortillas* in Castilian): vegetable, potato, cheese, fish, sausage, and mixtures of any or all of these. The possibilities add up to about sixty, plus another eight sweet omelettes for dessert: an excellent choice for a good light lunch or early supper. It's lively, noisy, crowded, and decorated with blow-ups of fashion photographs from the 1960s. At one time this gave a dated air to the place, but now with thigh-high skirts, pale lip gloss, and Mary Quant helmet-haircuts back in style, it's all very up to the minute. Prices run from 405 ptas to 1200; a hefty à la carte dinner could set you back us much as 2500 or 3000 ptas.

There are a lot of models swanning in and out, as many agencies are nearby, as well as an occasional photographer with black leather bags and tripods. Add to that many older, well-dressed gentry shopping in the smart surrounding streets, young working people nibbling at omelettes and picking up style tips from the models, and their bosses who neglect their lunch to stare at the beauties – an interesting mix every day. Open 12:00–01:30 in the *madrugada* – the early morning hours – seven days a week. A good choice for a Sunday lunch or supper. Closed on holidays. Visa, Amex, Mastercard.

Minerva

Minerva 6
Tel: 217 22 72
Metro: Diagonal (L3 or L5)

In the neighbourhood of c/ Neptù, a little enclave just south of the Gràcia, there are four or five expensive restaurants and one cheap

one: Minerva. We fell into it after recoiling from the prices elsewhere in the district. Minerva has a friendly, chatty waiter who
watches TV between courses. We had *judias con jamon* (white beans
with slivers of ham), a pâté *de casa* on toast, fine and spicy, sardines
and trout in a piquant red sauce, and salmon *ahumata* with lemon –
a Catalan equivalent of lox. Plus a lovely rosé by Tres Torres, and
flan and bananas for dessert. Cost: less than 1000 ptas. Closed
Saturday night and all day Sunday.

Batista

Córsega 337
Tel: 218 89 36
Metro: Diagonal (L3 or L5)

This old-fashioned restaurant on the eastern edge of the Gràcia
offers cloth napery and a slightly dowdy middle-class parlour
atmosphere, with prints of galleons and little oil landscapes dotting
the dining-room walls. Downstairs there's a friendly bar; the restaurant itself is half a flight up. We had enormous portions of
endivias a la roquefort and an *ensalada variada* of watercress and
endive; then *sesos a la romana* (brains, deep-fried) with lemon, and a
mixed grill *a la montaña*: rabbit, ham and sausage with *allioli* and
matchstick potatoes. Alongside, a good wine from a vineyard called
Sotofresno: the Ash Grove. And to follow, a truly lovely Catalan
dessert, *recuit amb mel i nous*: a soft fresh goat cheese with a layer of
honey and walnuts in a big eggcup. Everything came to about 4000
ptas for two, and the service was kindly and attentive.

Taberna Marcelino

Pça. del Sol 2
Metro: Fontana (L3)

Not exactly swanky, with no attempt at fancy dishes or decor, but
none the less acceptable. *Entrantes* (starters) are 225–850 ptas and
include *sopa de pescado, ensaladas* and such: a fairly tame salad costs
about 450 ptas. Grilled lamb chops (*cordero*) are 750 ptas, rabbit 650
– both with *allioli*, without which they would die of boredom. Served
with *patatas fritas*. A better choice might be *polpos alla gallega*: grilled

octopus with olive oil and cayenne. With wine for one of us and a *gaseosa* (mildly carbonated, semisweet lemon/lime soda, totally refreshing) for the other, and desserts, a very full dinner for two set us back 3750 ptas. It was dessert that did us in, both financially and morally: a *tarta Santiago* – a delicate almond tart served with a glass of fortified wine.

Cantina Mexicana

Encarnació 51
Tel: 210 68 05
or:
Torrent de les Flors 53
Tel: 213 10 18
Metro: Joanic (L4)

Two versions of the same restaurant, around the corner from each other, with pleasant rustic decor, a staggering variety of tequila on the shelves, friendly service, charming pottery plates, cups and bowls, and very good food whose only drawback is its skimpy portions. A chicken tostada, at 750 ptas, was about 10 cm in diameter and would have served as an appetizer. Fortunately they serve very good tortillas on the side, with a muscular salsa. Salads – an *ensalada mexicana* of lettuce, tomatoes, peppers, and avocado – are about 450 ptas. Other entrees include their versions of burritos and enchiladas, *truitas de blat de moro* (corn tortillas) stuffed with chicken and covered with molé sauce and cheese, tamales stuffed with pork and chilli, and plenty more. For dessert we had a refreshing *crema de mango*. Coffee is spiced with cinnamon, which will cause romantics to sigh and purists to recoil. Closed Sundays. No credit cards.

Sangita

Rabassa 37
Tel: 284 10 15
Metro: Joanic (L4)

Indian restaurants are making inroads in Barcelona, but most seem run of the mill. Sangita is exceptional: it's small, quiet, friendly,

simply decorated with a few Indian artefacts, and serves good
uncomplicated Indian food at very low prices. It's located just off
one of the prettiest squares in the Gràcia, the Pça. Rovira. We've
had *murghi mahkrani* – chicken in a gentle red sauce – at 600 ptas;
curried cauliflower at 450, Goanese chicken with coconut at 550,
chicken in a yogurt sauce, 650. Rice and parathas are about 200–
250 ptas, and there's a minuscule salad bar in one corner. Sangita's
cooking is refreshingly un-macho: no attempt to sear the tongue
with chillies. Open Tuesday to Saturday evenings 21:00 to 24:00,
and at weekends for lunch only, from 13:30 to 16:00.

Sa Lletuga

Mozart 4
Tel: 237 96 31
Metro: Diagonal (L3 or L5)

This Menorcan restaurant has charmed us from first to last. The
floors are red tile, the ceilings high and raftered, the walls white
bordered in bright green at the top and decorated with landscape
prints and maps of the tiny Balearic island. The patron – who does
most of the serving – is kind and attentive, and always seems to give
the right dish to the wrong person, without upsetting anyone. He
begins by serving a small dish of exquisite olives and little glasses of
gin and lemon to each table; the rest is up to you. A la carte, the
menu is priced at about 400–600 ptas for starters, 700–900 for
entrees, and includes *pebres* or *xampignons* or *tomàquets farçits de peix*
(green peppers or tomatoes with a delicate fish stuffing, mushrooms
stuffed with veal pâté), *formatge amb orenga al forn*, *macarronada*
(macaroni in red sauce), *llom de ses illes amb sobrassada* (loin of pork
smothered in soft Menorcan sausage), *mitjana xorigada flambejada
amb gin* (chicken in a sauce of langoustines), *conill amb pebres* (rabbit
with roasted green peppers). Plus very good bread and a bottle of
nice Rioja – all very wonderful, but what left our head spinning was
dessert, a *pastis de limón* – an enhancement on lemon cheesecake –
that redefines the word sublime. Or you might have a refreshing
sorbet of blackcurrants or (for the adventurous) *sobrassada amb mel*:
soft, spicy Menorcan sausage on toast with honey – yes, for dessert.

Rebost de la Plana

Braseria/Embotits
Gran de Gràcia 196–198 (Pça. Trilla)
Tel: 237 90 46
Metro: Fontana (L3)

The Pça. Trilla is a little oasis on the Granvia de Gràcia: nine palm trees symmetrically placed; the restaurant adorning a corner of the square. It's charming inside and out: a small bar at the entrance, a lovely garden behind. Two polite but inquisitive cats patrol the room. We had a quiet lunch here, beginning with an *amanida de toniya* (a tuna salad with red peppers), and *pollastre de pagès* – served 'farmer style', grilled with parsley and peppers, *allioli* on the side. Salads in a variety of dressings range from 350 to 500 ptas, entrées from 550 to 950: *botifarra de vic, tira de vidella, conill a la brasa, entrecot de vidella* were the choices. Open 12:00–16:00 and 19:00–01:00. Closed Sundays.

La Buena Tierra

Encarnació 56
Tel: 219 82 13
Metro: Joanic (L4)

A delightful warren of tiny dining rooms (including one with only one table and a window into the next room) that lead into a leafy garden in the back, roofed with vines. This is a vegetarian restaurant – but it doesn't carry health-consciousness to the point of blandness. It serves enormous portions of very good food, and at very good prices, with most dishes between 500 and 700 ptas. To give you an idea of the variety, along with perfectly seasoned large salads, La Buena Tierra serves *patatas salsa verde, sopa de cepolla gratinada* (a version of French onion soup), *blat de moro* (literally 'Moorish wheat;' actually corn) *a l'americana* or *salsa rosa, ensalada de agucate* (avocados) with *salsa rosa* or roquefort; then *canalons espinacs, porros* (leeks) *gratinats, endivias a la romana, espagettis napolitana* or *al pesto,* and *llibret de barenjena* – literally a 'book' of fried aubergine slices. Our salads and pasta were excellent, and the young woman who served us friendly and informative. Wine was expensive – the solitary drawback we noticed – so stick with beer or water. Open

Monday 13:30–15:30; Tuesday-Saturday 13:30–15:30 and 20:30–23:00; closed Sundays.

Ca l'Agusti

Verdi 28
Tel: 218 53 96
Metro: Fontana (L3)

A compact, unassuming place in one of the Gràcia's main shopping streets, two doors down from the Verdi Cinema – a trove of classic movies in 'V.O.', subtitled, not dubbed. Ca l'Agusti consists of a couple of rooms with tiled floors and marble tables, a teeming local clientele and quick businesslike service. The *menú* at 765 ptas is fairly standard, including an *amanida pequeñita* of grated carrots with raisins and lemon, or a very good *llentiles estoffades* (lentils in a sauce of ham and sausage); a plate of *verduras* (boiled potatoes and green beans); an excellent *vedella i rosillons* (tender veal in a sauce of big grilled orange-gilled mushrooms), or a *truita de toniya* (an unremarkable tuna-fish omelette); and a simple *flan* for dessert. Slightly more ambitious à la carte: *Amanida Ca l'Agusti* (a strange combination of lettuce, tomato, boiled egg, tuna and *embutido* – sausage!) for 775 ptas; *Amanida rapida* (tomato, onion, peppers, tuna, black olives) 425 ptas; or a *Ratllat d'anxoves* (toast with anchovies and chopped hard-boiled egg) for 525 ptas. Open 12:30–16:00 and 20:30–23:30; closed Wednesdays.

Niu Toc

Pça. Revolució 3
Tel: 213 74 61
Metro: Fontana (L3)

This restaurant begins as a bar and turns into a pale green dining room with a raised platform amidships, complete with piano and drumset. You can avoid the music at lunch (nothing begins until late evening) but you can't easily avoid the paintings around the edges of the room: the artist, when we were there, must have been blackmailing the restaurant owner. However, the food is good. We had *fideus* (the characteristic inch-long spaghetti of the region) in a delicious sauce of tomato and ground veal, and a *truita de pebres* (green peppers in an omelette), followed by *pastis de carn*, a fine meat loaf in a brioche-like terrine shell, with sautéed peppers and aubergine. Had we been more ambitious, we would have tried their *arroz negro* or *fideus negros*, rice and noodle dishes with squid in its ink. With dessert (peaches or custard on the day we were there), water, wine and coffee, the *menú del día* came to 750 ptas apiece.

Atzavara

---

c/ Francisco Giner 50
Tel: 237 50 98
Metro: Diagonal (L3 or L5)

This is a small, slightly bohemian and very casual Gràcia restaurant, run by two friendly women: one cooks, the other waits on customers, and together they create lovely food and a warm atmosphere. The room is long and narrow, a touch dilapidated but easy on the eye, with a changing show of contemporary prints on the walls – architectural drawings when we were there – and seats 20 people at the most. The kitchen dominates the centre, and if you sit at the bar you can chat with the cook.

Olives arrive at your table; then *petxina de gambes* (shrimps in their shells), *salmó fumat i succed de caviar* (smoked salmon in a roe sauce), *arroz amb salsa de rap* (rice with a sauce of monkfish), *farcelletes de vedella*, omelettes, a selection of *verduras* (including two kinds of spinach), five salads, three soups, a couple of pastas, very good wholegrain bread, all from about 450 to 1000 ptas à la carte, and all emerging from a tiny one-woman kitchen. Among the desserts is an incredible concoction of prunes in spiced wine, including, we think, lemon, coffee, thyme, rosemary, and possibly fennel. Atzavara has a high vegetable quotient: the more variety, the more likely there is some imagination in the food. It also has a pleasant and eccentric clientele. Late one rainy autumn evening – a slow night in the restaurant – we counted three of the seven customers humming along, at times alone, at times in unison, with the sentimental French and American songs that trickled out of the radio.

Cal Majó

c/ de l'Or 21
Tel: 217 48 26
Metro: Fontana (L3)

A lively, friendly Gràcia venue: the bearded, effusive patron seems
to be on first-name terms with all his customers, mostly a young
crowd. Two long, narrow rooms, joined by a servery in the rear,
well lit and very well air-conditioned (on cool evenings maybe a little
too well). When you're feeling overdosed on protein – when you've
had one too many meals of meat *a la brasa* – this is the place to make
for. A variety of big salads, *entrepans* (sandwiches of grilled big
bread), pâtés, and a few 'ordinary' dishes. Salads are enormous: two
can easily split an *amanida especial* – a salad of five sauces: from
vinaigrette or tomato-based to creamy cheese to a slightly bitter soy
dressing, with asparagus, sprouts, beets, carrots, lettuce as a vehicle.
We also had a pâté of *anec* (duck) with yellow peppers, fine-grained
and very good. Others were made with white wine or whisky, all
served on immense slabs of toasted bread. No *menú del día.* Hours:
19:30–01:00; no closing day. Credit cards: Visa, Mastercard.

Font de l'Estel

Francisco Giner 23
Tel: 218 14 19
Metro: Diagonal (L3 or L5)

This is a very large high-ceilinged room with a few farm implements hung on roughly plastered stone walls. With simple mission-
style furniture and tile floors, it has the look of a monastic refectory,
but a swarm of young, well-dressed and cheerful diners puts an end
to this impression. There's a 700 pta *menú del día*, available only at
lunch. We dined à la carte: an *amanida italiana* of fresh mozzarella
and tomatoes, oil and oregano was 490 ptas; then *fideus negros*,
which is pasta with squid in its ink, 850 ptas and the real reason for
our dropping in here: quite worth while. With bread, a beer, coffee
and tax, dinner set us back 1754 ptas. Closed Sundays. Visa, Amex,
Mastercard accepted.

Bilbao

Perill 3
Tel: 257 13 90
Metro: Diagonal (L3 or L5)

The Bilbao is an institution in the Gràcia, with a great convivial atmosphere. The air is thick with talk (and smoke). The lunchtime *menú del día* doesn't offer any startling choices, but it's very good value at 750 ptas all in: *sopa de verduras* (like a minestrone), *côtes brusellos* or *macarones* to start; *pollo rostit, pescadilla frita* or *hambourguesa* to follow, with wine, bread and dessert. If you're eating à la carte, it's easy to spend up to 2000 ptas, but for that you'll have a fine meal. We've tried mushrooms sautéed with young garlic; a thick and very rare fillet; rabbit in 'perfume' – predominantly thyme, subtle and delicious; wonderful bread; a wicked order of *lleonesas*: cream puffs in dark chocolate sauce. The menu is *cuina del mercat*, which means that what you get is what they liked best in their local (very good) market that morning. Open 13:00–16:00, 21:00–23:00, closed Sundays and holidays. Advice: get there promptly when the doors open at 13:00, before the neighbourhood crowds come swarming in, or have a *bocadillo* in a nearby bar and possess your soul in patience until 15:00.

El Glop

Sant Lluis 24
Tel: 213 70 58
Metro: Joanic (L4)

English-speaking travellers generally have been known to double over with laughter at the name of this very popular restaurant. However, the word *glop* does have a meaning: it's a sip or a swallow in Catalan. El Glop serves the traditional *pa amb tomàquet*, thick toasted bread smeared with tomato, olive oil and salt, with *botifarra, chorizos* and other traditional sausages and meats cooked on an open grill. Or you can eat more lightly, with big slices of tomato bread, served with cheese, anchovies, omelettes and so forth. Starters include salads – an interesting one is the very Catalan *amanida* of grilled aubergine with red peppers; or a lettuce, onion, hard-boiled egg and anchovy salad for 375 ptas; or a big dish of mixed olives, or a variety of hard cheeses or spicy dry-cured sausages. We've dined well and cheaply on grilled chicken, 500 ptas, and *botifarra negra* (black sausage), both with the ubiquitous bread-and-tomato embellishment. Desserts include home-made cakes – we had a *pastis de limon* at 350 ptas – as well as store-bought *crema catalana*, *flan* and Menorqueña frozen fruit and ice cream concoctions.

El Glop gets very crowded on weekend nights from about 21:00, so it's best to book for a meal after that time. Or go early – they open for dinner at a very reasonable 19:00. Open from 13:00–16:00, 19:00–01:00. Closed Mondays. They also have an annex (see below).

El Nou Glop

Montmany 49, torre
Tel: 219 70 59
Metro: Joanic (L4)

A less rackety version of El Glop, but only to be attempted if the parent restaurant is full. We had big slabs of peasant bread toasted and spread with *llonganissa* (a salami equivalent) or soft sausage, 325 ptas. A set of ribs (*asado de tir*) was 625 ptas, and *conill amb allioli* 425. To finish: *pressecs amb vi*, which is peaches in wine. Open 19:00–01:00, closed Tuesdays, Christmas and New Year's Eve.

Can Punyetes

Francisco Giner 8
Tel: 217 74 96
Metro: Diagonal (L3 or L5)

Like El Glop, also in the Gràcia, Can Punyetes offers *pa amb tomàquet*, served alongside grilled meat, traditional Catalan *amanidas* (salads) and plates of characteristically spicy Catalan sausages. Home-made cakes are good for dessert. It's very popular on Friday, Saturday and Sunday nights, so if you want to dine there after 21:00 it's best to reserve a table.

We are told that in the autumn you should seek out Can Punyetes for wonderful game grilled on the *brasa*, and a great variety of wild mushrooms from the local market.

At lunch, the average price is about 900 ptas; à la carte is as much as you care to spend. This pleasant neighbourhood restaurant is an offshoot of the original Can Punyetes, c/ Mariano Cubi 189. Both are open from 13:00 to 16:00 and 20:00 to 01:00; no closing day.

Restaurant del Teatre

Montseny 47
Tel: 218 67 38
Metro: Fontana (L3)

This spacious airy place is upstairs at the Teatre Lliure, literally 'Free Theatre', the home of an excellent Catalan repertory company. The room consists of a large open bar and a raised loft for diners; it's as big as a barn but subdued lighting and decor make it almost intimate. We have had some superb meals here. The menu varies often, as they announce that they cook *cuina del mercat*, always reassuring because it means that you will be offered what they considered the best choices in the market that day.

The *hambourguesa*, often thin, overspiced and overcooked in Barcelona restaurants, was perfect: thick, juicy, grilled to the right degree of medium rare, and best of all, pure beef with no minced onion or spices. If *conill a la mostassa* is on the menu, don't miss it – tender young rabbit in a sauce of mustard and white wine, with sautéed potatoes. Desserts are wicked; let yourself go to pieces here: exquisite lemon sorbet was our choice. The staff have a slightly bohemian look, are the soul of courtesy, and are happy to try out their English on you. The lunchtime *menú del día* is a very reasonable 850 ptas. A normal evening meal will cost about 2000–2500 ptas. Closed Sundays, Mondays and holidays.

Vineteria Verdi

Verdi 138
Tel: 415 39 96
Metro: Lesseps (L3)

This is, as its name indicates, a wine bar and restaurant – the amount of your bill will depend on the quality and quantity of the wines you choose. They range from very good and inexpensive

Catalan reds and whites from local vineyards, served in jugs, to the really fine wines that are making Catalonia's vintners increasingly famous.

Salads as starters are exceptional – try the one with crisp young endive, walnuts and local soft white cheese; it's called Groucho, for some reason. Or celery with blue-veined Catalan cheese and a spicy dressing. If *huevos revueltos con ajo* is on the menu, try it – it's scrambled eggs with young garlic tops, a very Spanish delicacy. Entrées are simple and thoughtfully prepared: we had chicken in a slightly peppery red sauce, subtle and delicious. The ice cream desserts, such as one made with rich creamy vanilla wrapped around dark chocolate and then rolled in toasted biscuit crumbs, are not to be missed (commercially made but very good – you order them by pointing at a colour photo). A dinner with a good, moderate house wine will be from 1000 to 1500 ptas – more expensive wines can bring it up to about 2200 ptas. Lunch, too, is à la carte only. Open 13:00–16:00 and 20:00–24:00, closed Sundays and all of August.

El Tastavins

Ramon i Cajal 12
Tel: 213 60 31
Metro: Fontana (L3)

The name means 'wine tasting', and as it indicates, this is a bodega – a place that decants wine from barrels into the customer's own bottle. It's a real neighbourhood place, with patrons who have been coming here since time out of mind. It stays open until 01:30, and is a centre for people who wander in for a glass of wine, some *tapas*, or a real meal.

The *menú del día* at lunchtime is 800 ptas, and offers fairly conventional Catalan food which varies according to what the owner found in the market that day. A la carte, you'll spend more money, but will have more choice.

The atmosphere of this family-run restaurant is casual, friendly, very typical of the Gràcia world.

Poble Sec

Can Margarit

Concòrdia 21
Tel: 241 67 23
Metro: Poble Sec (L3)

What once was the bodega – the wine warehouse – of a big old house in Poble Sec is now Taverna Can Margarit, one of the great pleasures of the neighbourhood. Enormous barrels and vats of wine still dominate the entrance hall: while you wait for your table you take a glass and drink whatever you choose, straight from the tap. It's disarmingly casual: the guests of the restaurant simply walk in and mill around. No one directs traffic and no one monitors your intake of wine. Eventually the patron herds you to your table in the restaurant proper, literally a barn of a room, with 6-m beamed ceilings, a few tiled wall surfaces, and wonderfully odd light fixtures: lanterns, illuminated glass grapes. Farm implements hang high on the walls. There's plenty of room for large groups at trestle tables in the middle and for smaller parties along the edges. The atmosphere is expansive and friendly, anything but solemn. The patron is constantly on the run, but always has time to chat with his guests. The room holds about 70 people and fills up, so make reservations before you go.

The menu is unpretentious but full of surprises. *Conill a la jumil-lana* (rabbit roasted with thyme, oregano, onions, whole garlic and salt) is a speciality of the house, and sublime. The same goes for *patatas al ajo cabañil* (sautéed potatoes in a terrific garlic sauce). We've also tasted a *pipirrana* of peppers, tomatoes and onions, grilled baby octopus, and lamb chops, all superb, and for dessert an exquisite *púding amb pressecs a liquor* – a confection of peaches, cake and brandy. Vegetables and starters – including the ubiquitous *pa amb tomàquet* – cost between 150 and 325 ptas; entrees between 700 and 1000 ptas, desserts about 250; but we've lately heard that prices have taken an upward jump. Closed Sundays and holidays.

Tres Xemeneias (Casa Jaime)

Vilà i Vilà 53
Tel: 241 30 78
Metro: Paral.lel (L3)

Casa Jaime is across the Av. Paral.lel from three looming abandoned smokestacks – one of the trademarks of Barcelona's urban
renewal process, which leaves intentional reminders of lapsed
industry in residential neighbourhoods. There's nothing at all
industrial about the restaurant itself, which is small, cosy and
charming. Here we had an absolutely delicious lunch of *anxoas*
(fresh anchovies) with *pa amb tomàquet*; a simple salad; a plate of
white asparagus with mayonnaise; an abundant *jarret de ternera*, a
joint of lamb, with potatoes in a succulent sauce. Total for two,
including wine, bread, water, coffee and tax: 4388 ptas. Closed
Sundays. Visa, Amex, Mastercard accepted.

El Settrill

Elkano 69
Tel: 442 82 67
Metro: Poble Sec (L3)

Restaurants in this neck of Poble Sec are few and far between. We
fell into El Settrill starved and footsore, and were rewarded with a
refreshing salad of red peppers and green tomatoes, 375 ptas, and
very good lamb chops (*mitjana de xai* in Catalan) for 650 ptas. El
Settrill is one of many Barcelona restaurants that cooks on an open
grill fuelled by firewood, and everything that comes off the *brasa* is
distinctively flavoured: it's like eating outdoors. Hours: 13:00–
16:00, 21:00–24:00; closed Sunday and Monday.

Pa i Trago

Parlament 41-bajo
Tel: 441 13 20
Metro: Poble Sec (L3)

This is a very typical Catalan restaurant, which means lots of grilled
fish and meat, good *entremeses* (starters) and spectacular desserts. Go
to Pa i Trago if you like hearty flavoursome 'organ meats' such as
sweetbreads, kidneys and liver, which are so neglected in England
and North America. The restaurant is decorated in rustic style, and
popular with business people at lunch and Catalan families who
enjoy fine traditional cooking at night. The lunch menu is 1500

ptas, which includes drinks and bread; at night, it's à la carte, and ranges up to about 2500 ptas for a three-course meal and drinks. Closed Mondays and holidays, so a good choice for Sunday lunch or dinner. Open 13:00–16:00, and 20:00–23:30.

Tibidabo/Pedralbes

Asador de Aranda

Av. del Tibidabo 31
Tel: 417 01 15
Metro: Av. del Tibidabo (FFCC)

The hills behind the city – Pedralbes, Sarrià, Tibidabo – are the lair of Barcelona's upper crust, and if you eat in these neighbourhoods you will pay upper-crust prices. Getting there is something of a project, too: you take a bus or FFCC (see page 30) to the Pça. John F. Kennedy, then walk up the Av. Tibidabo till you come to what looks like a medieval Moorish castle (it's actually Moderniste, built by a disciple of Gaudí, and is known as Frare Blanc, the White Friar, because it stands on the site of a vanished Dominican monastery).

Expect to spend between 3500 and 4500 ptas for a meal here, but it's money well spent. You will be offered fine Castilian – not Catalan – cooking, with superb grilled lamb chops, roast lamb, and dishes that transform mundane chorizo and morcilla sausage into cordon bleu fare. A specialty is *lechazo*, criminally young lamb roasted on a wood fire. Everything is beautifully cooked, and the setting itself breathtaking. In summer, you can have lunch on the terrace, among trees and businessmen. The dinner crowd is better mixed: families and couples. Open 13:00–16:00 and 21:00–24.00; closed Sunday night. Visa and Mastercard accepted; reservations necessary.

Elsewhere

La Bota de Raco

Av. Mare de Deu de Montserrat 232
Tel: 256 60 02
Metro: Guinardo (L4) or Maragall (L4 or L5)

It's best to go to the Bota in a large group, to share out portions of the enormous servings from one plate to another. If you are a twosome, you must both have huge appetites, or else be starving for dinner after a snack lunch, to get the most from this restaurant. They serve very good, very Catalan food, and two main dishes will cost you about 2000–2500 ptas – which works out much cheaper if you're part of a group splitting up the big servings. Open 13:00–16:00 and 20:30–24:00. Closed Mondays – so put this on your Sunday list if you can find a group of greedy friends to go along.

Recipes: Catalan food in your own kitchen

Mel i mató

The simplest sweet in Catalonia is undoubtedly the rich and voluptuous *turrón* – almond-studded nougat bars – of Xixona; the next easiest, and made in a minute, is soft white cheese with honey. Since you're unlikely to find *mató* outside Catalonia, substitute ricotta.

Serves 4
50 g (2 oz) pine nuts, lightly toasted under grill
300 g (11 oz) ricotta
100 g (4 oz) clear honey

Divide the ricotta among four pretty glass dishes, drip some honey over each, and top with toasted pine nuts.

 If you can't find ricotta, press good-quality cottage cheese through a sieve, rinse the sieve, and put the cheese back in to drain.

Escalivada

This most versatile dish is a Catalan cousin of ratatouille, with the tomatoes left out, and a freshness which comes from the relatively quick roasting. It is meant to be a starter course, but the quantities can be increased if you want to serve it as a vegetable with a bland main dish course such as cold roast chicken or tongue.

Serves 4, as a starter
225 g (8 oz) each of mild white onions, aubergines, sweet red peppers

100 g (4 oz) green peppers
A clove of garlic
Extra virgin olive oil

Preheat oven to 190°C (375°F), gas mark 5.

Put a little oil in a shallow dish and turn the vegetables over in it. Lay them on a large baking sheet and bake for about 40 minutes until soft. Remove and put the peppers in a paper or plastic bag, close tightly and let them stand for 10 minutes. Remove, peel and take out seeds.

Cut the aubergines and peppers into long strips; separate the onions into rings. Arrange them attractively on a serving plate and drip a little oil over them. Very finely mince (do not crush) the peeled garlic and toss over the vegetables. Cool.

Bolets al all (Mushrooms in garlic sauce)

Wild mushrooms are one of the delights of Catalonia – morels, ceps, *girolles* (chanterelles), often simply grilled on a charcoal fire under a light coating of olive oil. Oyster or shiitake mushrooms are now available even in English supermarkets and market stalls, and this very easy way to cook them takes only about two minutes. Serve them as a first course, or toss them into an omelette just before you fold it, and you have an approximation of *Truita amb bolets*.

Serves 4
225–300 g (8–10 oz) oyster mushrooms
2 large garlic cloves, peeled and very finely minced
3–4 tbs extra virgin olive oil
Small handful parsley leaves stripped from stalks, washed, dried, finely minced
1 small lemon, quartered
Salt, freshly ground black pepper

Wipe the mushrooms and slice if very large. Heat the oil and, keeping the flame high, cook the garlic and mushrooms, tossing them with a spatula, for about 2 minutes. Sprinkle with minced parsley and serve at once on hot plates. Serve with lemon quarters.

If there is any left (most unlikely), cool, cover, and spread on toasted French bread slices as a snack.

Sarsuela Barceloneta

Sarsuela (*zarzuela* in Castilian) literally means light opera, presumably, as Colman Andrews, author of the definitive *Catalan Cuisine*, remarks, 'the implication being that this is a sort of variety-show of a dish, not to be taken seriously.' However, given its ingredients and processes, it's not to be undertaken too lightly either. There are as many recipes for *sarsuela* as there are for gazpacho; some (which must have millionaires in mind) are made entirely with monkfish, some call for clams – very hard to get in England; one has three lobsters, one is made with crayfish instead. Colman Andrews flames his with rum, Jaume Barradas of Lleida adds anisette at the last minute. You see?

Serves 6
500 g (1 lb) firm fish – rockfish, redfish, monkfish – cut into
    serving-size pieces
6 large shrimps or prawns, unshelled
20 mussels, cleaned (see note)
500 g (1 lb) lobster, cleaned, cut across the tail pieces, claws cracked
Seasoned flour
Olive oil
2 cloves garlic, crushed
225 g (8 oz) squid rings
2 onions peeled and finely chopped
2 tomatoes, peeled and chopped, or 225 g (8 oz) (drained weight)
    tinned Italian peeled plum tomatoes
Bay leaf
Pinch of allspice
125 ml (4 oz) dry sherry
About 175 ml (6 oz) strained fish stock
Handful of parsley, washed, dried, leaves finely chopped
125 ml (4 oz) brandy
(Optional: *picada* sauce, made with 100 g (4 oz) white bread, cubed
    and fried in oil, blended in a food processor with 25 g (1 oz)
    toasted almonds and a large garlic clove, crushed)

Toss the fish pieces in flour to coat. Heat some oil in a large heavy saucepan and sauté the fish and the shellfish – except the squid and mussels – until lightly brown. Remove with a slotted spoon and set aside.

Cook the onion, garlic and tomatoes in the same pan, adding

more oil if necessary, until soft. Put the fish and shellfish back into the pan and reheat. Heat the brandy in a ladle or small pan, pour over the fish and set alight.

When the flames die down, add the bay leaf, sherry and allspice, and enough fish stock to come halfway up the dish. Simmer for about 8 minutes, add the squid rings and the cleaned mussels. Top up with water if needed.

Cook until the mussels open (discard any that do not), season with salt and pepper and sprinkle with parsley.

Provide each person with a deep bowl and put a large empty plate in the centre of the table for shells. Serve the optional *picada* sauce separately.

Note: mussels may be cooked separately, any that do not open discarded, the liquid strained and added with the opened mussels to the *sarsuela* just before serving.

Pa amb tomàquet

The essence of Catalonia: fishermen have it for breakfast, housewives eat it mid-morning returning from a bout of shopping in the *mercat* with a loaf of bread in hand, and a bag of ripe tomatoes bursting with juice and flavour. Tapas bars serve sophisticated versions of it topped with strips of anchovies, capers, artichoke hearts and translucent slivers of mountain ham.

The pure version for one person is just this: hefty slices of bread (*pa*) with (*amb*) tomato (*tomàquet*).

Two slices, thickly cut, of French or Italian bread, not too fresh, toasted
One medium-sized ripe tomato
Olive oil
Salt

Cut the tomato in half. Rub the bread on both sides with the tomato so that the bread is drenched with flavour. Trail a thread of oil over it, scatter with salt, lean over your plate, and discard your dignity: this is primal food.

If you can't lay hands on really flavourful continental-type tomatoes, don't settle for the tasteless red golfballs sold as 'rock hard salad tomatoes'. Instead, open a small tin of Italian peeled plum tomatoes, tip the contents into a sieve, drain off the juice, lightly crush the tomatoes with a fork, drain again, and press on to the bread.

Romesco sauce

You won't find real romesco peppers – sweet and mildly hot – in your market, but a very satisfactory version of this basic Catalan sauce can be made with a combination of readily available peppers.

Stir it into fish soup, serve it with poached or grilled chicken, put a small bowl on the table with any grilled fish, dollop it on to a hamburger, blend it with mayonnaise, try it with boiled beef.

2 large sweet red peppers
1 small hot dried red pepper, or a fresh red 'bonnet' pepper
2 large very ripe tomatoes, or 225 g (8 oz) tinned Italian plum
    tomatoes, drained
3–4 garlic cloves
75 g (3 oz) hazelnuts or blanched almonds
2 tbs red wine vinegar
About 100 ml (4 oz) extra virgin olive oil
Small handful parsley

Soak the dried hot pepper, if using, in water for 30 minutes. Handling it carefully, cut in half, take out the seeds, rinse well, dry and mince very finely.

Preheat oven to 200°C (400°F), gas mark 6.

Cut the fresh sweet and hot peppers in half (again taking great care with the hot ones), strip out the seeds and white veins, cut into narrow strips. Lay them and the unpeeled garlic cloves on an oiled baking sheet and roast near the top of the oven for about 20 minutes. The pepper strips should be brown but not black, and the garlic soft.

While they are baking, halve the fresh tomatoes, lay them on a sheet of foil one shelf below the peppers, and bake for 15 minutes. When cool enough to handle, squeeze gently to remove seeds, and peel. Tinned tomatoes should be lightly crushed and put in a sieve to drain.

Toast the nuts under a medium grill, watching them carefully.

Put the pepper strips in a paper or plastic bag, close tightly, let stand for 10 minutes. Then peel off the skins. Peel the garlic and chop coarsely. Put the garlic, peeled peppers (or the minced dried hot pepper) in a food processor or blender, and blend to a paste. Crush the nuts in a mortar or with a rolling pin between two sheets of plastic film.

Strip the parsley leaves from stems and add them with the nuts to the pepper paste. Blend well. Add tomatoes and blend again. With motor running, pour the vinegar into the paste, blend, and add enough olive oil to make a thick smooth paste. Season with salt.

Botifarra amb mongetes (Sausages with white beans)

Botifarra are pure pork, mildly spiced Catalan sausages, obtainable in England only through specialist Spanish grocers or delicatessens.

Failing the real thing, buy the best sausages, with or without herbs, you can find (Porkinson Bangers for choice, or those marked 95 per cent meat with as little filler of rusks and bread as possible). If you are within range of an Italian butcher or delicatessen, ask for fresh mild – not hot – Italian sausages.

Dried cannelli – white, long-shaped Italian beans – are often available in health food shops, and rather surprisingly, in Asian stores.

Serves 4
225 g (8 oz) white beans
4 large sausages or 8 small ones
1 clove garlic, peeled and crushed
Olive oil
Small handful parsley
1 medium tomato, peeled and chopped, or 100 g (4 oz) drained weight Italian peeled plum tomatoes
Pinch of cinnamon
Salt, pepper

Wash and pick over the beans, simmer in water to cover until tender. Drain. Gently fry the tomato, parsley and garlic in about a tablespoon of oil. Add the cinnamon and remove from flame.

Prick the sausages and sauté them in a little oil, or grill until medium brown and cooked through. Add the cooked beans to the tomato mixture and simmer for three or four minutes. Put the beans on a flat serving plate and surround with the sausages.

Lentil salad with lemon

Serves 6–8
350 g (12 oz) brown or green lentils, picked over, rinsed and
  drained
1 medium onion, peeled
3 cloves
3 tbs olive oil
1 tsp ground cumin
Salt, pepper
Small handful Italian flat-leaf parsley
1 large garlic clove, peeled and crushed
2–3 spring onions trimmed and coarsely chopped
100 ml (4 oz) lemon juice
1 hard-boiled egg white (optional)

To garnish: A finely chopped red sweet pepper and/or minced
spring onions

Put the lentils in a large saucepan and cover with water. Stud the
onion with the cloves and add it to the pot with the cumin and 3 tbs
of the olive oil. Season. Bring to a boil, skim off any scum that rises,
cover and simmer gently until lentils are tender. Pour off water and
throw away the onion. Let cool to lukewarm.
    While lentils are cooling, wash and thoroughly dry parsley. Run
through a food processor until finely minced, add the garlic and
spring onions, process again briefly. Scrape into a bowl.
    If using hard-cooked egg white, chop very fine by hand.
    Stir the lemon juice into the lentils and taste for seasoning;
mound in a bowl and scatter on the parsley and spring onion
mixture. Top with chopped egg white, red pepper and/or spring
onion rings. Pour on remaining oil.
    This salad can be made a day in advance and stored, covered with
plastic film, in the refrigerator.

Lenguado a la naranja (Sole with orange)

This is an elegant and worldly way to cook sole or plaice.

Serves 6
6 plump fillets of sole, skinned

Milk
Seasoned flour
2 tbs butter
1 tbs finely minced onion
150 ml (6 oz) orange juice
50 ml (2 oz) dry white wine
1 tsp grated orange peel
Salt, pepper
1 tbs butter, cut in slivers
1 large orange, peeled and cut in segments

Dip the fish fillets in milk, then dredge lightly in seasoned flour.
Heat the butter until it is sizzling but not brown, and cook the fillets
until lightly browned. As the fish is cooked, remove to a heated
platter and put in oven. Then wipe out the pan with kitchen paper
and add more butter.

Gently sauté the onion in the remaining butter until soft and
translucent but not even pale gold. Add the orange juice, wine,
orange rind, salt and pepper. Cook gently for 3 or 4 minutes. Strain
into a small saucepan and whisk in the butter slivers. Stir smooth,
then add the orange segments and heat for one minute more. Lay
the orange segments on the fish and serve at once.

Lenguado a la nyoka

Serves 4
4 small whole soles, skinned
Juice of one lemon
Salt and pepper
Seasoned flour
100 g (3–4 oz) butter
2 tbs olive oil
50 g (2 oz) sultanas
25 g (1 oz) pine nuts
25 g (1 oz) slivered almonds

Sprinkle lemon juice over the fish and season. Let it stand for about
an hour. Dredge with seasoned flour.

Preheat oven to 100°C (225°F), gas mark 2, and put a platter or
serving dish in it to warm.

In a large heavy frying pan, melt the butter with the oil until it sizzles, and sauté the fish, turning once, for about 5–6 minutes. Turn off the oven and put the fish on the warmed platter. Stir the raisins and nuts into the remaining butter–oil mixture and cook, stirring frequently, until the nuts are golden. Spoon over the fish and serve at once.

Pastel de natas y crema (Orange sponge cake with rum custard)

Serves 6
The cakes:
3 eggs, separated
50 g (2 oz) castor sugar
Scant tbs orange juice
Grated rind of one small orange
25 g (1 oz) plain flour
25 g (1 oz) castor sugar

The custard:
1 egg yolk, size 3
25 g (1 oz) castor sugar
Scant tsp cornflour
125 ml (4 oz) milk
Strip of orange peel
1 tsp powdered gelatine
Few drops vanilla essence
125 ml (4 oz) double or whipping cream
25 g (1 oz) icing sugar
1 tsp dark rum

Preheat oven to 180°C (350°F), gas mark 4.
Butter a 20 cm/8 in round cake tin and line the base with buttered greaseproof paper.

To make the cakes:
Separate the eggs. Put the whites into a large bowl and whisk to stiff peaks, then whisk in the orange juice and rind. In a smaller bowl, whisk the egg yolks with the sugar until thick and pale.

Stir about 2 tbs of the egg-whites into the egg yolk and sugar mixture to lighten it, then tip the egg yolk mixture on top of the egg whites and very gently cut and fold together.

Sift the flour over the bowl and gently fold together. Pour the mixture into two cake tins and bake for about 22–25 minutes or until the top of cake is firm to the fingertips.

Run a spatula around the edge of the cakes and turn out on wire racks. Sprinkle the top of one cake with the remaining castor sugar and set under a hot grill until sugar bubbles and begins to brown. Remove at once.

To make the custard:
Beat the egg yolks with the castor sugar and cornflour until thick and pale. Heat the milk with the strip of orange peel until it is almost boiling. Stir 2 tbs of hot milk into the egg and sugar mixture, beat well, then beat in the remaining hot milk.

Pour into a heavy saucepan and cook on low heat, stirring constantly, until the mixture is thick and smooth and coats the back of a spoon. Soften the gelatine in 3 tbs water and stir in to the custard. Add vanilla essence to taste. Stir then strain into a bowl and let cool until nearly set.

Whip the cream to stiff peaks with the icing sugar, and stir in the rum. Fold the cream into the custard and chill until almost set.

Cover the plain cake layer with the creamy custard, set the other cake on top, and chill well.

Patatas bunuelos

Serves 6
6 large potatoes (about 1000 g/2 lb)
2 eggs, size 3
25 g (1 oz) butter, softened
Oil for frying

Peel and quarter the potatoes. Cook in simmering salted water until soft but not falling apart. Drain well and return to pan, shaking them over low fire until they are dry. Mash until smooth. Whisk the eggs and beat them into the potatoes, then beat in the soft butter.

Heat oil to 190°C (375°F) and drop in the potato mixture by rounded teaspoons, half a dozen at a time. Fry until golden and crisp. Do not overcrowd the pan of hot oil, and keep the temperature up. Keep the *bunuelos* on kitchen paper until all are cooked and serve at once.

Peix espaza en safrà (Swordfish in saffron sauce)

Serves 4
750 g (1½ lb) swordfish steak, 4 cm (1 in) thick
3 cloves garlic, peeled
A thick slice of white bread, cubed
Small bay leaf
1 tsp parsley leaves
1 tbs olive oil
1 tsp saffron strands
200–250 ml (8–10 oz) water
To garnish: 100–150 g (4–6 oz) whole pitted green olives

Preheat oven to 175°C (350°F), gas mark 4.

Wipe and dry the swordfish steak and put in an oiled oval or oblong baking dish: it should fit snugly. Heat the olive oil in a frying pan and sauté the whole garlic cloves with the bread, parsley and bay leaf until the bread is golden. Remove bay leaf. Put the mixture in a food processor or blender and add water gradually to make a thin smooth sauce.

Pour the sauce over the swordfish and bake for about 30 minutes until the sauce is gilded and the fish flakes to the touch of a fork. Tuck olives around the fish and serve at once.

This can be made – even more extravagantly – with monkfish steaks.

Tapas Barcelona

While *tapas* – more than hors d'oeuvres or antipasto, less than a real meal – are not as typical of Barcelona as they are of Madrid, Seville or Granada, they do appear in many bars and small restaurants. They're marvellous as part of a buffet lunch, especially useful because they can be prepared well in advance.

One of the prettiest is *Ous romesco* – eggs in the classic mildly hot Catalan sauce. It will serve 8 as part of a tapas table. The recipe will give you enough sauce for the eggs plus a useful quantity to refrigerate and serve with steamed fish or chicken.

8 eggs, size 3, hard-boiled
2 spring onions

2 tbs flat-leaved parsley
2 rounded tbs mayonnaise
Pinch of salt
Dash of hot pepper sauce

Romesco sauce:
2 large sweet red peppers
3 tbs olive oil
2 small hot red peppers, or scant tbs dried red pepper flakes
2 tbs red wine or sherry vinegar
50 g (2 oz) hazelnuts or almonds, toasted
1 clove garlic, peeled and crushed
150 g (6 oz) tinned peeled Italian tomatoes (drained weight)
Salt

Preheat oven to 230°C (450°F), gas mark 8.

Cut the fresh red peppers into quarters and remove the seeds. Lay on an oiled baking sheet and bake for about 20–30 minutes, watching them carefully and turning over halfway through the baking time. Remove and put in a paper bag, close tightly and let them steam a few minutes. Peel the peppers and roughly chop.

If using dried hot peppers, carefully remove the seeds and mince. Put the fresh peppers in a food processor with dried chillis or red pepper flakes, oil and vinegar. With the machine running, add tomatoes, nuts, crushed garlic and salt, and blend smooth.

Cut the hard-boiled eggs in half and carefully remove the yolks. Press through a fine sieve into bowl and add minced spring onions, hot pepper sauce, mayonnaise and salt to taste. Stir in enough romesco sauce to make a firm mixture, and spoon or pipe it into the egg-white halves. Garnish with finely chopped parsley.

Store the remaining romesco sauce in a jar with a thin film of olive oil on top; tightly close the jar and refrigerate for up to a week.

Espinacs a la catalana (Catalan spinach)

Serves 4–5
900 g (2 lb) fresh spinach, or 450 g (1 lb) frozen leaf spinach
2 cloves garlic, peeled
2 tbs olive oil
25 g (1 oz) pine nut kernels
Salt, freshly ground black pepper

2 thick slices day-old bread, crusts removed
2 tbs butter
Scant tbs olive oil

Wash the fresh spinach very well and strip the leaves from their stems. Put it in a heavy saucepan with just the water that clings to the leaves, cover and cook on low heat until soft, stirring from time to time. If using frozen spinach, thaw with 1 tbs water in a heavy pan, stirring to break it up.

Drain the spinach very well in a colander under a plate, with a heavy weight on top; or press between two plates to squeeze out all the moisture possible. Chop finely (not in a food processor but with a knife). Drain again.

Crush one clove of garlic. Heat the oil and sauté the garlic until golden, stirring. Add the pine nuts and sauté one minute longer. Tip in the spinach and season. Stir and cook on medium heat for about 4 or 5 minutes, stirring often.

While the spinach cooks, heat the butter with the oil in a heavy frying pan until it begins to sizzle. Cut the bread into triangles and fry briskly on both sides. Lay it on kitchen paper to drain. Cut the remaining garlic in half and rub it over the bread quarters.

Put the spinach in a warmed dish and set the bread triangles around the edge.

Note: Arabella Boxer, in her *Mediterranean Cookbook* (J.M. Dent, 1981), has a recipe much like this, but adds a very Catalan touch with a tablespoon of currants thrown in with the pine nuts.

Samfaina

A Catalan cousin of ratatouille – infinitely versatile, as it may be served not only as a vegetable, but as a sauce with grilled chicken, poured into an omelette, stirred up with beaten eggs, or in one of the many ways suggested by Colman Andrews in his *Catalan Cuisine*. It can include aubergines or leave them out, be innocent of garlic or sweetly redolent. It keeps well for about four days with a thin layer of olive oil poured over the top, tightly sealed with plastic film and refrigerated.

450 g (1 lb) sweet Spanish onions
75 ml (3 oz) olive oil
2 large red sweet peppers, seeded

450 g (1 lb) aubergines
450 g (1 lb) courgettes
450 g (1 lb) peeled tomatoes, or drained contents of a 1 lb/400 g tin
   of Italian peeled plum tomatoes
2 cloves garlic, peeled and crushed
Salt and pepper

Cut the onion in half and slice very thin. Heat the oil in a large
heavy frying pan and gently sauté the onion until it is soft but not
brown. Cut the peppers into thin strips. If using fresh tomatoes, cut
them up roughly; very lightly crush drained tinned tomatoes with a
fork. Cut the aubergine into 1 in (2.5 cm) cubes. Add the vegetables
to the softened onions, stir in the garlic, turn over to coat with oil,
and cook gently for about 10 minutes.

Cut the courgettes in cubes and add to the pan, stirring well.
Season. Cover and cook for another 10 minutes until the liquid has
evaporated and the vegetables are soft.

Gambes en all (Prawns in garlic)

Serves 4
3 cloves garlic, peeled and finely chopped
75 ml (3 oz) extra virgin olive oil
675 g (1½ lb) uncooked, shelled prawns
Salt, freshly ground black pepper
Small handful parsley leaves, finely chopped

Heat the oil in a heavy frying pan and very gently sauté the garlic
until it is very pale gold. Add the prawns and cook gently for about
5 minutes, stirring often. Season, sprinkle on the parsley and serve
at once, with thick slices of French bread, or one of the coarse
Italian breads such as ciabatta or focaccia.

This is a perfect quick lunch or light supper dish. It can be made
with freshly cooked prawns – stirred with the garlic for 2 minutes or
less – but not, please, with tasteless frozen shrimps or prawns.

La Nit *(Nightlife)*

You can arrange to spend all your Barcelona time in bars (and unfortunately a visible minority of tourists do just that). They are all-hours, all-purpose settings: for stand-up coffee breaks, quick meals, informal meetings, recuperation from shopping, passionate kissing, profound reading, resolute drinking, and wild times in general.

Almost every street in the city has several bars, and all seem to be crowded at certain times of the day. Some open at 08:00, a few are serving coffee at 07:00 for early birds on their way to work. Mothers drop in early, children in tow, for a quick coffee and a *croixant*; teenagers frequent the bars at mid-morning break around 11:00, and swarm in again after school for a Coke and a snack. Older people linger over a *café con leche*, and enjoy the warmth and the company. People drop in to use the phone or consult the *Pàginas Grogues* (the *Yellow Pages*). For the traveller they're indispensable: a place to rest your feet, read the paper, park your shopping, make a phone call, look over the *tapas*, go to the loo, restore your energy with coffee and a drop of *conyac*.

Every neighbourhood bar serves *bocadillos* (simple sandwiches), tortillas, variations on *pa amb tomàquet*, and (usually) *tapas* throughout the day. Many turn into unpretentious restaurants at mid day, turning out quick simple dishes for the office crowd. Others of various degrees of elegance and exclusivity cater only to the late-night set. Some denominations:

Bodegas are technically wine cellars: they sell wine and spirits by the glass or by the litre, often from huge spigoted wall-mounted vats. They may also sell coffee and snacks or light lunches, and some, like Can Margarit, have evolved from private cellar to bustling restaurant. In the neighbourhood of c/ San Salvador, on Verdi and Alzina, the bodegas open at 07:00 for coffee and rolls.

Granjas are milk-bars – originally dairies – and specialize in coffee and light pastry, along with yogurt, *nata* (thick sweet cream), ice cream, *mel i matò*, *flan* and such; they may or may not sell alcohol, and since they cater to the breakfast and *merienda* (late morning or afternoon snack) crowd, they tend to open and close earlier than proper bars.

Barres are bars: smoky cavernous working-class saloons; tiny, chatty neighbourhood holes-in-the-wall; elegant and expensive nightspots where the Barcelonese obsession with design ascends into heaven. The variety of fad and fashion is dizzying: nostalgic, Moderniste, leather, Fellini, stainless steel, classical music, tarot, psychedelic, rock 'n' roll, Fifties, samba, disco, bohemian, tango, video, intellectual, gay, circus, yuppie, cowboy, Woody Allen, flamenco, biker, aristocratic, English, Brel-and-Piaf, Satanist. Most are open from 19:00 to 03:00, and either closed Sundays or open only till midnight. And if you can't get into one, there are always plenty of others nearby. For the enthusiast, there's an exhaustive guide to the Barcelona scene, in Catalan: *Nits de Bars*, published by Parsifal Edicions, Barcelona, and available in bookshops for 1100 ptas. For the not-so-enterprising, a few suggestions:

Xampanyerias

Cava is the Penedès version of champagne, and *xampanyerias* are where you'll find it. Best known outside Catalonia are Cordoniù and Freixenet, but there are plenty of others worth indulgence: Castellblanch, Hill, Juve i Camps, Marqués de Monistrol, to name a few of the hundred or so available. Go for the *bruts* and *brut natures*. Naturally there are bars that specialize in nothing but *cavas*:

Artcava Fusina
Fusina 6

La Cava del Palau
Verdaguer i Callís 10

La Xampanyeria
Provença 236

Xampanyeria Ca La Manyos
Muntaner 18

El Xampanyet
Montcada 22

Xampú-Xampany
Gran Via 702

Bars

Be advised that serious drinking in Barcelona is not for
cheapskates. Although a glass of the house *tinto* in a bodega won't
lighten your pockets by more than a hundred or so pesetas, you can
blow thousands on a few simple daiquiris in the more exquisite
venues. Consider the bar scene as spectator sport, and nurse your
drink. Among the more spectacular:

Boadas

Tallers 1

Deco intellectual.

La Fira

Provença 17

Funfair relics.

Harlem

Comtessa Sobradiel 8

Jazz.

Nick Havanna

Rosellón 208

'The ultimate bar.'

Paraigua

Pg. de l'Ensenyança 2

Classical music.

Pastis

Sta Mónica 4

Nostalgia.

Soweto

Sócrates 68

Afro, reggae, salsa, merengue.

Velvet

Balmes 161

High design, high fashion, high prices.

Velódromo

Muntaner 213

Faded snooker.

Woody

Pça. del Sol 7

Woody as in Allen.

Zeleste

Almogávares 122

Assorted trendiness.

Zsa Zsa

Rosseló 156

Unfaded elegance.

We can't resist listing a bar called Drinking in the Rain, Av. Sarriá 50. This bar serves aperitifs, coffee and cocktails. It's open seven days a week from 11:00; in the evenings it's a piano bar. We've never been there. But what a great name.

Espectacles
(Sights and sounds)

The Barcelonese eye delights in fun and fantasy, the odd, the obscure and the eclectic. With a fat economy at the turn of the century, the city was able to indulge its vagaries and produce unparalleled architectural *jeux d'esprit* – Gaudí's shimmering explorations of the grotesque, Domènech i Montaner's buoyant art nouveau inventions, Puig i Catafalch's neo-Gothic palaces: the overlay of frill and filigree on the stolid high-bourgeois mansions of the Eixample.

Barcelona's great *fin de siècle* architects were among the elite of the city's intelligentsia: they consorted with poets, painters, philosophers and musicians, and were steeped in the politics of Catalanism. Domènech's work, particularly – for all its whimsy – was a radical attempt both to liberate architecture from its dowdy nineteenth-century norms, and to create a distinctive Catalan style, modern but with clear medieval roots. The measure of its success is that it is still radical today.

At about the same time, the city's Moderniste painters – notably Ramon Casas and Santiago Rusiñol among many lesser lights – were returning from Paris with peculiar Barcelonese twists on post-Impressionism. The streets, squares and parks began to fill with an astounding variety of sculpture: bronze statues with umbrellas, spectacles, picnic baskets. Barcelona's infatuation with display continues to this day: the city is loaded with stylish galleries, fresh public statuary, over-the-top graphics and outer-space architecture; and much of it is as politically charged as it was at the turn of the century.

Architecture

If you need an excuse to visit Barcelona, it would have to be the city's architecture. There are two approaches: to wander the streets at random and drink them in, with no notion of the historical context or stylistic evolution of what you see; or to map out the high points, educate yourself about the details, track down the most promising spots, and draw conclusions about the people who built and inhabit this hothouse of architecture. If you choose the first method (which is a perfectly good one, in our view), you need no help from us; if the second, a few pointers and some examples:

The two great periods of architecture in Barcelona are late medieval, packed into the Ciutat Vella, and nineteenth-century Renaixença, concentrated in the Eixample Dreta (see Getting around, pages 38–9). There are scatterings of noteworthy baroque and eighteenth-century structures in odd corners of the city, and a number of worthy contemporary buildings, but what most delights the eye is the results of the city's early and late efflorescences.

I. Early

Medieval Barcelona was built on Roman ruins atop Mont Tàber, the gentle rise whose summit, if it can be called that, lies between the Cathedral and Pça. Sant Jaume. Traces of Roman walls, palaces and temples are scattered throughout the quarter, and although nothing substantial is left, it has remained the centre of ecclesiastical and political life in Barcelona for 1500 years.

The Cathedral dominates the scene: an agglomeration of Romanesque and Renaissance architecture, with a Paleochristian basilica beneath it, an apse and three naves of equal height, Catalan Gothic towers above, and a twentieth-century neo-Gothic doorway in front, facing the Pça. de la Seu. The present version of the Cathedral was begun in 1298 on the remnants of its eleventh-century Romanesque predecessor, but most of it, including the main altar, dates from the fourteenth century, though the exquisite cloister with its fountain and its flock of geese was built in the fifteenth.

All but a few of the Romanesque buildings of Barcelona's first Golden Age – the eleventh and twelfth centuries, when the Beren-guer Counts ruled – were replaced by even more extravagant archi-tecture in the fourteenth. Among the survivors are the church of Sant Pau del Camp, south of the Ramblas – a marvel of strength and symmetry – and the simple, elegant façade of the Capella de Santa Llúcia – patron saint of the blind, of seamstresses, and more recently of electricity – alongside the Cathedral.

What captures the eye in the Ciutat Vella is the frozen remains of Barcelona from the fourteenth to sixteenth centuries, the city at its peak of empire during the reigns of Jaume II and Pere III, dizzy with wealth, and in two subsequent centuries of decline. Some indications:

The Palau Reial Major, in the Pça. del Rei, was originally the site of the Praetors of the Roman colony; next, the headquarters of the Visigoth conquerer Ataulfo; then the castle of the tenth- and eleventh-century Counts of Barcelona. But little of those days remains. The palace was remade (like most of the city) in the fourteenth century by the Aragonese count-kings. The star turn is the Chapel of Santa Àgata, an austere room overlooking the Pça. del Rei, accessible from the Museu d'Història de la Ciutat, and leading into the barnlike Saló del Tinell, the ceremonial chamber in which Ferdinand and Isabella are said to have received Columbus on his return from his first voyage (and also the fifteenth-century headquarters of the Inquisition in Barcelona).

The Palau del Lloctinent is appropriately next door to the Palau Reial, attached below the empty windows of its watchtower. It housed the viceroys of the Kings of Aragón (it now holds the Aragonese archives), and was built in 1549: a Renaissance interior court behind a simple Gothic façade, with a coffered ceiling over the courtyard staircase.

The side entrance to the **Ajuntament** (the city hall) on the c/ de la Ciutat: preserved Gothic, leading into a sixteenth-century courtyard and up a black marble staircase to the Saló de Cent, the fourteenth-century seat of Catalonia's parliament, remodelled in neo-Gothic style in the early twentieth century but still retaining its graceful columned windows and beamed ceiling. When nineteenth-century remodelling reduced the size of the Gothic portal, the main entrance to the Ajuntament was moved to the neo-classical façade on the Pça. Sant Jaume.

The Palau de la Generalitat, opposite the Ajuntament on the Pça. Sant Jaume, is actually a series of connected buildings: a fifteenth-century palace, between cs/ Sant Honorat and Bisbe; an open-air stairway surrounded by a raised gallery; the Capella de Sant Jordi (Saint George, Catalonia's patron saint), an example of Catalan *flamígero* style; an interior courtyard of orange trees (sixteenth century), and a seventeenth-century façade facing the Plaça – the only complete Renaissance structure in Barcelona. The Generalitat is open to the public only on Sundays, from 10:00 to 14:00.

Drassanes, the covered dockyards at the bottom of the Ramblas, were begun in the fourteenth century – at the height of Catalonian empire-building – and continued to evolve into the eighteenth; but the basic pattern is medieval, and they retain the atmosphere of a giant Gothic factory: three bays on the Rambla side and eight more behind them, just high enough to enclose a complete galley. The fact that they're now about a hundred meters away from the harbour should give you an idea of how the landscape has changed over the centuries. The Drassanes now house the Museu Marítim (see page 159).

Santa Maria del Mar: stark perfection of Catalan Gothic architecture, set squarely in the Born district, itself redolent of the medieval city. It was built fairly quickly in the mid-fourteenth century, and as a result reveals the architecture of the period at its purest: no baroque renovations, no modern afterthoughts. Even the saints' niches that line its sides are devoid of the stagy effects and excessive ornamentation that mar the insides of many Spanish churches. The niche that houses Sant Joan Ante Portam Latinam, for example, is almost modern in its austerity: simple marble altar and plain wood effigy. The church is lofty and airy, with three naves and stout well-spaced columns, and no central sanctuary to occlude the interior. It is often host to visiting performers – an American gospel choir, for instance – and these occasions are not to be missed. But even when deserted it is well worth visiting.

II. Late

The hallmark of Moderniste building – the flowering of architecture that occurred in Barcelona's moneyed districts at the turn of the century – is an obsession with design. There are thousands of five- and six-storey apartment buildings in the Eixample, none of them alike. Their decoration ranges from almost subliminally faint *graffito* – a delicate floral tracery on stucco – to lacy ironwork balustrades and delicate stained-glass windows, to massively ornate stone carving, gaudy explosions of tile, faux-medieval turrets and castellations, and ultimately to the writhing, convulsive stone constructions of Gaudí.

You'll find most of the city's Moderniste landmarks in the Quadrat d'Or, the 'golden square' of a hundred Eixample blocks bordered on the north and south by Pg. de Sant Joan and Aribau, and on the east and west by the Ronda de Sant Pere and the Diagonal. Their concentration here was a simple matter of money, which flowed in torrents into the area around the Pg. de Gràcia in the middle of the nineteenth century. The great trio of architects Domènech i Montaner, Gaudí, and Puig i Catafalch, along with scores of their contemporaries and followers, were commissioned by the city's merchant-princes to redesign the mid-century palaces that lined the Gràcia, and by developers to design new apartment buildings from the ground up for the *haute bourgeoisie*. Here are some of the best:

Casa Amatller

Pg. de Gràcia 41
Metro: Pg. de Gràcia (L3 or L4)

Architect: Puig i Catafalch, 1900

The centrepiece of the block known as Mansana de Discòrdia (the Apple of Discord) flanked by Montaner's Casa Morera, Sagnier's Casa Mulleras, and Gaudí's Casa Batlló. Unmistakably 'Gothic', with an enormous stair-step roofline, and each row of windows elegantly and distinctively spaced, giving a sense of lightness to this solemn building. Walk through the doorway and you find yourself in a skylit entrance hall at the foot of a swooping stone balustrade, straight out of Ivan the Terrible (Part I).

Casa Batlló

Pg. de Gràcia 43
Metro: Pg. de Gràcia (L3 or L4)

Architect: Gaudí, 1906

Visits by arrangement: tel: 204 52 50

With its droopy, hooded window embrasures and snake-eye balconies, articulated bone-like columns, a scaled carapace of blue tile and a single turret like a melted mushroom, this is undiluted Gaudí, entertaining, off-beat and just a bit creepy. You'll find the serpent-imagery mirrored in the interior hall and stairwell if you venture inside.

Casa Calvet

Casp 48
Metro: Urquinaona (L1 or L4)

Architect: Gaudí, 1900

Gaudí's first apartment building in the Eixample, with ironwork balconies that extend outward like prows, and topped with a pair of rounded half-domes, elaborately ornamented. More conventional than his later work, but full of his exquisite characteristic detail: sinuous door handles, railings, doors and banisters.

Casa Ramon Casas

Pg. de Gràcia 96
Metro: Diagonal (L3 or L5)

Architect: Rovira i Rabassa, 1899

We like this house because it once belonged to the great Moderniste painter Casas (not every artist was a pauper) and because it's now inhabited by the great ultramodern gadget shop Vinçon. The ground floor is totally redone in black (which nicely sets off Vinçon's glittering displays), and the first floor is restored turn-of-the-century, dramatic high-ceilinged rooms full of trendy, expensive present-day furniture.

Casa Comalat

Diagonal 442 and Còrsega 316
Metro: Diagonal (L3 or L5)

Architect: Valeri i Pupurull, 1911

Modernisme at its most baroque, with carved stone garlands, encrusted balcony supports, frilly ironwork, and an immense, curvy cornice topped with a giant stone knob. The Còrsega side, with its ranks of shuttered windows, looks dark and unlived in; its ground-floor doors and windows are low to the ground and lend a mysterious subterranean effect. But look up and you'll see bursts of bright ceramics under the balconies and the roofline. And the interior is the Moderniste equivalent of Disneyland: a fantasy of colour and shape.

Casa Fuster

Pg. de Gràcia 132
Metro: Diagonal (L3 or L5)

Architect: Domènech i Montaner, 1911

Ornate and curvaceous, with plenty of pillars and Venetian-style windows, a mansard roof, and a projecting tower at one corner.

Palau Güell (Museu de les Arts de l'Espectacle)

c/ Nou de la Rambla 3
Tel: 317 20 78
Metro: Liceu, Drassanes (L3)
Hours: weekdays 10:00–13:00 and 17:00–18:00; Sundays 10:00–13:00.
Admission: 100 ptas

Architect: Gaudí, 1889

The house was built, very expensively, for Gaudí's constant patrons the Güell family, and sits incongruously at the edge of the Barri Xinès, a precinct less than savoury. It's a combination of the opulent and the austere, faced with greying white stone and furnished inside with glistening grey marble. It's also Gaudí's spookiest house, full of reptilian motifs. Its entrance is a cavernous, horseshoe-shaped interior driveway, with stairs that lead up to a sombre mezzanine. One flight further up and you are in a series of galleries that surround the central Sala d'Actes – a domed theatre at least three times as high as it is wide, the dome itself narrow and bullet-like, pierced to let in daylight: a pronounced Moorish effect. Along the west gallery, overlooking the street, is a series of overlapping columns and arched window embrasures, subtly rounded and elegant. Upstairs is a warren of perfectly proportioned little rooms, each with a fireplace of sleek, organic marble. And throughout are the small details, from intricately carved ceilings to door handles and light fixtures, that indelibly mark Gaudí's creations.

The Palau Güell houses the city's theatre museum and archives, and temporary exhibits are shown on the ground floor; upstairs, in the main floor galleries, turn-of-the-century posters and theatre-related paintings by Casas, Rusiñol, Andreu and others are worth the trip in themselves. The house is a gem, and not to be missed.

Casa Lamadrid

Girona 113
Metro: Verdaguer (L4 or L5)

Architect: Domènech i Montaner, 1902

Squat stone pillars support the façade; lacy iron grillework adorns the balconies. The window frames have a subtle art nouveau flavour, and the roof is decorated with ornate stone carving.

Casa Macaya

Pg. de Sant Joan 108
Metro: Verdaguer (L4 or L5)

Architect: Puig i Catafalch, 1902

The varied spacing of windows on each floor, arcaded above and below, is characteristic of Puig, and so is the medieval-transplant effect. The fantasy is played out with elaborate sculpted balconies, delicate tracings on stucco surfaces, and a set of doors that would look good on a monastery. The building is owned by the Caixa de

Pensions, one of Barcelona's many enlightened banks, which occasionally opens it up for exhibitions.

Casa Milà (La Pedrera)

Pg. de Gràcia 92
Metro: Pg. de Gràcia (L3 or L4)
Hours: Monday–Friday 10:00, 11:00, 12:00, 13:00, 16:00, 17:00, 18:00; Saturdays 10:00, 11:00, 12:00, 13:00; Sundays 11:00, 12:00, 13:00.

Architect: Gaudí, 1910

Gaudí's last and most outlandish apartment building, and the back of his hand to Ildefons Cerdà: the undulating stone balconies and wave-shaped roofline defy and conquer the straight edges of the Eixample. The rough, 'eroded' surface of the stone mocks the refinement of this patrician district, and the twisted, tiled chimneys are totally idiosyncratic; the entrances are like cave mouths. The interior space is surprisingly simple and flexible: a pair of internal wells lead through columned rooms to outside balconies with twisted, nightmarish grilles. Stairways tunnel through, several leading in what seems the same direction but arriving at different levels. Every detail, from door handles to lift cages, has the Gaudí touch. Laundry hangs out to dry at the back, as in every other house in Barcelona.

Editorial Montaner i Simón (Fundació Tàpies)

Aragó 255
Metro: Pg. de Gràcia (L3 or L4)

Architect: Domènech i Montaner, 1886

If you can still notice anything after the shock of haywire sculpture on the roof, the building is full of surprises. The exterior is formal and symmetrical, a brick-and-glass façade that betrays its Mudejár influence in its arched windows and doorway. Inside all is light and air, and not just because it has been totally remodelled: you can still see the exposed cast-iron columns that support the roof and the enormous skylight that illuminates the hall: turn-of-the-century high-tech. For notes on Tàpies, whose work is exhibited here in profusion, see page 163.

Casa Lleó i Morera

Pg. de Gràcia 35
Metro: Pg. de Gràcia (L3 or L4)

Architect: Domènech i Montaner, 1906

This rich, ornate fantasy now houses the headquarters of the Ajuntament's Patronat de Turisme on the first floor, and (unfortunately for architecture buffs) a branch of Loewe's on the ground floor, which, decades ago, replaced Domènech's exquisite stonework with plate glass. The exterior has the look of a Venetian palace, surmounted by a lacy dome on stilts. Inside and upstairs (if you can manufacture an excuse to visit the office of the Patronat) is an extravaganza of 'medieval' art nouveau stonework, wood carving, and abundant stained glass. The conference-room of the Tourist Bureau is a panorama of pastoral scenery in glass and tile, glowing with filtered light.

Palau Baró de Quadras

Diagonal 373
Metro: Verdaguer (L4 or L5)
Hours: Tuesday–Sunday 09:00–14:00; closed Mondays.
Admission: 200 ptas.

Architect: Puig i Catafalch, 1906

Stone façade, a rounded, grilled doorway which takes up almost half the front, an ornate balcony that runs the length of the first floor, and a different set of windows on each of the four upper storeys. All these elements are resolved in simplicity and austerity. Inside, in the stairwell, all hell breaks loose: a pillared and porticoed extravaganza of tile, like an opulent Turkish bath. The Palau Quadras houses the Museu de la Música, so no ruses are required to explore it.

Casa Antoni Salvadó

Casp 46
Metro: Urquinaona (L1 or L4)

Architect: Batllevell i Arús, 1904

Next door to Gaudí's Casa Calvet, very un-Moderniste: classical lines, ornate balconies, a fine arcade at the fifth floor which pulls it all together, and an added sixth floor which absolutely negates the effect (a misfortune that has befallen more than a few of Barcelona's turn-of-the-century houses).

Casa Miquel Sayrach

Diagonal 423–425
Metro: Verdaguer (L4 or L5)

Architect: Sayrach i Carreras, 1918

An odd combination: Gaudí's influence is unmistakable in the yawning corner windows, while the two street sides are relatively restrained. What really sets this building apart – for better or worse – is the bizarre conical spire that flies out of the roof on curved pillars.

Casa Terrades (Casa de les Punxes)

Diagonal 416–420
Metro: Verdaguer (L4 or L5)

Architect: Puig i Catafalch, 1905

Punxes are thorns, and you can spot this thorn-palace from blocks away by its six pointed fairytale towers.

If these whet your appetite, there are plenty of others worth tracking down, including:

Casa Francesc Cairó
Enric Granados 106

Architect: Boada i Piera, 1907

Casa Antònia Costa
Rambla de Catalunya 122

Architect: Domènech i Estapà, 1904

Casa Esperança Isern
Girona 67

Architect: Cot i Cot, 1910

Casa Enric Laplana
Pg. de Sant Joan 6

Architect: Martorell i Puig, 1909

Palau Ramon de Montaner
Mallorca 278

Architect: Domènech i Montaner, 1893

Casa Francesc Pastor
Provença 258

Architect: Sagnier i Vellavecchia, 1898

Casa Isabel Pomar
Girona 86

Architect: Rubió i Bellver, 1906

Casa Thomas
Montaner 291–293

Architect: Domènech i Montaner, 1898

Public buildings of the Renaixença

Palau de la Música Catalana

c/ Sant Pere més Alt
Metro: Urquinaona (L1 or L4)

Architect: Domènech i Montaner, 1908

The triumph of Modernisme: technically on the leading edge of the architecture of its time, its arches and capitals are supported by steel beams (and even the glass lends support); acoustically superb; and visually radiant. Inside and out, the simplicity of its structure is masked by the opulence of its ornamentation. Although the hall is anything but enormous, it's crammed with decoration – cascades of stone carving (including immense Pegasuses that leap out of the walls), hundreds of red and yellow ceramic roses that grow downward between the rafters, and lavish expanses of stained glass along the sides and forming a huge inverted bubble in the ceiling. Despite all this the room feels open and expansive, and daylight sparkles with rose and gold as it filters through the glass.

Hospital de la Santa Creu de Sant Pau

Metro: Hospital de Sant Pau (L5)

Architect: Domènech i Montaner, 1902

Hospitals are generally the last places you want to visit in your travels, but make an exception for this one. The Sant Pau consists of about thirty buildings in an area the size of nine Eixample-sized blocks; the main entrance is at the junction of Av. de Gaudí and c/ Sant Antoni. It looks more like a pastiche of Gothic sensibility than a working hospital: whimsical and elaborate 'medieval' brickwork, brightly tiled domes, cupolas and minarets, Arab arches. It also thumbs its nose at the checkerboard Cerdà plan of the Eixample: the whole complex runs diagonally against the horizontal planes of 'uptown' Barcelona; and where Cerdà's rigid pattern enforces straight edges, Domènech's loose array of buildings, with paths and plantings between them, allows for infinite variations on a theme of roundness.

An added attraction is the perfect view of Sagrada Familia from the steps of the main entrance of the hospital: a straight shot *diagonally* through the Eixample along the Av. de Gaudí, which neatly bisects four Eixample blocks. It seems that every rule in Barcelona has an exception.

Sagrada Familia

Metro: Sagrada Familia (L5)
Hours: 09:00–19:00
Admission: 300 ptas

Architect: Gaudí, begun 1882

Gaudí's unfinished masterpiece: melted Gothic. He took over the project two years after its inception, and ultimately it became his obsession – the result of his spiritual conversion on 3 November, 1883. It was to be an expiation of the sins of Barcelona, imbued with passion and packed with symbolism. Stretched tendons of stone frame the southern entrance; immense hollow lacework spires erupt at the north. They have become icons of Barcelona. Every surface is encrusted, bulges and flowers with detailed decoration. Narrow stairways wind up between walls. Alleys coil off, leading to other staircases, rooms and viewpoints, giving a feeling of being enmeshed in architecture. Given the grimness of these stones, their agonized twists and shrieking descents, Gaudí's mystical vision of 1883 must have been singularly lacking in bliss.

A lift (75 ptas) takes you up to the arch at the north entrance: walk out between the central towers for dizzying views of the city. In the crypt is a Gaudí museum (as well as the architect's tomb), with scale models of parts of the cathedral and sample carvings of its decorations, plus old photos of the architect's earlier buildings. The plaça across from the Sagrada has a small children's play area, and stalls selling modern jewellery in art nouveau style, postcards and posters (600–4000 ptas), and 3D cardboard replicas of Gaudí's buildings.

Gaudí died in a traffic accident in 1924 and, since he left no detailed plans, a team of architects is proceeding on fragments of his old models and a certain amount of guesswork. Construction continues at a leisurely pace: no one expects miracles.

Columbus Monument

Pça. Portal de la Pau
Metro: Drassanes (L3)

Architect: Gaietà Buïgas, 1888

Not quite as hideous as the Albert Memorial in Hyde Park, but close. The column was raised on the occasion of the Universal Exhibition of 1888; the idea had been floating around since 1852 'to highlight the importance of Columbus's achievement and to perpetuate the significant part paid by Catalonia in the discovery, conquest, and civilization of America.' An ironic notion because the discovery of America more or less bankrupted Catalonia: the Atlantic replaced the Mediterranean as a focus of trade.

The structure consists of a pedestal surrounded by iron lions; allegorical figures representing Catalonia, Aragón, Castile, and León, plus extra sculptures of historical figures connected with the discovery; a 51-metre column with further allegories at its base, and a bronze statue of Columbus on top (pointing east, for some reason). There's a lift inside which takes you up to the mirador: open 24 June–24 September, from 09:00 to 21:00 hours daily; restricted hours during the rest of the year, and closed Mondays.

Parks and outdoor art

Barcelona doesn't just have parks, it has battlegrounds for controversy. The city's design-conscious planners have a tradition of extremism to uphold, and every newly inaugurated or freshly refurbished park is both an experimental landscape and a home for experimental art. Since the death of Franco the city has built or revived more than a hundred parks and plaças, scattering among them 72 major sculptures: compensation for decades of neglect under the old regime. The results are mixed: some charming (Joan Brossa's 'visual poem', for example – stone punctuation marks scattered on the grass outside the Velòdrom d'Horta); some awe-inspiring (the Parc Crueta del Coll, with Eduardo Chillida's 'Elogi de l'aigua', an immense stone claw suspended over water); and some to be avoided at all costs (the big Parc de Joan Miró and its unfortunate Miró sculpture, which together demonstrate that size isn't everything).

The fiascos are few, however, and serve to quicken both the landscape and the endless debate about it. What is most interesting about the city's efforts to build parks and open spaces is the choice of sites and their integration with urban themes. Some are moulded around the existing elements of old industrial areas (la Crueta was a quarry, Clot a railway roundhouse), and others incorporate striking (or discordant) synthetic components (like the watchtowers in the Parc de l'Espanya Industrial) in more or less natural settings. Interesting too is the city's decision to preserve the cold chimneys of dismantled factories: giant brick towers that rise incongruously above the neighbourhoods of Gràcia and Poble Sec.

If post-modernist parks aren't to your taste, there are plenty of classical landscapes to be found in Barcelona, and (of course) the Parc Güell, which fits into no category. What you *won't* find are *central* parks: the medieval centre of town grew up long before the notion of urban greenery caught on; and besides, Catalonians like to stick close together, and still build their houses with as little intervening space as possible.

When the Eixample came along in the nineteenth century, its designer, Ildefons Cerdà, wisely intended to leave two sides and the interior of each block, as well as the *chaflanes* (the angled corners), as open squares and gardens. Overpopulation and the mad rush to settle the district put an instant end to that idea, and as a consequence most of the city's parks fell into areas too steep or too distant to be colonized (such as Tibidabo) or whose former inhabitants had gone out of business (such as the barracks of La Ciutadella).

Among the best (and worst) of Barcelona's parks:

Parc de l'Espanya Industrial

Metro: Sants Estació (L1 or L5)

Just east of the railway station, a very peculiar combination of the classical and the industrial-modern. Its lake has a statue of Neptune stranded high and dry, looking totally out of place; its western edge is guarded by what look like prison watchtowers; and at one end there is a children's slide in the shape of a giant bat-winged dragon, the stuff of nightmares, probably the scariest piece of playground equipment ever devised.

Parc Pegaso

Metro: Fabra i Puig (L1)

Features a paved square with sculpture by Ellsworth Kelly, woodlands and a small lake.

Parc Crueta del Coll

Metro: Penitents (L3)

An old quarry, it now has an artificial beach, with sculpture by Ellsworth Kelly and Roy Lichtenstein.

Parc del Clot

Metro: Clot (L1)

A *clot* in Catalan is a pit, and this park was partially built out of a natural amphitheatre. It also contains sculpture by Bryan Hunt, a disused factory chimney, and the roofless remains of an old brick-and-stone roundhouse – with a waterfall somehow incorporated into its structure.

Parc de Joan Miró

Metro: Tarragona (L3) or Pça. d'Espanya (L1)

A commemoration of Joan Miró with his 20-metre concrete sculpture, 'Dona i Ocell' (Woman and Bird), surely the master's most hideous work. The park itself is a concrete wilderness, and makes you wonder whether it hasn't been cursed by its previous incarnation as the Parc de l'Escorxador – the site of the city's abbatoir.

Parc de Pedralbes

Metro: Palau Reial (L3)

Formal, classical accompaniment to the King's Barcelona residence, and very French in its abjuration of grass in favour of gravel. A tranquil and dignified garden, far removed from the ruck: appropriate terrain for the monarchists who inhabit the hills above it.

Estació del Nord

Metro: Arc de Triomf (L1)

Built alongside a former train station which now houses a bus depot and a new community sports centre. Features an enormous, undulating blue and white ceramic construction by Beverly Pepper. Next door, construction is underway for a new home for the Archives of the Crown of Aragón, a National Theatre, a Municipal Auditorium, and a Plaza of the Arts: revitalization of one of the city's bleakest neighbourhoods.

Parc de la Ciutadella

Metro: Arc de Triomf (L1) or Ciutadella or Jaume I (L4)

If Barcelona has an 'official' park, this is it: not particularly big, and packed with public buildings and museums, commemorative statuary, grandiose monuments, formal gardens, a tranquil pond, an artificial waterfall and a zoo – but for all that it feels both wide open and removed from the commotion outside its walls. The site of the park is the grounds of the old Citadel, the eighteenth-century barracks of the Bourbon army of occupation. In the 1860s the land was ceded back to the city, and in 1888 it was redesigned and rebuilt to house the Universal Exhibition.

The best entrance to the park is through the wonderful brick Arc de Triomf at the west end of the Pg. de Luís Companys – complete with balustrades and lamp standards by Gaudí. At the base of this promenade, along the south wall of the park, are Domènech's Castell dels Tres Dragons (now the Zoological Museum; see page 165), the glass-roofed Hivernacle and Umbracle (former botanical conservatories). In the centre of the park is a round lagoon complete with rowing boats (135 ptas an hour), a lilliputian island, and a motley collection of ducks and geese; and behind this lies the old Parlament de Catalunya, currently the home of the Museu d'Art

Modern, facing the formal Pça. d'Armes. Here a little lotus-filled pond holds 'El Desconsol', the sublime sculpture of Josep Llimona, one of the emblems of the city. And filling the north-east corner of the park is the Zoo: for the most part pleasantly open, with egrets and ibises casually mingling on the lawns with yaks and emus, but with the usual bitter complement of lions and bears in straitened circumstances. Admission to the Zoo is a stiff 600 ptas, regardless of age.

Parc de Montjuïc

Metro: Pça. d'Espanya (L1 or L3) and bus No. 61 to Pça. Dante; or Paral.lel (L3), then funicular to Av. Miramar and telefèric to Castell de Montjuïc.

Montjuïc is the big hill that drops down to the sea just south of the city proper. The name is an ancient reference to Barcelona's Jewish population, of whom no trace remains on the hill but a few broken tombstones in a corner of the old fortress. Montjuïc has seen everything: a Roman ritual centre, an Arab garden, a Jewish cemetery, a Bourbon military stronghold, an exposition centre, a sports complex, a tourist attraction. Here you can see the worst surviving examples of Noucentiste architecture – the barren neo-classical formalism that followed the Moderniste movement in the 1920s. The pavilions erected for the International Exposition of 1929 – the Palau Nacional, the Pavelló de la Ciutat, the Pavelló de les Arts Gràfiques (now the Archaeological Museum), the Fuixarda Stadium – have a dowdiness uncharacteristic of Barcelona. The Exposition was a triumph for the dictator Primo de Rivera, and almost bankrupted the city.

Among the attractions that dot the hill:

● The recently reconstructed **Mies van der Rohe pavilion**, which had been demolished after the 1929 Exposition: simple, austere, perfect.
● **Poble Espanyol**, a mini-Disneyland, with every Spanish town in cameo, architecturally correct, squeaky clean and totally artificial. Entrance fee: 500 ptas.
● The **Montjuïc Parc d'Atraccions**, a fun fair à la Tibidabo, first stop on the telefèric on the way to the Castell.
● **Castell de Montjuïc**, the eighteenth-century fortress that crowns

the hill, a symbol of oppression. Now the site of the Military Museum (see page 166).

● A slew of specialized **gardens**: ornamental, botanical, cactus. The best is the Maragall gardens, attached to a little royal villa. It's open only on Sundays and holidays, 10:00–14:00.

● **Teatre Grec**, recreation of a Greek amphitheatre and scene of summer festival activities; brochures available at the Palau de la Virreina on the Ramblas.

● **Fundació Miró**, repository of the artist's works (see page 162).

● **Olympic stadium**, swimming pools, baseball diamond, rugby and football pitches, tennis courts, dog track.

● **Archaeological** and **Ethnological Museums**, housed in old Exposition pavilions.

● A large and boring **cemetery**.

Parc Güell

Metro: Lesseps (L3), then north on Travesera de Dalt to c/ de Larrard; or bus No. 24 to Av. Santuary Sant Josep or c/ de Larrard.

The Güell and the Ciutadella split the title for Quintessential Barcelona Park. Ciutadella is formal and urbane, Güell wild and exotic. Parc Güell is Gaudí in a fanciful mood: the main entrance is through a tile-encrusted wall, past a pair of stone pavilions topped with a fantasia of blue and white ceramic chips: battlements, a steeple, a minaret. Immediately inside the walls is a double staircase presided over by a giant lizard, water dribbling from its mouth. Then a covered hall (it was to be the marketplace of a little garden-city intended for the park, never completed or even properly begun) supported by massive columns, and roofed with an open plaza surrounded by Gaudí's famous serpentine tile benches. Nearby, the Casa Museu Gaudí, a jewelbox of a house where Gaudí lived for a time: his bedroom was a tiny monastic cell.

The housing project that never quite got off the boards (it was abandoned in the 1920s) left most of the hillside in a semi-natural state: rocky knolls, dense thickets, rugged vegetation, narrow trails, and no attempt at cultivation. All in all, a complete anomaly.

Parc del Labyrint

Metro: Montbau (L3)

This very non-Barcelona park is in some ways its most beautiful: a series of Italianate formal gardens, classical and serene, rising in terraces; goldfish ponds, bridges, niches, colonnades, a real hedged labyrinth, culminating in a grotto – all quite small and tidy and very peaceful. To get to it you walk through the grounds of the Velòdrom d'Horta (a giant Mussoliniesque stadium) and past the mock-fortress of the Marques d'Alfarràs, who built the gardens in the eighteenth century.

Art in public places

In many cities the only art that graces the streets and squares is graffiti, and while Barcelona has plenty of that too (especially in the more Catalanized sectors) it abounds in outdoor sculpture. If it jars the eye or the sensibilities (for better or worse), it's probably contemporary. If it's commemorative or sentimental, and perhaps provides the occasion for a small fountain, it generally dates from the nineteenth century. Our favourite few: the seated Angel Guimara, complete with bronze spectacles and a benign, quizzical expression, in the Pça. Josep Oriol; the flower girl Raquel Meller, basket over arm, an unofficial patron saint of the Raval district, across the Paral.lel from the Apolo theatre; the delightful Dama del Paraigua, in Victorian bustle, sporting a parasol, in a corner of the Ciutadella next to the Zoo; the dignified, life-sized statue of Antoni Rivora, seated on a park bench in his own square in the Gràcia. You'll find plenty of other examples in unexpected corners of the city.

Museums

Museu d'Art Modern

Pça. d'Armes
Parc de la Ciutadella
Metro: Barceloneta (L4), Arc de Triomf (L1)

Hours: Tuesday–Saturday 09:00–19:30; Sundays and holidays 09:00–14:00; Mondays 15:00–19:30.

Admission: 400 ptas; students 100 ptas.

The museum's bland exterior (by Barcelonese standards) conceals a fabulous horde of Barcelona's Moderniste painting and sculpture, with some interior design thrown in. The paintings and drawings of Ramon Casas (1866–1932) rightly dominate. The Paris influence on his work and that of his colleague, Santiago Rusiñol, is pervasive: cool greys and blues threaded with vibrant colour, homage to Degas. And Casas's charcoal portraits of his contemporaries – Pau Casals, Domènech, Picasso, Puig i Catafalch, and the wonderful dandy Pere Romeu, co-founder of Els Quatre Gats (the Chat Noir of its day in Barcelona) – are brilliant. Look also for the paintings of Galí and Sunyer, charming woodblocks by Eric Ricart, Rodinesque sculpture by Josep Llimona, and three small, bizarre figurines by Ismail Smith Mari. Plus: architectural drawings, furniture and furnishings by Gaudí and others, clothes, and jewellery, depending on the curators' whims. The museum is a direct channel to the roots of Barcelona's Renaixença, not to be missed.

Museu d'Història de la Ciutat

Pça. del Rei s/n
Metro: Jaume I (L4)

Hours: Tuesday–Saturday 09:00–14:00, 15:00–20:30; Sundays and holidays 09:00–13:30; Mondays 15:30–20:00.

Admission: 200 ptas (includes entrance to the Saló del Tinell and the Chapel of Sta. Àgata).

Housed in the Casa Padellàs, a fifteenth-century palace, this collection rises chronologically from a basement excavated out of Roman ruins, through early Christian, Jewish, Arabic, and medieval relics, and upstairs through the centuries to the present. Most interesting to us are the maps and map overlays that register the gradual (and sometimes sudden) evolution of the town: the imposition of the Eixample, the Via Laietana, and the Ramblas on the urban landscape. A scattering of eighteenth-century portraits; charcoal studies of street life; diagrams of various sieges and bombardments. A second-floor landing leads through the austere Chapel of Sta. Àgata (consult your hagiography for *her* gruesome story) and into the Palau Reial Major (eleventh-fourteenth century), the palace of the former Kings of Aragón and Counts of Barcelona. An anteroom leads into the Saló del Tinell, a hall the size of a barn, built in the fourteenth century under Peter the Ceremonious. The room now houses important temporary exhibitions. If you're interested only in what's on show at the Tinell, the statistics are:

Saló del Tinell
Pça. del Rei 9
Metro: Jaume I (L4)
Hours: Tuesday–Saturday 09:30–14:00 and 16:30–21:00; Mondays 16:30–21:00; Sundays 09:30–14:00.
Admission: 100 ptas.

Museu Marítim

Portal de la Pau 1 (foot of the Ramblas)
Metro: Drassanes (L3)

Hours: Tuesday–Saturday 09:30–13:00 and 16:00–19:00; Sundays and holidays 10:00–14:00; closed Mondays.

Admission: 150 ptas; students and children under 14 free.

The medieval Drassanes Reiales (the Royal Dockyards) of Barcelona, now home to a profusion of nautical documents and artefacts collected by the Barcelona Nautical College: a life-size replica of a seventeenth-century royal galley dominates the scene (thirty banks of oars, 180 rowers). Plus model boats in wood, bone and ivory, made by sailors and prisoners; a few real fishing skiffs and yachts; navigational instruments, ship fittings, tools, artillery, figureheads; and a map collection that includes a chart once owned by Vespucci. For aficionados, a replica of Columbus's Santa Maria is moored in the harbour across the way. The museum's souvenir shop sells brass keyrings with anchors, navigation lights or bells for 600–1180 ptas.

Picasso Museum

Montcada 15–19
Metro: Jaume I (L4)

Hours: Tuesday–Saturday 10:00–20:00; Sundays 10:00–15:00; closed Mondays.

Admission: 400 ptas; students 200 ptas.
Museum and temporary exhibition: 600 ptas.

Picasso spent his late adolescence in Barcelona, and only dropped in occasionally thereafter, but the city put its stamp on him, and has devoted this pair of adjoining palaces in La Ribera, the artist's old neighbourhood, to his work. The collection, founded on massive donations by Picasso's friend and familiar Jaime Sabartés, chronicles his development from juvenilia onward: prolific paintings, ceramics, drawings – notably a room full of his chalk pastiches of Velasquez's 'Las Meninas'. A formidable labyrinth of a museum. Set behind the entrance courtyard is a clean, bright, expensive cafeteria (1500 ptas. for the set lunch, less for snacks – but at least you need not have paid museum admission to get in). A souvenir shop sells posters for 600–700 ptas, reproductions (1500–3000), scarves (4000) and T-shirts (1300), and scores of postcards. (Paupers will find the same postcards cheaper elsewhere.)

Museu Tèxtil i de la Indumentària

Montcada 12–14
Metro: Jaume I (L4)

Hours: Tuesday–Saturday 09:00–14:00 and 16:30–19:00; Sundays and holidays 09:00–14:00; closed Mondays.

Admission: 200 ptas; children free.

In other words, the Costume Museum, and under no circumstances to be scorned. It lends a touch of poignancy and immediacy to the city's history: you can sense the people long vanished from under these layers of doublets, bustles, pantaloons and Empire gowns.

The clothes and accessories run from the elegant seventeenth-century to some embarrassing numbers of the 1970s, and are fascinating in themselves: beautifully embroidered and decorated dresses, elaborately ornamented shoes, fans, purses, gloves, parasols and lorgnettes. But it is the unspoken presence of their bygone owners that gives us the chills: a tiny ballroom, cordoned off, populated by a score of mute and headless mannequins, each in perfect eighteenth-century apparel, all facing the viewer, like refugees who didn't quite escape the guillotine. The quiet of the rooms in this converted Gothic palace does nothing to dispel these phantoms.

Museu Frederic Marés

Pça. St. Iu s/n
Metro: Jaume I (L4)

Hours: Tuesday–Saturday 09:00–14:00 and 16:00–19:00; Sundays and holidays 09:00–14:00; closed Mondays.

Admission: 200 ptas.

Like the Museu d'Història de la Ciutat, this one proceeds chronologically from the crypt in the basement and the pre-Roman artefacts on the ground floor to the twentieth century in the attic. But the resemblance stops there: the Marés is the most obsessively bizarre museum on the planet, and the higher you go, the stranger it gets. On the second floor, after endless vistas of medieval Christian sculpture – acutely uncomfortable saints and martyrs, mostly – you find yourself in a side gallery devoted to manifestations of the Black Madonna of Montserrat: paintings, sculpted icons, newspaper cartoons, rosaries in every conceivable medium, and you begin to glimpse the mind at work in this palace of trivia. On the third floor all pretence of seriousness is lost: fans, reticules, combs, parasols, pipes, cigar bands, cigarette cards, playing cards, scissors, dolls, bicycles, meerschaum pipes, matchboxes, theatre cards, theatre tickets, shells and flowers under glass, fashion plates, hat pins, mechanical instruments, toys, shoes, pin-ups, telephones, phonographs, menus, photos of arrivals at a ball and actors in costume: all the debris of post-turn-of-the-century Barcelona in profusion, under glass. And not just one of each, but *hundreds*. The courtyard of the museum is light and airy, quiet and refreshing. When exhaustion drives you from the Marés, this is the place to rest your eyes and feet.

Fundació Miró

Pça. Neptu s/n
Parc de Montjuïc

Hours: Tuesday–Saturday 11:00–19:00 (Thursdays 11:00–21:30); Sundays and holidays 10:30–14:30; closed Mondays except holidays.

Admission: 400 ptas; students 200 ptas.

Bus No. 61 from Pça. d'Espanya, corner of Av. Reina Maria Cristina, every half hour. The funicular from Paral.lel Metro station to Pg. de Miramar runs daily in summer, otherwise Sundays and holidays only.

A private foundation created by Joan Miró in 1971, it houses large numbers of his works, many on permanent exhibition; plus other artists' shows, films, videos, recitals of contemp music, lectures and seminars. It's primarily a repository for hundreds of Miró paintings, sculpture, textiles, the complete graphic works, and thousands of drawings: through sheer volume of production, Miró had an unofficial lock on the post of Great Municipal Artist. Some of his most hideous accomplishments adorn the city's public places (notably the 'Dona i Ocell', a gaudy giant saltcellar in the Parc Joan Miró, and a garish mosaic on the Ramblas). But some of his early works are full of charm, and you may be able to winkle them out at the Fundació. The building was designed by Josep Lluis Sert, and is full of light and space. It also houses Espai 13, a gallery in the basement, with floating exhibitions of contemporary art, mostly by unknowns; a shop with postcards, books and T-shirts (2000 ptas), posters (600–4000 ptas); loos, phones, lockers. Plus an expensive café – but the grounds are a good place to picnic.

Museu del Perfum

Pg. de Gràcia 39
Metro: Pg. de Gràcia (L3 or L4)

Hours: 10:00–13:30 and 16:00–19:30; closed Saturdays, Sundays and holidays.

Admission: free

Perfumeria Regia is a perfectly ordinary shop on the Pg. de Gràcia, not a clue on the outside to the treasure within. You walk through the shop itself, and through a little private makeover room into a warren of dimly lit glass cases jammed with the impedimenta of the perfume business: mortars, pestles, alembics, scales and scent containers dating from the sixth century BC to the present. It's the biggest collection of perfume bottles in the world, religiously collected and meticulously labelled. Many are works of art, some by Dalí, others by Lalique, Daum and Tiffany. For older visitors it opens the floodgates of memory: Jungle Gardenia by Tuvaché, Schiaparelli's Shocking in the Dalí bottle, Countess Maritza, Prince Matchabelli. Scents from places you'd never suspect of such frivolity: Yugoslavia, Russia, Israel, Cuba. Our favourite is called simply Irving W. Rice, from the United States. The only pleasure denied you is the one you crave most – to pull the stoppers for an instant and risk a massive nostalgia attack.

Fundació Tàpies

Aragó 255
Metro: Pg. de Gràcia (L3 or L4)

Hours: Tuesday–Sunday 11:00–20:00; closed Mondays.

Admission: 400 ptas; students 200 ptas.

From the outside, this is one of the great anomalies of Barcelona. A striking example in glass and red brick of Domènech i Montaner's Catalan Modernism, this former publishers' office is built around a skylit courtyard, supported by iron columns and steel beams – very advanced for its time. Now it's crowned with a heap of what looks like a stainless-steel bird's nest, and if you're unaware of the sensibilities of the artist whose work is housed within, it makes no sense at all. Inside, the exterior vision is resolved. Tàpies's paintings, lithographs and constructions are stark, sombre, sometimes disjointed or ironic, and like a desert landscape both spiked and severe. A permanent collection of his work is housed in the basement; the beautifully redesigned upper floors contain temporary exhibitions which, if you're lucky and Tàpies's work is on show, will give you an idea of this extraordinary Catalan artist's mastery of the austere.

Museu de la Ciència

Teodor Roviralta 55
Metro (Generalitat): Av. del Tibidabo
Bus: Nos. 17, 22, 58, 73

Hours: Tuesday–Sunday 10:00–20:00; closed Mondays.

Admission: 450 ptas, plus 300 ptas for the Planetarium; students 300 ptas.

The provinicial government, in its eternal spirit of contrariness, runs its own little underground system, the Ferrocarrils de la Generalitat, with stations and ticketing separate from the Metro (see page 30). The quick way to the Science Museum from the centre of town is to catch the Generalitat's Tibidabo train at Pça. de Catalunya or Provença, get off at the last stop, and walk up the Av. del Tibidabo. Take a left turn at c/ Roman Macaya, then right on c/ Teodor Roviralta and follow the signs to the museum: about ten minutes all told, and all uphill. Along the way you'll pass some of the rich villas of the last age, now mostly given over to private schools. The museum itself is in a refurbished turn-of-the century building by Domènech Estapa, and is quintessentially hands-on: ingenious experiments that demonstrate the laws of physics, especially optics and perception, equipped with enough buttons and levers to occupy the attentions of small fry on the rainiest of afternoons. There's also a submarine, a copy of Foucault's Pendulum (the machine, not the book), and a Clik dels Nens – a room equipped for under-10s only, with a door too small for grown-ups.

Museu de Zoologia

Pg. Picasso s/n
Parc de la Ciutadella
Metro: Arc de Triomf (L1)

Hours: Tuesday–Sunday 09:00–14:00; closed Mondays.

Admission: 200 ptas.

This was a café-restaurant built for the Universal Exposition of
1888 by Domènech i Montaner, and was then known as the Castle
of the Three Dragons, after a play by the echt-Barcelona playwright
Frederic Soler (aka 'Pitarra'; see restaurants, page 95). Its bare brick
and exposed ironwork are characteristically Moderniste, as is the
neo-Gothic romanticism. The restored building now houses a dusty
collection of stuffed animals (a baby giraffe and a baby elephant
among them, by some lapse of taste) and racks of preserved insects
under glass. It really should be called the Museum of Taxidermy.

Autòmates del Tibidabo

Parc d'Atraccions del Tibidabo
Metro: FFCC to Av. del Tibidabo; then Tramvia Blau and funicular
to Tibidabo.

Hours: April–September 11:00–20:00 daily; October–March
11:00–20:00 Saturdays, Sundays and holidays.

Admission: 450 ptas.

This very peculiar collection of nineteenth-century automata is
buried inconspicuously among the everyday rides and games of the
Tibidabo funfair, but it's the only one worth investigating, and you
don't have to pay the all-attractions admission to get in. It consists of
thirty or so robots, most in working order, electrically activated:
fortune tellers, marionettes, wrestlers, tumblers, boxers, ballroom
dancers, a Sleeping Poet, a vision of Hell. Each in its own glass
booth, and more than a little sinister.

Museu Militar

Top of Montjuïc
Metro: Montjuïc telefèric from the Pça. Dante on Montjuïc.

Hours: Tuesday–Saturday 10:00–14:00 and 15:30–20:00; Sundays and holidays 10:00–20:00; closed Mondays.

Admission: 50 ptas.

This eighteenth-century fortress known as the Castell de Montjuïc has endless galleries of guns and knives from the Marés collection and donated by the Army. The building itself was a military prison under Franco – the execution ground of Lluís Companys, president of the Generalitat, and many others who got on the wrong side of El Caudillo. Franco gave it to the city in 1960. Incongruously, in a cell on the ground floor, are the pathetic remains of the ancient Jewish cemetery: a few inscribed stones, with attempts at decipherment on pasteboard, sometimes just a name or a couple of words. From the battlements of the castle are terrific views of the harbour, but overall it's a melancholy place, haunted by its past.

Others you might find interesting or amusing:

Museu Arqueològic
Pg. de Sta. Madrona s/n
Parc de Montjuïc

Paleolithic, Neolithic, Bronze, Iron and every other age.

Museu d'Art de Catalunya
Palau Nacional, Montjuïc

The region's Romanesque and Gothic art: twelfth to fourteenth centuries.

Museu del Calçat Antic
Pça. Sant Felip Neri s/n

The shoe museum.

Museu de Carrosses Fúnebres
Sanco de Avila 2

Funeral carriages.

Museu Etnològic
Pg. de Sta. Madrona s/n
Parc de Montjuïc

Relics of the family of man.

Col·lecció d'Indumentària i Accessoris de Bombers
Pg. Nacional 67

Souvenirs of the Fire Department.

Museu del Monestir de Pedralbes
Baixada del Monestir 9

A Catalan-Gothic convent for the Poor Clares, complete with church, chapter house and three-storey cloister.

Art Galleries

The galleries of Barcelona – a city that prides itself to the point of vanity on its visual sense – are concentrated in the c/ Consell de Cent in the Eixample and in the Born: the equivalents of Madison Avenue and SoHo in New York, or the Matignon and Saint-Germain in Paris. The following is just a sampling: there are 100 art galleries in Barcelona, and another 15 just for photography. Most are open Tuesday to Saturday, 11:30–14:00 and 17:00–21:00, and of course admission is free.

Eixample:

Sala Gaspar

Consell de Cent 323
Metro: Pg. de Gràcia (L3 or L4)

Artists: Rainer Borghoff, Antoni Clavé.

Galeria Ciento

Consell de Cent 347
Metro: Pg. de Gràcia (L3 or L4)

Artists: Heiner Blum, Angel Bofarull.

Dau Al Set (Galeria Salvador Riera)

Consell de Cent 333
Metro: Pg. de Gràcia (L3 or L4)

Artists: Reiner Fetting, Leonardo Sciascia.

Galeria Eude

Consell de Cent 278
Metro: Pg. de Gràcia (L3 or L4)

Graphics by Appel, Hartung, Hockney and others.

Galeria Subex

Mallorca 253
Metro: Pg. de Gràcia (L3 or L4)

Magic realism by Josep Comes i Busquets.

Born/Ciutat Vell:

Galeria Benet Costa

Comerç 29
Metro: Jaume I or Barceloneta (L4)

Artists: Sol Lewitt, Wolfgang Luy.

Galeria Berini

Pça. Comercial 3
Metro: Jaume I or Barceloneta (L4)

Artists: Ludger Gerdes, Christiaan Bastiaans, Antonio Sosa.

Galeria Maeght

Montcada 25
Metro: Jaume I (L4)

Artists: Max Neumann, Calder, Braque, and plenty of other 'names'.

Lino Silverstein

Antic de Sant Joan 3 baixos
Metro: Jaume I or Barceloneta (L4)

Group shows: photography.

Galuchat/Barcelona

Calders 4
Metro: Jaume I or Barceloneta (L4)

Modernisme, Art Deco, *'funcional'* design.

Elsewhere:

Galeria Taché Editor

Joan Sebastià Bach 22
Metro: La Bonanova (FFCC)

Artists: Rebecca Horn and others.

Galeria Alejandro Sales

Ganduxer 33
Metro: La Bonanova (FFCC)

Artists: Moreno Meyerhoff and others.

Cinemas

Although most foreign films are dubbed, you can generally find
original-language versions (labelled V.O.) in the artier theatres:

Alexis
Rambla Catalunya 90
Tel: 215 05 06
Metro: Diagonal (L3 or L5)

Arcadia
Tuset 14
Tel: 237 14 83
Metro: Diagonal (L3 or L5)

Arkadin
Travessera de Gràcia 103
Tel: 218 62 42
Metro: Diagonal (L3 or L5)

Capsa
Paul Claris at Aragón
Tel: 215 73 93
Metro: Pg. de Gràcia (L3 or L4)

Casablanca
Pg. de Gràcia 115
Tel: 218 43 45
Metro: Diagonal (L3 or L5)

Malda
Pino 5
Tel: 317 85 29
Metro: Liceu (L3)

Verdi
Verdi 32
Tel: 237 05 16
Metro: Fontana (L3)

The Guía d'Ocia has a separate listing of V.O. movies. Admission is generally 500 ptas, but each house has its discount days – 300 or 350 ptas on Mondays or Wednesdays, sometimes holidays. Showings are generally between 16:30 and 22:30 (and plenty of people do opt for the late show).

Bullfights

Barcelona tolerates the corrida, but doesn't encourage it: perhaps because it's such a 'Spanish' custom. There are occasional ads in the (Catalan) newspapers decrying its cruelty – but there are enough fans in the city to support two arenas (only one of which is used regularly) and a bullfight museum. The season is from March to September, Sundays at 17:30, at the Plaza de Toros Monumental, Gran Via between c/ Lepant and Padilla – which is also where the museum is located. If you don't think there's already enough gratuitous killing in the world, you can check the newspapers for details and seek it out for yourself.

Music/theatre/dance

The best source of information on current productions is the Centre d'Informació in the Palau de la Virreina, Rambla 99: racks of brochures on seasonal events in all the arts. They're open Monday to Saturday, 10:00–21:00 and Sundays from 10:00 to 14:00.

Plenty of Barcelona's major cultural events take place under festival umbrellas: Grec (aka Festival d'Estiu), which runs from late

June to early August, and the Festival de Tardor, the Fall festival, currently known as the Olimpiada Cultural.

Grec has fewer events but more interesting venues: small-scale operas and plays in the open-air Teatre Grec on Montjuïc; chamber music in the Hivernacle (a former winter conservatory) on the edge of the Ciutadella; dance and experimental theatre performances in the Mercat de les Flors on the edge of Montjuïc; rock concerts in the Velòdrom d'Horta.

The Festival de Tardor incorporates events at almost every theatre and hall in town, in a scattering of churches, plus free open-air performances on the Ramblas, some of them definitely fringe. Curiosity alone would take you to performances by Hinchables Al Victor ('$NO_2ACO_2HO_2$ . . . *i no tenim res més ma afegir*') or Las Katalítas ('*Seràaamaravilloooso viajal-astaMallorca's ssin necesidàsss de tomal el tasisss o l'aviooonn . . . Viaje al Planeta Skip*').

Barcelona's major musical events take place at:

Gran Teatre del Liceu

Rambla dels Caputxins 65
Tel: 318 91 22
Metro: Liceu (L3)

Opera, ballet and concert season: September to June. Grand productions, major artists, serious prices (5000 ptas and up for good seats, but less than 500 for the gods). Tickets on sale for the day of the performance are in the fourth and fifth tiers of the balcony only. Catalans, regardless of class and income, are music lovers, and you'll find the Liceu packed to the rafters with all walks of life.

Palau de la Música Catalana

Amadeu Vives 1
Tel: 301 11 04
Metro: Urquinaona (L1 or L4)

Home of the Orquestra Ciutat de Barcelona, with plenty of guest spots and recitals for visiting artists. Sunday morning and Wednesday evening concerts are very cheap, but tickets can be scarce. Pick them up on weekdays between 11:00 and 13:00 or 17:00 and 20:00.

Less grand but not to be sneezed at:

Zarzuela, the domestic light opera of Spain. You can find it at:

Teatre Victoria

Av. Paral.lel 67
Tel: 241 39 85
Metro: Paral.lel (L3)
or

Teatre Infantil de Sants

Sants 71
Tel: 421 21 20
Metro: Pl. de Sants (L1 or L5)

Saturdays at 18:00.

Banda Municipal de Barcelona

Centre Cívic Cotxeres de Sants
Tel: 431 49 11
Metro: Pça. de Sants (L1 or L5)

An old-fashioned official town band, in uniform, performing two or three concerts per month of light classics (and some local modern music). Sundays at 11:30, free.

Teatre de l'Aliança del Poblenou

Rambla del Poble Nou 42
Tel: 309 08 90
Metro: Poblenou (L4)

The likes of Laurie Anderson and Cecil Taylor, with excursions into music from Zaire and Kenya, Algeria, Mali and Jamaica.

Església de Santa Anna

c/ Ribadeneira 3
Metro: Catalunya (L1 or L3) or Liceu (L3)

Occasional gospel groups from the States: a perfect marriage of voices and acoustics.

Ars Studio

c/ Atenes 27
Tel: 417 65 95
Metro: El Putxet or Pàdua (FFCC)

Contemporary European jazz.

International Jazz Festival

End of October or beginning of November

Performances generally in the Palau de la Música by a variety of artists: the likes of W. Marsalis, S. Grappelli, McC. Tyner and D. Gillespie, the MJQ.

Theatre

The city fairly bristles with theatres. A sampling of the hottest, in order of heat:

Teatre Romea

Hospital 51
Tel: 317 71 89
Metro: Liceu (L3)

Shakespeare directed by Tabori; Ibsen directed by Bergman; Kleist directed by Syberberg. Tickets from 800 to 1300 ptas.

Teatre Lliure

Montseny 47
Tel: 218 92 51
Metro: Fontana (L3)

The Gràcia's neighbourhood playhouse, with high standards:
Schiller, Guimerá, Goldoni, Strindberg. Plus concerts, dance performances and poetry readings.

Teatre Malic

c/ de la Fussina 3
Tel: 310 70 35
Metro: Arc de Triomf (L1)

Food for thought in the Born. Visiting productions: La Cantatrice
Chauve from Paris; Puppet Theatre Triangel, Holland; Assondelli
e Stecchettoni, Italy. Tickets about 800 ptas.

Teatre Adrià Gual (La Cuina)

Sant Pere més Baix 7
Tel: 317 20 78
Metro: Jaume I (L4)

Cortazar and Ghelerode.

Sala Beckett

Alegre de Dalt 55 bis
Tel: 219 79 27
Metro: Joanic (L4)

Beckett productions, lectures, conferences, films, videos. Price
ranges from free (for lectures and readings) to 1000 ptas (full
productions).

Mercat de les Flors

Lleida 59
Tel: 318 85 99
Metro: Pça. d'Espanya (L1 or L3)

Once the municipal flower market, now holds dance and theatre troupes in large experimental productions, mostly local, generally three or so per season.

Music halls

These old-fashioned entertainments are still alive and well in Barcelona. Try:

Bodega Bohemia

Lancaster 2
Tel: 302 50 81
Metro: Drassanes (L3)

Where Stars Are Born, and no one on stage is under seventy years old.

El Molino

Vilà Vilà 99
Tel: 241 63 83
Metro: Paral.lel (L3)

It's been around for fifty years, and nothing has changed. 'Con el *genial cómico Tony Rama, Rosita Amores "la bomba de El Molino", la sexy boom Lorena Bell, el fantastico ballet de El Molino . . .*' and much more. Tuesday to Sunday at 18:00 and 23:00, Saturdays at 10:30 and 01:00.

Dance halls

La Paloma

Tigre 27
Metro: Universitat (L1)

La Paloma is a contender for the Best Show in Town. It's a big, gaudy hall with an immense dance floor surrounded by booths and tables, and la Gran Orquestra La Paloma on stage – an orchestra that can play positively *anything*, from torch songs to salsa, and make it danceable. The floor only looks big at the beginning of the evening; by midnight it seethes. In its early days La Paloma catered to the help – the maids and butlers of Barcelona – who had such a good time that pretty soon all the world showed up. It still maintains an atmosphere of democratic joy. Open Thursday, Friday, Saturday nights. Go late.

If La Paloma palls (unthinkable to us) try also:

Tango
Diputació 94
Metro: Rocafort (L1)

and

Apolo
Nou de la Rambla 113
Metro: Paral.lel (L3)

And don't forget:

The Circus

Every autumn at the Plaza de Toros Monumental
Corts Catalanes at Pg. de Carles I
Metro: Marina (L1) or Sagrada Familia (L5)

¡Leones! ¡Tigres! ¡Chimpoancés! ¡Perros futbolistas! ¡El Mayor Espectáculo del Mundo!

Street scenes

Sardana

The national dance of Catalonia: a ring of anywhere from four to fifty people and of every generation, their coats and bags heaped in the middle, hands joined, gracefully, lightly lifting on toes and landing on heels. The music is provided by a *cobla* – eleven solid citizens equipped with reeds, brass, tiny drums, a thin melody that wavers between gay and melancholy. The dance itself looks simple: a few steps and lifts and light bounces, nothing acrobatic, but it is rhythmically very complex, and pride is taken in performing it correctly. The Sardana is a celebration of Catalanism and in hard times a quiet protest against repression, a very serious dance indeed. You can watch it or attempt it in front of the Cathedral any Sunday at noon, or in the Pça. de Sant Jaume on summer Sundays and holidays at 19:00, and in winter at 18:30. Also in the Pça. Sant Felip Neri, the first Sunday of each month at 18:00.

Street fairs and festivals

Every district has its **Festa Major**, an annual street fair with masses of food and drink, music, children's shows and games, costumes for adults and children, grand balls and street dances, fireworks, parades, and an annual decorative theme: recently in the Gràcia, for example, the streets were 'underwater', with streamers of sea-weed and plenty of mermaids. The festas last for several days and nights, until everyone is totally wasted. The best ones are in July (Barri del Raval) and August (Barri de Gràcia) but there are plenty of others in every neighbourhood from June to September.

And then there are the **Festivitats** that celebrate patron saints, local and national holidays, local trades and businesses, in fact any excuse at all. The biggest:

1–5 January: Festa i Cavalcade dels Reis d'Orient, when Barcelonese children celebrate the gifts of the Magi with sweets and toys.

7–13 February: Festes del Carmestoltes, or Carnival, banned in Barcelona between 1936 and 1980, and now back with a vengeance.

The main event is a giant parade on the Rambla de les Flors.

23 April: Festivitat de Sant Jordi, the Dia del Llibre i de la Rosa, when gentlemen give roses to ladies, and ladies give books to gentlemen: a courtly tradition in the Born neighbourhood that spread throughout the city.

11 May: Festivitat de Sant Ponç, in the c/ Hospital: a natural food fair, with herbs and such for New Age mystics and vegetarians.

23 June: Revetlla de Sant Joan, when the citizens get rid of old clothes and furniture, fill themselves with sweet *cocas* stuffed with pine nuts and fruit, and celebrate with fireworks on Montjuïc.

11 September: Diada Nacional de Catalunya, the celebration of a defeat: the fall of Barcelona to the Bourbons in 1714. The festivities take place in the Fossar de les Moreres, just outside the Church of Mare de Déu de la Mercé.

24 September: Festivitat de la Mare de Déu de la Mercé, the patron saint of Barcelona, celebrated with music and theatre outdoors in the Pça. de Sant Jaume, in front of the Cathedral, and the Pça. Reial. Plus a Ball de Gegants and a release of the creatures of Hell, complete with fireworks.

Check with the Ajuntament's Tourist Office for more specifics on dates and places. They also publish an annual list – in fact a book – of *Manifestacions Ciutadanes*.

Botigues i magatzems
(Shopping)

Shopping in Barcelona is always a pleasure but rarely a bargain, and some of the city's more sumptuous shops rightfully belong in the Museum section of this book. You're as likely to walk out with what they sell as with one of the Meninas in the Museu Picasso. The peseta has been gaining on us, and a handful of pound notes or dollar bills doesn't have the dazzling effect it had a decade or so ago. But don't despair, there is a multitude of ways for you to make the most of your spending money, and when all else fails you can window-shop.

Hours

Most shops are open from 09:00 or 10:00 to 13:00, and reopen from 16:00 to 20:00; clothes shops may stay open an hour later. The department stores (Galerías Preciados and El Corte Inglés) are more accommodating: 10:00–20:00 or 21:00, Monday to Saturday. Many small shops close for several weeks in August. Some close on Mondays, most close on Saturday afternoons, and all, with one exception that we know of, close on Sundays. The exception is:

Drugstore

Pg. de Gràcia 71

Open 24 hours, with a variety of little shops including a supermarket, a cafeteria, a tobacconist, and a restaurant.

Etiquette

In every transaction you make in Barcelona, a smile and a valiant attempt at Castilian or Catalan will generally see you through. The city's shopkeepers are thoroughly professional (they've had centuries of practice) and will make you feel at home, figure out what you want, and do their best to provide it. As in other continental cities, it's good manners to keep your hands off the merchandise: ask for what you want and let the salespeople find it for you. Unless you're in the bargain basement of a department store or in the open-air market at Sant Adrià, it's impolite to rummage through the sweaters.

You'll find the queuing system in crowded shops less defined than in the Anglo-Saxon world, but it does exist: each customer keeps track of everyone else's comings and goings, and knows exactly when to come forward when the salesperson cries '*Quien es el ultimo?*'. In department stores (as in cafés), where the rules of succession are even more muddled, you say (or shout) '*Oiga, por favor*' to attract attention. On rare occasions you'll come across a particularly myopic sales assistant, someone who's convinced of your invisibility and wouldn't help you even if he could see you. On these occasions it pays to take nothing personally: you can't possibly get the upper hand, and there's no point in making a scene. Instead, think back to the fate of the Armada in 1588. You won't get better service, but you'll feel better.

For shopping on a grand scale, the areas to explore are the Pg. de Gràcia and the Rambla de Catalunya between Pça. Catalunya and the Diagonal; the Diagonal itself from Balmes west to Pça. de Francesc Macià; and various chunks of the Ciutat Vella. Within these precincts you can find the big department stores, the *luxe* clothiers and furriers, the great furniture design outlets, the cutest and priciest gift shops, the slickest shopping malls. In short, look but don't touch.

What you won't find in these areas are discounts for travellers. There are no little perfume, gift, and handbag shops in Barcelona like the ones in Paris which offer discounts of 20–25% for purchases in foreign currency. We've never found a place where you can buy last season's couture model dresses, or famous-name men's suits at less than full price. There seems to be no equivalent of 'dress agencies' with smart slightly used clothes, not even an Oxfam or thrift shop for the skint shopper. You pay full price or you go without.

However, for the intrepid shopper, there are two annual sales seasons when you might pick up a bargain in the department stores: *Rebajas de Invierno*, from the end of January through February, and the *Rebajas de Verano*, all of July and the first part of August. On these occasions the rules of shopper etiquette are suspended.

In the c/ de Trafalgar, near the Ciutadella, and in the winding streets just west of c/ Princesa in the Ciutat Vella you'll come across rows of *confeccionistas*, on-the-spot manufacturers and wholesalers of ready-to-wear clothing, and word has it that cunning Barcelonese who 'know somebody' can pick up bargains here. But tourists aren't part of the network, so don't get your hopes up.

If you're helplessly drawn into variety stores – the Monoprix and Prisunic in France, Standa in Italy – the Barcelona equivalents are Sepu (Rambla Estudis 120) and Sumago (Ramble Estudis 113). Both offer cheap clothes, housewares, the bare necessities. Unlike their French and Italian equivalents, they demonstrate no flair, no peculiarly Spanish trait, and none seems to be expected – but good for a cheap shopping fix.

Clothes

Fortunately for the travelling pauper, Barcelona has a very relaxed dress code. While Madrileños dress to impress each other, Barcelonese dress for their own comfort, and if they can get away with jeans and a jacket, so can you. On the boulevards of the Eixample Dreta you'll spot plenty of elegant outfits and expensive coiffures, but the emphasis is on austerity rather than flash, and you won't feel out of place or compelled to compete.

Barcelona has two department stores (*grans magatzems*) each with two big branches:

El Corte Inglés

Pça. Catalunya 14 and Diagonal 617–619

and

Galerías Preciados

Portal de l'Angel 19 and Diagonal 471–473

Of the two, El Corte Inglés is somewhat more upmarket, and the Diagonal branch of El Corte is the most grand. Both carry everything you'd expect of a department store: clothes for men, women and children, luggage, linen, kitchenware, furniture – all at department store prices.

Barcelona's slickest shopping malls (the *galeries*) are the three branches of **Bulevard Rosa**:

Pg. de Gràcia 53–55
Diagonal 474 (the 'Diagonal' branch)
Diagonal 609–615 (the 'Pedralbes' branch)

They're great places in which to learn how the other half lives, each consisting of several layers of incredibly de luxe clothes shops, and the newest of them all, the Bulevard Rosa Pedralbes, is the most splendid and the least affordable.

Clothing speciality shops

Camper

Four branches:
Pau Casals 3
Valencia 249
Bulevard Rosa Pedralbes at Diagonal 609–615
Muntaner 248

Informal shoes at informal prices.

Galon Glacé

Roger de Llúria 87

Clothes and accessories from the 1940s, 1950s and 1960s.

La Manual Alpargatera

Avinyo 7

The ultimate source of handmade *alpargatas* – traditional rope-soled, canvas-topped casual shoes – in a score of styles and colours.

Menkes

Gran Via 646

Flamenco gear and dancewear: dresses, shoes, castanets, mantillas, combs, the works. Plus traditional Catalan dance costumes: skirts, sandals, lace doo-dads, hairnets.

La Mirada Encantada

Roger de Llúria 89

More retro clothes.

Perla Gris

Balmes 285
Consell de Cent 300
Rambla Catalunya 112

Spectacular socks at astronomical prices.

E. Sole

Ample 7

Thirteen varieties of espadrilles, 175–1225 ptas. Plus boots, hip-bags and shoes in raw leather.

Sombrereria Obach

Avinyo 1

Hats for men, including traditional red Catalan peasant headgear and black *boines*, the Catalan equivalent of the Basque beret.

El Transwaal

Hospital 67

One of several vendors of chefs' uniforms and *ropas de trabajo* along c/ Hospital.

Books

BCN Books

Aragó 227

Tiny, eclectic, central.

Happy Books

Pça. de Gràcia 77

Lively, brightly lit, full of remainders and other sale books, including some in English. Art books, natural history, cookery books. Also, for some reason, chocolates, whisky, marmalade.

Institut Català de Bibliografia

Rambla Estudis at Portaferissa

All subjects, mostly rather dull administrative records of the Catalan provincial government. Some surprising finds include children's books, exhibition catalogues, filmographies. Posters for about 400 ptas, including a series that illustrates Catalan vocabulary.

Llibreria Come-In

Provença 203

Specializes in textbooks for teachers of English, but fortunately these include a mammoth collection of Penguin Classics, and a fairly good choice of contemporary writers in paperback. The mark-up is fairly stiff, so don't attempt to buy in bulk.

Llibreria Francesa

Pg. de Gràcia 91
Muntaner 224

The speciality here is books in French, with a wide variety of continental magazines and newspapers, plus big sections of travel guides, art books, and cookery books. A sliding-wall bookcase near the entrance displays a fairly good selection of English and American bestsellers, interspersed with classics, at very fancy prices. Not for the voracious reader, but centrally located if you can't walk another fifty paces without something to read.

Millà

St Pau 21

Theatre books.

Simons and Ko.

Granja 13

An almost-invisible storefront in the south-west corner of the Gràcia, near the Pça. de Lesseps, and refuge for those who feel naked when they run out of books. Used English and American paperbacks with emphasis on the novel, and good sci-fi and mystery sections. Excellent prices, a merciful trade-in policy, and charming proprietors.

Totem

Pça. St. Josep Oriol 4

Old comics.

Gifts and miscellany

Artespania

Rambla de Catalunya 75

Upmarket crafts in wicker, wood and clay.

Beardsley

Petritxol 12

and

Akeora

Petritxol 3

Both good sites for paper goods and writing implements, house gifts, cookery books, kitchen towels, gadgets, baskets, well-priced *objets*, all eminently presentable and portable.

La Caixa de Fang

Freneria 1 (behind the Cathedral)

Plats, olles, cassoles, gerres, bols, vaixelles, jocs de sangria . . . tot de fang. (*Fang*, by the way, is clay.)

Ceramica Artistica

Llibreteria 18

Pots, plates and tiles, some good, some touristy. They specialize in copies of fifteenth-century Catalan *ofici* tiles: colourful depictions of the ancient trades of the city and the countryside.

Cereria Subirà

Baixada Llibreteria 7

Founded in 1761, it's the oldest shop in Barcelona. Candles for all occasions: votive for church, decorative for the home, kitsch for all other occasions. The shop itself is an antique, well worth dropping into.

Coses de Casa

Pça. Josep Oriols

Quilts and woven bedspreads in exquisite colours.

Dos i Una

Rosselló 275

A little of everything: designy T-shirts, a cabinet of exquisite earrings and silver trinkets, intricate toys, trendy posters and postcards, a few books, smiling salespeople.

Gimeno

Pg. de Gràcia 102

Pipes, lighters, gewgaws from a few hundred to tens of thousands of pesetas.

L'Herbolista del Rei

Vidre 1

This is (we think) the oldest herbalist in the city: the Barcelonese alternative to socialized medicine. You'll come across others, generally musty little nooks but fully operational, scattered throughout the neighbourhoods.

Jocs i Coses

Gran Via 519

Toys and games.

Jutglar

Verdi 38

Glass and rustic pottery. Casserole dishes from 200 to 500 ptas for paella, lasagne, etc. Blown glass pitchers. Bowls with holes (for roasting chestnuts, traditionally). Planters, bottles, vases, cups – simple cheap pottery at very good prices.

Magicus

Diputació 274

Magic for amateurs and professionals.

Mallart

Jaume I 17

A vast array of illustrated decks of cards and chess sets, one based on a Gaudí design.

No Name

Travessera de Gràcia 128

Baskets and small wood items, stools, cutting boards, and very beautiful black and red striped shopping bags.

Pepa Paper

Paris 167
and
Muntaner 183

Every species of decorative paper.

La Poterie

Travessera de Gràcia 130

Big white pots, all handmade, from all over Spain: some 'antique' (over 100 years old), some merely 'old'. Also to be found: glassware, blue and white plates, amphorae, a number of articles that resemble agricultural equipment, and two big affectionate dogs (NFS).

Servicio Estación

Aragó 270–272

Three floors up, two down, solidly packed with household, garden and industrial fittings: plastic, glass, wood, brass, iron: everything from a doll-sized screwdriver to a roll of kitchen flooring. The building itself is Neobrutalist in style, perfectly adapted to its contents, but from the second-floor garden patio you can gaze at the rear of Gaudí's Casa Batllo on the Pg. de Gràcia. To buy something, you get a chit from the salesperson, take it to the cashier, return to the sales counter and pick up the stuff. They must have learned this method from GUM in Moscow.

El 7 Peus

Travessera de Gràcia 142

Muebles antiguos, porcelanas, libros, relojes, cuadros, bronces, pisos completos.

Spectacles Diplomados

Pallac 6

Antique and modern specs and sunglasses.

Toll

Ferran 31

Knives, scissors, secateurs, razors, candle snuffers, chain mail gloves and aprons for enthusiastic knife-wielders.

Vinçon

Pg. de Gràcia 96

Nobody leaves town before stopping in at Vinçon: the ultimate in designer gadgetry and ultra furniture. The shop windows themselves are works of art, and seem to change daily. Downstairs are gadgets and gizmos, pens, knives, calculators, torches, stationery; then lamps, linen, desks, kitchenware, bathroom fittings, hairbrushes, combs, scissors: everything for the techno-freak. A soapdish in chrome or white that fits triangle-shaped into a corner, or a roll-topped bathroom cabinet (no doors to swing out and hit you in the face). For practical and space-saving ideas, a display kitchen. The house once belonged to the Moderniste painter Ramon Casas, and the upstairs has been beautifully restored: lush old rooms in sombre colours, now full of ultramodern pointy furniture, very decorative but highly uncomfortable.

Furniture design

After you've experienced Vinçon, listed above, take a stroll through the following. Leave your credit cards at home.

BD Ediciones de Diseño (Barcelona Centre Disseny)
Mallorca 291–293

Insolit
Diagonal 353

Pilma
Diagonal 403
and
Valencia 1

Nancy Robbins
Pau Claris 181

Markets, flea and otherwise

Els Encants

Pça. de les Glòries
Metro: Glòries (L1)

Mondays, Wednesdays and Saturdays from 08:00 to 17:00. Walk
under the Corts Catalanes to the block between Dos de Maig and
Independència. On the fringe of the market is a scattering of
people selling odds and ends: an old radio, a pair of shoes, out-
grown children's clothes spread on a cloth. The market itself is the
same but more so: specialist stalls with jeans at 1500 ptas, shoes,
casual and second-hand clothes, stationery, comics, old magazines,
videos, cassettes. Stalls with assorted junk: radio valves, household
bric-à-brac, corsets, old spectacles, bits of crystal from old chandeliers, old chandeliers with bits of crystal missing, pottery, coins,
banknotes, medals, porn magazines, books, caged birds, cloth by the
yard, kitchen equipment, wrecked typewriters, sewing machines – a
magpie's delight.

Mercat Gótic d'Antiguitats

Pça. del Pi
Metro: Liceu (L3)

Thursdays (if not a holiday) from 09:00 to 20:00. The Pças. del Pi
and Sant Josep are quiet and bright after the alleys of the Barri
Gòtic, and the Thursday antique fair adds a little excitement. All

sorts of oddments are on display: old books (one on how to make alcoholic drinks by distillation, infusion, and fermentation), lace bobbins, postcards, cameras, fountain pens, dolls, doorknobs, brass light switches, china, glassware and jewellery. One stall sells only lacework and lace-decorated clothes. A very tiny flea market but worth a quick spin.

Mercadillo Sant Adrià

Near Pça. Vila, Sant Adrià de Besòs

Tuesdays from 8:00 to 13:00. Bus No. 544 from c/ Valencia to Barri Besòs. The bus crosses Barcelona's northern border, the Riu Besòs, and immediately makes a right turn into the suburb of Besòs. Get off at either of the next two stops (or simply follow the crowd). The market fills an enormous space under the motorway.

Sant Adrià is a vast open-air market for cheap clothes, costume jewellery and shoes. Everything is new, and much comes complete with counterfeit brands. It's not a flea market, but if you're aggressive you can pick up some bargains: socks for 100 ptas, shirts for 500, T-shirts for 200-plus. You can find jeans, leather belts, lamps, bags, dried flowers, pyjamas, bras and corsets, woollen goods, ribbons. The market is mobbed, chaotic and noisy. Sales are negotiated by hissing, grabbing, shouting, sharp claps of the hands. Prices are rarely listed, although some stalls announce *todos por 100*. The market is permeated by gypsy families displaying goods on a blanket or bare ground, or carrying a handful of items through the crowds: a few pairs of stockings, a bag of garlic. It's the best open-air theatre in Barcelona.

Pça. Reial

Metro: Jaume I (L4)

On Sunday mornings this elegant eighteenth-century plaça turns into a market for old coins, medals and stamps. It's full of avid collectors and a few cops at the north-east corner nabbing the lowlife.

Centre d'Antiquaris

Pg. de Gràcia 55, 1st floor
Metro: Pg. de Gràcià (L3 or L4)

A parcel of antique shops, mostly full of heavy old stuff, with a few bad art galleries interspersed and some quite interesting shops with small *objets*. We were looking for bronze lizards, and ultimately found one stratospherically priced at 52,000 ptas. Also: Dinky toys, model airplanes, religious art, art nouveau lamps, all too expensive but fine for rainy-day browsers.

Mercat Sant Antoni

Comte d'Urgell
Metro: Poble Sec (L3)

Surrounded on Sundays from 10:00 to noon with books (few of any value), comics, magazines, movie posters and stills, coins, medals and stamps. Postcards (some old and interesting) are 25 ptas up. Mobbed.

Flowers

Outside the Mercat de Concepció
Valencia between Bruc and Girona
Open year round, except Christmas Day.

Rambla de les Flors
Flower stalls on the Rambla de Sant Josep, between c/ Hospital and c/ Carme. Flowers in profusion.

Food

Barcelona's covered markets are treasure troves, not just for the odd bite to carry you through a morning's walk, but for edibles to take home as gifts or stock up your own kitchen. However, before you dive into the markets, check your own country's regulations about what kinds of foods you can bring in: some don't permit meat of any kind, even preserved or dried. Others have a ban on fruit, in case you were thinking of carrying home a last-minute punnet of perfect strawberries.

The best-known of Barcelona's great public markets is the **Boqueria** on the Ramblas, a great, shadowy, crowded place. The stalls are bright with giant strawberries in May – their perfume scents the air. In October wild mushrooms of fantastic shape and colour spill off stalls in the vegetable section. One delicatessen stand has twenty-three kinds of olives, capers, pickled vegetables in trays, two dozen kinds of dry sausages and salamis.

Many sell fresh green herbs as well as herbs dried and tied in bunches. In one place, in the spring, you can find green young asparagus as thin as chopsticks, in others the asparagus is ivory-white and incredibly thick. There are potatoes from Mallorca, tomatoes from Holland, apples from America, tangelos and mandarins from Israel.

The centre of the Boqueria is silvery with fish, and scores of food writers have exhausted their adjectives over the incredible variety. Everything is slithering fresh, looking as though pulled flapping from the sea a few minutes ago.

In the autumn, the game stalls are like Dutch still-life paintings, with guinea hens and pheasants in their feathers hanging on racks, venison still in fur, boars' heads glowering down upon you. Either you revel in the richness or it turns you into an instant vegetarian.

The Boqueria opens at about 08:30, six days a week, and begins to wind down around lunchtime; part of it reopens after siesta time, but the best of it is in the early morning.

Every district of the city has a covered market of its own where fresh fruit, vegetables, fish, meat and such oddments as capers, olives, pickled vegetables, sweets and prepared dishes are sold. Front stalls often show their best and give you their worst; those toward the centre of the market are better but more expensive.

Among the older and more redolent *mercats* are Santa Caterina (1848), Clot (1879), Barceloneta (1887), Sant Antoni (1884) and Llibertat (1897); but the ones we've enjoyed most are the Boqueria itself, on the Rambla Sant Josep, the Gràcia market on Travessera de Gràcia at Torrijos, and the Concepció market on Valencia between Bruc and Girona. There you can find:

● a great variety of **olives** – tiny Joquillos, little grey-green ones from Arbeca, huge greeny-brown Obregons from Andalusia – they make wonderful gifts. In even the smallest local market you'll find at least fifteen kinds. Buy screw-topped plastic containers (Servicio Estación, the fantastic DIY shop on Aragó near the Pg. de Gràcia, has them in all sizes) and tip your olives into them.

● **dried herbs**, wonderfully fragrant, a real temptation, but keep in mind that they're fragile and crumble easily. Wrap carefully in newspaper packets . . . although even crumbled they're a thousand times more flavourful than the expensive ones you get in jars in your home-town supermarket.

● **dried mushrooms**, available on the same stalls that sell the incredible variety of fresh ones. The best selection is in the autumn.

● the dry, spicy **sausages** of Catalonia, a perfect gift for friends with a taste for the pungent. At the market stall just point to what you want: ask for anything from 100 grams to a kilo. Or buy a whole one such as thin smoky *fuet*, and divide it up for gifts when you get home. Avoid the softer ones like *morcilla* and *sobresada*, as they don't keep well and are apt to ooze all over the contents of your suitcase.

● **jamon serrano**, the incomparable Spanish mountain ham, extremely luxurious. Every market has whole ones hanging up, complete to the cloven hoof.

● Spanish **cheese**, most interesting though not nearly so well known as Italian or French. Explore those available on the cheese-counters of any market: look for mild Quintana, Cabrales, a goat cheese lightly streaked with blue veins, or Azul Danes, another goat cheese. Others are fresh Queso de Burgos, Manchego Seco (hard), deep-flavoured Vall d'Aran, or La Garrotxa.

You can taste a range of Spanish cheeses at the Cannes Bar, c/ de Doctor Joaquim Pou near the Cathedral. And just outside the Boqueria is the Casa Guinart. We're told their cheeses are varied and distinguished, but as there's always a queue outside the door we haven't been able to get in to follow this up.

For other Catalan delicacies, look into local *charcuterias*, which are usually open Tuesday to Saturday. Try:

Angel Jobal

Princesa 38

Azafranes (saffron) is the most portable and most appreciated of presents from Spain. AJ sells it in all quantities from a gram to a kilo. The shop is redolent.

Colmado Pijoan

Perez Galdo 49

Open seven days a week from 10:00 to 22:00.

Here you can put together the makings of a picnic – ham croquettes, cold roast chicken, lovely cooked vegetables like fried *albergínies* (aubergines), sometimes with anchovy fillets.

Craccrac

Castellnou 44

Dried fruit and nuts (what else would a store with this title sell?).

Fargas

Boters 16

Freshly made – and very expensive – chocolates, among the luxuries of Barcelona. It has other branches, but in this original shop chocolate is still ground, as it has been forever, on a dark Satanic mill.

Mauri

Provença 241

Pastry that's as much a treat for the eye as for the tongue. If Barcelona had a branch of Fauchon, this would be it.

J. Murria

Roger de Llúria 85

In a lush art nouveau exterior are preserved truffles, olive oils, olives, anchovies, red peppers, breadsticks, wines and liqueurs.

Planelles Donat

Portal de l'Àngel 25

Purveyors of *turrón*, the super-rich sweet made of almonds and olive oil and sugar. It's traditionally a Christmas delicacy, but you can find it year-round in Barcelona. Some varieties are thick with sliced almonds, others smooth and unctuous, some even chocolate-coated.

The Tea Centre of Barcelona

Travessera de Gràcia 122

These people not only consume tea, they are consumed by it. Over a hundred varieties, including four blends of their own invention, and perfumed blends of fruit, flowers, herbs, spices.

Olive oil from Spain is, of course, a glorious gift – but it's only available in glass bottles (breakable) or in tins (heavy). The rich opulent taste of Spanish oil isn't to everyone's taste, although we love it poured on coarse bread and sprinkled with sea salt or trickled over a ripe tomato that has been squashed on to toasted peasant bread.

If you want to take home some of the great Catalan white wines, or brandy, or *anís*, our advice is to wait and pick it up in the duty-free at the airport: prices are lower than in shops in town.

Barcelona pràctic
(Staying afloat)

Animals

Barcelonese like big dogs; they like to keep them in their apartments, and park them on their balconies, where they can bark. They rarely take them into restaurants or other public places.

Cats seem to belong to the neighbourhoods: like most Barcelonese they're well fed, well cared for, independent, and not particularly outgoing with strangers. If you're fascinated by feral cats, the place to find them is the zoo in the Parc de la Ciutadella: not the exotic varieties behind bars, but the nomads who slink everywhere through the grounds, coexisting with the imported birds and beasts of the zoo's open areas.

Apart from the zoo, live animals in cages are concentrated at the top end of the Ramblas: birds and bunnies for sale as pets. The neighbourhoods of Barcelona are full of birdsong – the balconies are crowded with caged canaries who sing to each other across the *carrers* – and this is the source.

Babysitters

They're called *guarderias* or crèches, and you can find them in the *Yellow Pages* – the *Páginas Grogues* or *Páginas Amarillas*. Or ask the patron of your hotel or hostal for a recommendation.

Books (in English)

See Shopping, page 185.

Car hire (but first see Driving, below)

The usual famous names, Hertz, Avis and so forth, are available at the airport to rent you a car. Book from England and well in advance in the summer.

Spanish hire companies through which you can rent before leaving England are:

Atesa
65 Wigmore Street
London W1M 9AG
Tel: 071 224 0504

Melia
273 Regent Street
London W1R 7PB
Tel: 071 499 6493

Trans-Hire
Unit 16
88 Clapham Park Road
London SW4 7BX
Tel: 081 978 1922

We ourselves have never rented a car in Spain, and certainly have never needed one for Barcelona and the coast around it. Those who have say that driving – especially in summer months – takes a lot of the fun out of the holiday.

The most committed traveller-by-car we know suggests: stick to public transport if you are going to be mainly in and around Barcelona. He advises, however, that if you want to strike off away from the coast, into some of the fascinating and little-explored towns of the Catalan hinterland and on into the foothills of the Pyrenees, a hire car is a good idea. Arrange for it beforehand, pick it up at the airport, get all the insurance you can, and bypass the city completely. After your Catalan journey, turn the car in, catch the train into town, and you're free to use the very good public transport in Barcelona without strain.

Clothing sizes

Women:
Clothes

British	10	12	14	16	18	20
American	8	10	12	14	16	18
Spanish	38	40	42	44	46	48

Shoes

British	4½	5½	6½	7½
American	6	7	8	9
Spanish	37	38	40	41

Men:
Clothes

British/American	35	36	37	38	39	40
Spanish	36	38	40	42	44	46

Shirts

British/American	14	15	16	17	18
Spanish	36	38	40	42	44

Shoes

British	7	8	8½	9½	10½
American	7½	8½	9	10	11
Spanish	41	42	43	44	45

Cultural institutes

Good sources of free entertainment: films, exhibitions, concerts. Drop by for a schedule of events.

Institut Alemany de Cultura
Gran Via 591
Tel: 317 38 86

Institut Britànic
Amigó 83
Tel: 209 63 88

Institut Francès
Moià 8
Tel: 209 59 11

Institut Italià de Cultura
Ptge. Méndez Vigo 5
Tel: 317 31 74

Driving in Barcelona

The best advice we can give is the most obvious: don't do it. The
Spanish, and those who live and drive in Barcelona, drive fast and
with dash. We have been told that the accident rate for foreign
drivers is high. Public transport is superb and taxis are cheap.
Parking is difficult if not impossible. If you want to get out of town,
to Montserrat or any of the pretty Costa Brava resorts, use the
excellent trains (see Day trips and getaways, page 238). You'll live
longer and come home more relaxed.

A particular menace for driver and pedestrian alike is the buzzing
swarm of Vespas and other small motorbikes and scooters which
charge through the city – they can turn, swerve, ride up on the
pavement, cut in front of slower-moving vehicles, all but climb
trees. For the native driver, they are like being swarmed over by
ants; for the foreign driver, simply hell.

If you must take a car into Spain, be sure you have all the
documentation needed: International Driving Licence (if yours isn't
the standard EEC three-part printed licence, get it from the AA or
the RAC, or take your current licence to the nearest Spanish Consulate for a translation). Vehicle registration papers. Insurance
policy. Above all, check your insurance before you go. Don't assume
that just because you have comprehensive insurance it will give you
all the protection you need when driving abroad – especially in
Spain. Legally, all you have to do is tell your insurers that you're
taking a car abroad.

Many companies are unwilling to extend your coverage without
selling you a Green Card, which gives you extended coverage at a
cost from £20 up depending on your length of stay.

Other companies have other rules:

General Accident will issue you a card free if you're a policyholder for up to 45 days, then charge you £15 for every 15-day period after that for up to 90 days.

Norwich Union gives policyholders five weeks' use of a Green Card free.

The AA Green Cards for their members are free, for up to 45 days, and they strongly recommend that you have one. As they point out, an internationally recognized insurance certificate eases a situation greatly at the time of an accident when, *ipso facto*, tempers are easily lost and reason can go by the board. This is especially important in Spain – it's hard enough to argue logically in English, much less in Castilian.

This brings us to the important question of bail bonds. In Spain, if you're in a car accident, the rule seems to be all parties are considered guilty until they can prove their innocence. Therefore, GET A BAIL BOND if you are taking a car to Spain, or thinking of hiring one there.

Spanish police can impound both you and your car unless you hand over a heavy deposit, in cash or traveller's cheques. This cash-down policy is their way of ensuring that you will show up if the matter goes to court.

Arrange for a bail bond with your insurance company, or with the AA or RAC. If you're nicked for a traffic offence, as distinct from an accident, a cash payment on the spot will reduce the fine by 20 per cent, the Spanish Tourist Office in London says.

Electricity

220 or 230 volts AC, with round-pin, two-point plugs.

Embassies

See Emergencies, page 230.

Entrances and exits

Tancat = closed
Obert (or *oberta*) = open
Spanish doors open inwards.

Guide books and background reading

Barcelona Design Guide

Juliet Pomés Leiz and Ricardo Feriche
Editorial Gustavo Gili, Barcelona 1990

Architectural itineraries and venues for architects and designers, with shops, hotels, restaurants and night-spots of special interest thrown in. In Castilian and English.

Nits de Bars

Angel Juez and Oriol Comas
Parsifal Edicions, Barcelona 1990

A staggering collection of Barcelona's bars and night-spots, described in joyous detail. In Catalan.

Argot Barceloní

Antoniu Sánchez, Rafel Taixés and Rafael Tasis
Parsifal Edicions, Barcelona 1991

Street-talk, much of it from the lower depths, and if you can interpret the Catalan translations, wicked and witty.

Barcelona

Andrew Eames, ed.
Insight City Guides
Apa Publications (HK), 1990

Profusely illustrated, well written and intensively researched by a team of writers and photographers. A lovingly-written introduction to the history, culture, and streets of the city, with good notes for travellers at the end of the book.

Barcelona: A Thousand Years of the City's Past

Felipe Fernández-Armesto
Sinclair-Stevenson, 1991

A thorough and dispassionate history of the city from the emergence of the Counts to the International Exhibition of 1929, and a refreshing read: although he sympathizes with the city's recurring reversals of fortune, Fernández has little patience with Catalanism and its attendant histrionics. He actually considers Barcelona as part of Spain.

Catalan Cuisine

Colman Andrews
Macmillan, 1988, paperback edition Headline

Plenty of uniquely Catalan recipes (including some very bizarre concoctions indeed), and plenty of background detail, devoutly catalogued: three pages on the life and times of *bacallà* (salt cod) alone, followed by another seven pages of salt cod recipes. Five different recipes for *allioli*. A treatise on the varieties of sausage. Loving and obsessive.

The City of Marvels

Eduardo Mendoza (trans. Bernard Molloy)
Collins, 1988

La ciudad de los prodigios is a Horatio Alger novel (in which virtue plays no part) about a country boy who muscles his way into a fortune in the city between the World Fairs of 1888 and 1929. An excellent guide to the history of corruption in Barcelona. Very funny and rather nasty, with a piquant dab of magical realism.

Coping With Spain

Garry Marvin
Basil Blackwell, Oxford 1990

Useful and detailed: how to survive internal travel in Spain, the telephone and post offices, emergencies and medical matters, money questions, technical hints on restaurants and hotels, and extensive notes on how not to make a fool of yourself at a bullfight.

Homage to Barcelona

Colm Tóibín
Simon & Schuster, 1990

An Irish journalist's essays on the history, art, politics and popular culture of the city – knowledgeable and affectionate.

The Quadrat d'Or

Albert Garcia Espuche, ed.
Olimpíada Cultural and Ajuntament de Barcelona, 1990

A catalogue of 150 Moderniste houses in the 'Golden Square' of the Eixample, with photos (old and new) of each, and an excellent introduction to the cultural and artistic forces that produced them.

The Spaniards: A Portrait of the New Spain

John Hooper
Penguin, 1987

Economy, politics, the army, the monarchy, education, media, the arts, the church, the sexes, the regions.

Hairdressers

There are almost as many *perruquerias* (*peluquerias* in Castilian) as there are citizens of Barcelona, and location seems to determine price and degree of fashion.

Health (see also Emergencies, page 226)

Catching cold is inevitable in the autumn: half the city has a hand-kerchief to its face. Pollution exacerbates whatever bugs are in the air. Throat complaints are common. There's no avoiding it if you spend your time on the streets or in places where contagion is easy – such as hotels and restaurants. The *farmàcias* are full of exotic nostrums and friendly advice, and the ones that are open at night and weekends – a roster that changes by rotation – are listed daily in the newspapers under *Farmàcias de Guardia*. Or you could try a herbalist (see pages 188–9).

Better news is that since Catalan food is relatively simple and rides easy on the stomach, you're unlikely to come down with a *crise de foie*, the ghastly result of too much rich food that inevitably takes down travellers in France. But it doesn't hurt to keep an eye on what you eat – especially *tapas*, which have a tendency to lie in wait all day, unrefrigerated, for the unsuspecting traveller. If it doesn't look fresh, don't eat it.

Hitch-hiking

Hitch-hiking is not looked upon with favour in Spain; very few drivers, understandably enough, will stop to pick up a stranger. However, Auto-Stop, the international organization which puts together travellers without cars and people who can take passengers, has an office in Barcelona. There's a set fee for each journey. Take your passport and look respectable or you haven't a hope. Barnastop, c/ Pintor Fortuny 21, near the Ramblas. Tel: 318 27 31.

Holidays, festivals and hours

* 1 January	Any Nou
* 6 January	Reis Mags (Epiphany)
*19 March	Sant Josep
23 April	Sant Jordi (the patron saint of Catalonia)
* 1 May	Festa del Treball
11 May	Fira de Sant Ponç
24 June	Sant Joan
*15 August	Assumpció
*11 September	Diada (national holiday of Catalonia)
*24 September	La Mercè
*12 October	Hispanitat (national holiday of Spain)
* 1 November	Tots Sants
* 6 December	Dia de la Constitució
* 8 December	Immaculada Concepció
*25 December	Nadal
26 December	Sant Esteve

Movable feasts:
*Dijous Sant   Maundy Thursday
*Divendres Sant   Good Friday
*Pascua de Resurecció   Easter
*Dilluns de Pascua   Easter Monday
*Corpus Christi

*public holidays

If a public holiday falls on a Tuesday or Thursday, you can count on local businesses to stay closed on the preceding Monday or following Friday: the *puente*, or bridge, between holiday and weekend.

Business is now almost as important as pleasure in Barcelona, and as a consequence the traditional Spanish siesta has all but vanished here. Everyone takes a long lunch break, and no one goes to bed before midnight, but otherwise the city is more or less on a northern schedule, with many businesses on eight-hour shifts.

Shops are generally open from 09:00 or 10:00 to 13:00 and 16:00 to 20:00 Monday to Friday, Saturdays from 09:00 or 10:00 to 14:00. Department stores open from 10:00 to 20:00 or 21:00, Monday to Saturday.

Business offices are usually open 09:00–14:00 and 16:30–19:00 Monday to Friday.

Banks: 09:00–14:00 Monday to Friday, and 09:00–13:00 on Saturdays.

Information sources

Patronat de Turisme (municipal service)

Moll de la Fusta
Hours: 09:00–15:00
15 June–30 September: 08:00–20:00
Tel: 310 37 16
and
Sants Estació vestibule
Hours: 08:00–20:00
Tel: 325 52 35

Oficina de Turisme (run by the Generalitat of Catalonia)

Gran Via 658
Hours: Monday–Friday 09:00–19:00; Saturdays 09:00–14:00
Tel: 301 74 43
and
El Prat airport
Hours: Monday–Saturday 09:30–20:00; Sundays 09:30–15:00

American Visitors Bureau

Gran Via 591
Tel: 301 01 50

Palau de la Virreina

Rambla Sant Josep 99
Tel: 318 23 83

Racks of free brochures on current cultural events: music, theatre, art, dance, lectures, festivals of the arts.

Casacas Rojas

Peripatetic information sources, dressed in red and white, displaying the letter 'i' on their uniforms. They patrol the Barri Gòtic, the Ramblas and the Pg. de Gràcia from 09:00 to 21:00, between the end of June and the end of September.

Telephone information

010   the Citizen Information Service: 24-hour info on everything
094   weather
003   directory enquiries

Insurance

Which? magazine covered the subject of travel insurance thoroughly in its February 1991 issue. If you're not a subscriber, look it up in your local library well before you set off.

If you're a UK citizen travelling in an EEC country, you should get Form E111 from the post office or the DHSS, and cling to it through thick and thin; it will provide a certain amount of medical coverage, but you'll have to pay at least 20 per cent of the total cost, and remember that it won't be luxurious or even comfortable if you're landed in hospital for more than a day or two.

A really good comprehensive insurance policy should insure for medical costs of £250,000 for European travel – which sounds like a lot, but will give you complete coverage for medical, dental and hospital bills, and even provide for flying you and an escort home by air ambulance if the worst happens.

This same policy should provide cancellation insurance for your flight, prepaid hotel bills, car hire, or whatever – in case you or a close relative are ill before your departure date, or if your house catches fire, or you lose your job, or if your house has been burgled and you are asked to stay put by the police, or even if you have to cancel to serve on a jury.

Be sure that the policy covers you for loss of money and personal belongings. And read the fine print: make sure that your definition of money – cash, traveller's cheques, credit cards, Eurocheques – is the same as the insurance company's, and check to see that if travel tickets or passport are lost or stolen you can claim on your policy for replacement costs.

Also, if your flight is unavoidably delayed for more than 24 hours, your policy should allow you to cancel and get a refund of your air fare. A good policy will also pay you at least £20 for a flight delay of 12 hours or more, to cover food and at least a portion of a hotel bill.

If your luggage is wandering around Europe without you for more than 12 hours, you should be able to claim at least £50 for urgent replacements.

Pay for everything you can with credit cards, keep all receipts, and send your claim in as soon as you get home – on the off chance that the policy will pay out before you get the credit card bill.

When you've charged your travel tickets on credit cards, you get some automatic coverage – but it's no substitute for really adequate comprehensive insurance, and you can't claim on more than one policy.

A good policy for a holiday of up to two weeks shouldn't cost more than about £15. Banks often issue policies, but make sure you see the actual policy or a detailed brochure. We found that four central London branches of one of the most famous banks had no brochures, and in each case the overworked clerk at the Foreign Exchange window could only assure us that the policy covered 'everything'. (It turned out that although the cost was the same as some of the comprehensive policies issued by other companies, the medical coverage was only a tenth as much.)

Travel agents and tour operators often offer policies, but don't accept one unless it touches all the bases described above. Here as always, it pays to be sceptical.

We have heard good reports of policies issued by the five companies listed below. (All were among the 'Best Buys' in the *Which?* article.) Contact them in good time to get their brochures and arrange for coverage.

Whiteley
Tel: 0422 348411

MKC
Tel: 0268 590658

Perry Gamble
Tel: 081 879 1255

Accident & General
(your nearest branch)

Crispin Spears
Tel: 071 480 5083

BUPA subscribers can take out a very good comprehensive policy at fairly low cost – roughly £15 for 12 days. There's no age limit, but you must get the policy seven days before travelling. Tel: 071 352 5212.

PPP (Private Patients' Plan) subscribers can get International Emergency Medical cover for up to £35,000 at no extra cost – and have an SOS Alarm Centre operational 24 hours a day with instant advice. In addition, they can provide you with the name of an English-speaking doctor near you. For details, phone 0323 410515, or write to them at Upperton Road, Eastbourne, East Sussex BN21 1LH.

Laundry

The norm is next-day service, *lavar y secar* (clothing washed and dried for you) by the kilo. Prices are about:

5 kilos	850–885 ptas
6 kilos	980 ptas
7 kilos	1015 ptas
10 kilos	1400 ptas

Self-service coin-ops scarcely seem to exist in Barcelona, and they're not that much cheaper than having your laundry done for you. We've only found one, in the Barri Gòtic:

Autoservicio Lavanderia ROCA
c/ Rauric 20

A load of 5 kilos takes 40 minutes in rather dilapidated machines, and costs 700 ptas. The same establishment will do your laundry for you at 980 ptas for 6 kilos, a surcharge of 23 ptas per kilo, if you keep track of such things.

Left luggage

Look for the *consigna*, the left luggage lockers in Sants Estació, open from 07:00 to 23:00, about 200 ptas per day. (There's no left luggage service at the airport.)

Lavatories, public

Public loos in Barcelona are rare, but they do exist: in Sants Estació and other public buildings, in department stores (but surprisingly grotty in our experience), and (if you can manage to look as if you belong there) in the big hotels. At the Hotel Colon, for instance, march straight ahead from the entrance and you'll see well-marked *servicios*. Museums are all equipped with loos but (with the exception of the Picasso Museum) you will have had to come up with the price of admission before taking advantage of them. There are a few coin-op lavatories on the more populous streets: at the bottom of the Ramblas, near Drassanes, for instance, but a) they're never there when you want them, b) they're even smaller than airplane WCs, and c) they're too overused to be particularly clean. More are promised for the Olympic year.

The best alternative is to take advantage of the good nature of café owners. If you stumble into a café or bar and ask for the *servicios* you'll never (in our experience) be turned away. It would be polite at least to have a snack or a cup of coffee before you leave, but it's not obligatory.

Generally the more upmarket the place, the cleaner and better equipped the facilities, but since you won't always find yourself among the gentry, it's a good idea to carry a bit of lavatory paper (*papel higienico*) at all times. And don't be surprised if the WC is missing its seat. Somewhere in Barcelona there must be a warehouse full of purloined toilet seats, and we'd like to know where it is.

The most charming lavatory we know is in the La Xicra, the chocolateria in the Pça. Josep Oriol. Exquisite tiles, creamy soap, and the only really hot hand-drier in the world. Their cheesecake is fabulous, too.

Manners

Barcelona is a big city and a businesslike one, and its inhabitants have developed the carapace of all big-city dwellers: they're intent upon their own affairs, and rarely spare a passing glance for strangers. Generally, in the course of everyday transactions, they're direct and helpful; and if you become an established figure in the neighbourhood, even for a few days, you'll be recognized and welcomed, and your regular habits (a *cortado* and a *xuxo*, or the daily *Vanguardia*) anticipated and immediately served. One of the great pleasures of travel is to watch the barriers crumble, even when alien language and culture seem to be insurmountable.

Occasionally, though, you'll be treated with blank indifference, even a crust of hostility. You can only assume that this shop or café has been roughed up by waves of drunken northern yobs from the Dark Ages onward, and nothing you can do will warm up the atmosphere. In which case, shrug it off and find somewhere more congenial.

If you're fortunate enough to meet the Barcelonese as friends or friends of friends, your relationship will be flooded with warmth and attention, and the least you can do is reciprocate: with flowers or a *turrón* when you're invited to lunch, or an honest attempt to pick up the tab when you go out to dinner.

Barcelonese like to shake hands on all occasions, from casual encounters on the street to formal meetings in the office. If you find yourself sharing a table at lunch with strangers, you're likely to be drawn into conversation, and when you or they depart there are handshakes all around.

Money

See also Preliminaries, page 11, for thoughts about how much to take with you.

The denominations

coins: 1, 2, 5, 10, 25, 50, 100, 200, 500 ptas
(a 5 peseta coin is traditionally called a *duro*)
notes: 100, 200, 500, 1000, 2000, 5000, 10,000 ptas

To give you an idea of what these are worth:

1 pta will get you nothing; useful as ballast
25 ptas is enough for a local phone call
75 ptas will buy you a newspaper (in Catalan)
100 ptas will buy you a *cortado* – warm coffee (with milk) in a shot-glass
200 ptas is the cost of admission to the Museu d'Art Modern
450 ptas will buy you a T-1 10-trip Metro/bus ticket, or a roll of film
500 ptas will get you from the harbour to the Gràcia in a taxi
600 ptas will get you into the Zoo
750 ptas will buy you a good lunch (on the *menú del día*)
1000 ptas will buy you a large gin and tonic in a trendy bar
3000 ptas will give you a good night's sleep in a hostal

and so on . . . till you've spent it all.

Barcelona banks: the money printers

Banks in Barcelona are scattered as thick as confetti: there has been nothing like it since Beirut in the 1960s. Almost always the banks are superb edifices with high ceilings, gentle music, marble floors and walls, sofas, coffee tables, soft lights. How can they afford it all?

It's simple: they're rolling in the commissions they charge travellers for converting foreign currency into pesetas. **Barclays** for example, at Pg. de Gràcia 45, will be glad to change your Barclays traveller's cheques for you – for a minimum commission of 750 ptas per transaction. That's about £4 at the autumn 1991 rate of exchange. For a £50 cheque, they pick up about 8 per cent in fees – in addition to the 2 per cent you paid when you bought the cheques. They'll be happy to cash a personal cheque on your English Barclay account – for another 750 ptas, please. They will cash these cheques up to £100 a day, with your chequebook, passport and Barclaycard. Barclays branches, if you're still with us, are also at Diagonal 419, Ronda de la Universitat 27, Gandúxer 10, and Pça. de Sant Jaume.

Natwest charges a minimum of 500 ptas for cashing their own traveller's cheques, and the same for cashing cheques on your personal Natwest account in England (up to £100 per day). The central office is at Pg. de Gràcia 67, with branches at Balmes 195, Valencia 327, and other ritzy locations.

Other English-linked banks: Lloyds at Rambla de Catalunya 123, and Midland at Diagonal 427. We haven't checked their rates.

Spanish banks such as Sabadel, Santander, Banco Central and others, can set their own commission rates: a typical one in the Ramblas charges a fee of 500 ptas minimum for exchanging dollars or pounds (cash) to pesetas. One hundred ptas is the minimum for cashing American Express traveller's cheques here, which seems a gentle bite. For 'big sums such as 50,000 ptas' the rate drops to a kind 1 per cent. Spanish banks will not cash English or American personal cheques, even with your bank card and passport.

Banesto, across from the Pg. de Gràcia Metro station, has a 500 ptas minimum charge for Amex traveller's cheques or foreign cash. But it has beautiful REAL Barcelona chairs designed by Mies van der Rohe, oriental rugs, gentle lights, and it's open from 08:30 to 16:30 Monday to Thursday from September to June. A great place to write postcards, meet friends, read your mail, shelter from the rain. But don't think about changing money there.

Commercial **cambios** such as ExacChange in the Ramblas let you off a little easier, with a 300 pta commission for cashing Amex traveller's cheques, or changing dollars or pounds (cash) into pesetas. But their exchange rates will not be quite as good as those at the bank.

Now for the good news: **American Express** traveller's cheques cost you just 1 per cent to buy, and for cashing the cheques at the Amex office in Barcelona, it's a mercifully low 1 per cent commission per transaction. The same goes for changing pounds or dollars (cash) into pesetas. You can change that last lonely £20 note for just 20p. The fee for $100 is a dollar. You swan out feeling rich, and very kindly inclined toward Amex.

Their hours are good, too: 09:30–18:00 Monday to Friday, 10:00–12:00 Saturdays. Everyone speaks English/French/German/Portuguese and probably Urdu and Arabic as well.

Giro Bank: The National Giro Postcheque scheme allows British customers to take money out of their UK accounts, in pesetas, at main post offices in Spain. Get up-to-the-minute information, and cheques, from your local National Girobank office. There is a charge for each cheque you use, plus a commission charge at the Spanish post office, but it's a convenient and safe way of drawing money abroad.

Banking hours

Most banks open at 08:30 and close at 14:30 on weekdays, 08:30–13:00 Saturdays. They are closed on Saturdays in the summer (15 June–15 September). Some stay open until 16:30 one day a week, autumn to spring.

Our advice about taking money into Spain can be summed up in about twenty-five words. Enough pesetas bought in England to start you off. The rest in Amex traveller's cheques. Nothing in Barclays or Natwest traveller's cheques. Your own personal chequebook and bank card as a last resort.

Note: almost all Barcelona banks have 24-hour automatic cash machines in outside lobbies. You get through the locked door by slipping your credit card in a slot. Once inside, tap in your PIN number with your card to get a cash advance which will appear on your next statement (plus interest from the date of withdrawal). At Barclays and in other English-based banks, you can get information on the machine in English or Castilian. Spanish cash-dispensers will only speak to you in their own language.

Newspapers and magazines

The international editions of the *Financial Times* and the *Independent*, and the *International Herald Tribune*, are available daily in the kiosks around the Ramblas and the Pg. de Gràcia, but they'll cost you between 165 and 200 ptas.

La Vanguardia: local, established, conservative, monarchist, written in Castilian but pro-Catalan nationalism; good coverage of the arts.

El País: Barcelona edition of the liberal national daily, in Castilian. Best for international news.

El Diari de Barcelona: locally known as *El Brusi*. In Catalan.

El Periódico: local, leftish, mass appeal, in Castilian.

Cinco Dias: local, Castilian.

Avui: conservative, Catalan nationalist, in Catalan of course.

Vivir en Barcelona: a slick monthly devoted to social and cultural goings on about town, written half in Catalan, half in Castilian.

Guía del Ocio: the weekly arts and entertainment guide, covers Friday to Thursday, and includes everything from opera reviews to sex shop ads. Its extensive restaurant section is invaluable, as are its sections on art galleries, films, and concerts.

Blanco y Negro: current affairs.

Cambio 16: weekly newsmagazine.

¡Hola!: gossip.

Nuisances

Noise

Barcelona can be deafening. Traffic is the worst offender, especially during rush hours when everyone leans on the horn. Motorbikes, which seem to outnumber both cars and pedestrians, are particularly obnoxious. The only defence, if you like to sleep late or take naps when everyone else is trying to get home, is to seek out an inside room in your hotel or hostal. Your window may look out on an airshaft, but at least you'll get some sleep. For insurance, take ear plugs.

As in every big city, noise is a fact of life in Barcelona. You simply can't escape the little electronic ditties of the slot machines in cafés ('La Cucaracha' is the universal theme), the roar of Gaggia coffee machines, the constant wail of ambulances mopping up after rush hour, and the normal exuberance of Barcelonese conversation. But remember that you didn't come here for tranquillity.

Pollution

The concomitant of traffic, it's at its worst on hot, heavy days. Palliative: head for the beach, even if only the beach at Barceloneta, where you stand a chance of a Mediterranean breeze.

Beggars

Less visible than formerly, but those who have survived the clean-up of the city have established turf: a few musicians, not very musical but highly skilled in the pathetic arts, at the top of the Ramblas and on the Pg. de Gràcia; occasional sad and passive beggars at central Metro entrances; a handful of gypsies near the Cathedral, intrepidly nailing tourists with carnations. The city employs many of its disabled citizens as ticket sellers for the Onze lottery – on street corners, in the Metro, and in kiosks the size of call-boxes all over town: less than meaningful work, but a giant step above beggary.

Numbers (in Castilian)

Cardinal

Uno, dos, tres, cuatro, cinco, seis, siete, ocho, nueve, diez
1, 2, 3, 4, 5, 6, 7, 8, 9, 10

Once, doce, trece, catorce, quince, dieciseis, diecisiete, dieciocho, diecinueve
11, 12, 13, 14, 15, 16, 17, 18, 19

Veinte, treinta, cuarenta, cincuenta, sesenta, setenta, ochenta, noventa, cien
20, 30, 40, 50, 60, 70, 80, 90, 100

mil: thousand

Ordinal

Primero, segundo, cuarto, quinto, sexto, séptimo, octavo, noveno, décimo
first, second, third, fourth, fifth, sixth, seventh, eighth, ninth, tenth

But when specifying a date, say:
El diez de mayo, not *decimo de mayo*.

Post

The central post office is in the Pça. d'Antoni López, at the foot of the Via Laietana. Office hours are approximately Monday–Friday 09:00–14:00 and 16:00–20:00, and Saturdays 09:00–14:00 (the hours are approximate because each window has a speciality, and its own set of hours).

If you play your cards right, you can avoid setting foot in this rather Kafkaesque *Administració Principal de Correus*. Instead, buy your stamps from the ubiquitous little shops (*estancos*) marked *Tabacs S.A.* These outlets of the state tobacco monopoly also sell stamps (*sellos* or *matasellos* in Castilian, *segells* or *timbres* in Catalan). You can then post your cards and letters in the yellow pillar-boxes, commonly known as *buzons* and found at pivotal intersections.

It currently costs 45 ptas to send a postcard to Britain and the rest of the EC, and 45 ptas for a letter up to 20 grams. Postcards to the US and Canada are 64 ptas, airmail letters 69 ptas for 15 grams or less. Some technical terms (in Castilian):

Letter = *carta*
Postcard = *tarjeta postal*
Airmail = *correo aéreo*
postal code = *número postal*
general delivery = *lista de correos*
postal order = *giro postal*
parcel = *paquete pequeño*
post office = *oficina de correos*

If you plan to receive mail in Barcelona, you can have it sent to:

American Express
Pg. de Gràcia 101
08008 Barcelona

or to the central post office:

Lista de Correos
Barcelona 08002

Pronunciation

See also Vocabulary, page 244.

You can't spend five minutes in Barcelona without noticing that Catalan contains some pretty bizarre combinations of letters: on menus, street signs, shop fronts, everywhere: cabs are *lliure*, *magatzems* are open on *feiners* but *tancat* on *dimiunge*, *pa* is served with *tomàquet*, *croixants* are good but *xuxos* are *més bo* . . . You can work some of them out from the context, and from the remnants of your Castilian and French, but others are both incomprehensible and unpronounceable. Here are a few tips to get you over your word-shock. Fortunately, mispronunciation is not an issue (as it is in France): Catalan has undergone endless mutations over the centuries, and no one has a lock on the rules.

x is pronounced approximately 'sh': *xocolat* = sho-co-laht
ig at the end of a word is pronounced 'tch': *puig* = pooch
c and ch are pronounced 'k': *Catafalch* = cah-ta-fahlk
ç is pronounced 's', as in French: *plaça* = plah-sa
ll is pronounced 'y': *lliure* = yee-ure
l.l is pronounced as an English double l: *paral.lel*
Castilian ñ is Catalan ny, as in *Espanya*
r is trilled as in Castilian or Italian, but silent at the end of a word:
carrer = carr-eh
ei is pronounced 'eye': *feiners* = feye-nairs
j is usually pronounced 'h': *judias* = hu-di-as; but occasionally like
an English 'j': *Montjuïc* = mont-ju-eek
u is silent, unless written ü: *querida* = ke-ree-da; *Güell* = gu-ay
ou is pronounced 'ohw': *noucentisme* = nohw-sen-tis-meh

Railway information

See page 23.

Religion

Barcelonese are ambivalent, to say the least, about their religion. Spain is overwhelmingly Roman Catholic (especially since 1492, when it threw out the Jews) but the coupling of Catholicism and central government made for some violent anticlericalism in the periods when Barcelona was most at odds with its overlords in Madrid. The exquisite church of Santa Maria del Mar owes some of its stark and beautiful austerity to the Anarchists who torched the interior in 1909 and 1936.

Although it has plenty of conservative bastions – notably Opus Dei, the powerful Catholic political action group – the Church has mostly diversified its political interests, and you can happily attend Mass in Barcelona without a partisan thought in your head. Or try one of the alternatives:

Communidad Israelita de Barcelona

Porvenir 24
Tel: 210 90 47

St George's Church

Sant Soan de la Salle 41

Anglican. Annual jumble sales and plenty of other services for expatriates, too.

Parroise Française

Anglí 15

Roman Catholic (masses in French on Sundays, and also in English on alternate Sundays).

Slang

Barcelona is the centre of Catalanism and, after thirty years of its suppression under Franco, Catalan is spoken with a vengeance. Franco also promoted mass immigration of non-Catalans into Barcelona, as a means of diluting Catalan nationalism, and the result is a linguistic free-for-all, a mix of regionalisms and neologisms and what purports to be Catalan. A cosmopolitan attitude and a lively underworld also contribute to the city's penchant for slang.

Catalanglicisms: *autsider, bitnic, beibi, bai, blacaut, esquater, establixmen, estar, estrip-poker, frilans, jevi* (as in *jevi metal*), *jipi, kitx . . .*

Smoking

Ubiquitous among young and old of both sexes although there is said to be a mild antismoking groundswell. *No es bò*, a few posters in the Metro discreetly advise, and behind the ticket kiosk in one Metro station there's a giant replica of a crushed butt, in the manner of Claes Oldenburg: striking but not particularly effective. Restaurants (and especially cafés) can be positively blurred by smoke, although buses and Metro trains are smoke free.

Ducados (strong *tabaco negro*) and Fortunas (mild *tabaco rubio*) are the best-selling cigarettes. Cigars come in all strengths, sizes and varieties – including some good inexpensive ones from the Canaries – and there are still plenty of restaurants where you can order one to top off your meal.

Telephones

Dial slowly and deliberately. The sound of a ringing phone is long intermittent tones; a busy signal more rapid.

All Spanish provincial prefixes begin with 9, followed by the number in the province. These prefixes must always be used when calling from another province. When calling Spain from another country the provincial 9 prefix is dropped.

To make calls from Spain to another country, dial 07 followed by country code, area code minus the initial zero, and number. The dialling code from Spain to the UK is 07 44; from the UK to Spain, 010 343.

If you plan to make a long international call, best go to the public office of the Telefonica in the Pça. Catalunya (cheaper than the one in Sants). At the telefonica you can pay with bills after you make your call. Rates depend on time of day: cheapest is between 22:00 and 08:00.

Tarifa A (normal rates)
Monday–Friday 14:00–20:00

Tarifa B (reduced)
Monday–Friday 00:00–08:00 and 20:00–24:00
Saturday 00:00–08:00 and 14:00–24:00
Sundays/holidays 00:00–24:00

Tarifa C (high)
Monday–Saturday 08:00–14:00

Blue public phones, located in outdoor kiosks, are tricky. You load your coins (5 or 25 pta pieces) in a little ramp which holds them until you've dialled and the connection is made; the coins then drop in as needed. For some reason – possibly a local gravity failure – the coins rarely drop in and the phones rarely work. For anything other than a local call, use one of the newer green or red phones in bars: they have proper slots, and indicate by LED display how much you've put in and how much credit you have left. The ones that take 100 pta coins are the only reasonable ones to use for long distance.

Generally the classier the bar, the better your chances of finding a
phone isolated in an alcove – where you can speak without shouting
and hear without plugging your free ear.

Time

Barcelona is one hour later than GMT: when it's 11:00 in London,
it's noon in Barcelona.

Tipping

Service is included in all restaurant bills, but in practice it's civilized
to leave another 5–10 per cent in restaurants and bars. (Fortunately
the percentage goes down as the bill goes up.) In recent years
English-speaking tourists have picked up a reputation as slim tip-
pers, and you will be rewarded with profound thanks (and sometimes looks of utter disbelief) when you leave something. Taxi
drivers and hairdressers should get 10 per cent; for lavatory attend-
ants, doormen, theatre and movie ushers, 25 ptas.

Traffic

If you're British or Australian or Japanese, it doesn't hurt to
remember that Spanish traffic runs on the right-hand side of the
road. Apart from that, there are no rules.

Water

How can anything be edible if the water tastes so bad? Barcelona
water won't make you sick, but it's so full of purifying chemicals that
you will inevitably drink bottled water. Fortunately there's plenty to
choose from – *con gas* or *natural* – among the abundant springs of
Catalonia.

When you order water in a restaurant, it will be bottled, and it will cost money – 100 ptas or so for a small bottle. The *menú del día* will generally include *vi o aigua* in the price of a meal; if you want both, it's extra.

A large plastic bottle of still water from any supermarket costs between 65 and 95 ptas, and is a useful furnishing for your hotel room: for knocking back aspirin, accompanying snacks, or whenever you're thirsty (Catalan food, heavy on salt and spices, has a way of making you thirsty). And in summer, when you can be seriously dehydrated by the heat, it's indispensable.

Wheelchair access

Minimal. Most of the hotels and hostals in this book have lifts, but you're likely to encounter a series of steps before you get to them, and the lifts themselves are almost always small, ancient and awkward. The pavements in many of the city's more interesting precincts are too narrow even for the ambulatory, and access to the kerb is routinely blocked by parked cars.

Urgències (Emergencies)

Medical emergencies

To call an ambulance, dial the Red Cross (Creu Roja) at 300 20 20, or either of the two municipal ambulance numbers: 329 77 66 or 329 97 01.

Emergency wards (*Urgències*) in the main hospitals are best equipped for medical emergencies:

North-west Eixample

Hospital de Sant Pau

Sant Antoni Maria Claret 167
Metro: Hospital Sant Pau
Tel: 347 31 33

South-central Eixample

Hospital Clinic Provincial

Casanova 143
Metro: Hospital Clinic
Tel: 323 14 14

Barceloneta/Olympic Village

Hospital Mare de Deu del Mar

Pça. Doctor Pont Freixas
Metro: Ciutadella
Tel: 309 21 12

Emergency clinics

Clinic Teknon
Lazaro Cardenas 4
Tel: 201 25 11

Clinic Quiron
Av. Mare de Deu de Montserrat 9
Tel: 214 12 00

Theft

See also Knavish Tricks, page 234.

Although the city is essentially safe, you needn't abandon common sense altogether, especially in the rough or excessively touristed precincts. Don't go around with the edge of your wallet sticking out of your back pocket, or with the front flap of your handbag flipped open and a handful of traveller's cheques clearly visible (we saw this one day in front of the elegant Loewe's shop in the Pg. de Gràcia). It makes no sense at all to lay down a sheaf of pesetas on a café table while adding up a restaurant bill. And don't hang your camera by the strap on a café chair . . .

Cross your handbag and carry nothing of value. A handbag is a place to carry tissues and sticking plasters and such; important things should stay in your room, or in your pockets. Thieves prefer to take purses on the run; muggings are rare. The common thief is called a *descuidero*: he takes what you leave unattended: if you don't take care of it (*no te cuidat*), he will.

Of course you'll have the wit to lock your hotel or hostal room door when you go out for the day, and leave the key at the desk.

Most hotels will put real valuables in their safe for you. It's sensible to keep passport and traveller's cheques with you, but buried either in a money belt or deep inside a zip pocket if you can. But that said, it's senseless to worry about what might happen and probably won't.

Lost passport

Keep a photocopy of the relevant pages in your room. If you lose your passport, report it immediately to the police (see Police, below), and then head for your consulate (see Stranded, below), who will issue you a temporary document that will get you in and out of most countries, or at least home.

Lost money

Report it to the police, as for passports, and then borrow enough for a couple of stiff brandies. See Police, below, and Insurance, page 210.

Police

There are four varieties, each with their own turf. The **Policía Nacional** (formerly khaki uniforms, now blue) patrol the streets (and those of every other city in Spain, too) on foot and by car. They are only interested in crime. The **Guàrdia Urbana**, the municipal force (blue uniforms, white-chequered band on hat and sleeve) deal with traffic and municipal infractions. The **Guàrdia Civil** (green uniforms, black bat-wing hats) watch the borders and immigration points and cruise the rural areas. And the **Mossos d'Esquadra** (blue uniforms, hats with red insignia) are the provincial Catalonian police, who mostly stand outside the Palau de la Generalitat.

In an emergency (other than traffic-related) that requires police assistance, the ones to call are the Policía Nacional. Dial 091 and give your location and the circumstances. To report a theft or an assault (which you *must* do if you want to file an insurance claim), visit their headquarters at Via Laietana 49 (corner of c/ Comtal) or the police station at Ample 23 (at c/ d'en Carabassa). Both have English interpreters during the summer.

The Guàrdia Urbana – the city cops – maintain a multilingual agency, Turisme Atenció, at Rambla 43 (just off the c/ Nou de la Rambla) specifically for tourists in trouble, with medical assistance, legal advice, facilities for reporting crime or loss, help with temporary documentation, and a phone for family contact or cancellation of stolen credit cards. It's open round the clock in summer and at Christmas and Easter, otherwise during regular business hours. Tel: 301 90 60.

Traffic accidents

Dial 092 – the Guàrdia Urbana – to summon the cops.

Traveller's cheques

The company that issues your cheques will have given you a set of receipts, with cheque numbers, when you bought them, and you should check them off as you use them. If you lose the remaining cheques, get in touch with the issuing company immediately (American Express and the bigger British banks have branches in Barcelona).

Credit cards

Keep track of numbers and expiration dates. If your cards disappear, call the issuing bank or agency immediately (a local call if there's a Barcelona branch; otherwise, see information on international phone calls on pages 223 and 235). Generally there's a limit to your liability, but speed counts, and policies vary. You can also insure your credit cards against loss and fraudulent use. Check with the issuer.

Travel insurance

See page 210.

Stranded

If you find yourself without money, traveller's cheques, or transport home because of loss, theft, or other damage, call on your embassy. If they are convinced that you are a genuine victim of circumstances, they can arrange to get you home, and you must agree to pay them back as soon as you reach a source of funds.

Australian Consulate
Gran Via Carles III 98
Tel: 317 58 82

British Consulate
Diagonal 477
Tel: 419 90 44

Canadian Consulate
Via Augusta 125
Tel: 209 06 34

Irish Consulate
Gran Via Carles III 94
Tel: 330 96 52

United States Consulate
Via Laietana 33
Tel: 319 95 50
It's on the fourth floor and not easy to find.

Appendix A:
The List of Pamela Carewe

Dear Miles,

A youngish woman I met through Oxfam used to work as a travel courier, escorting groups by coach and by plane, to Spain and Portugal.

Her family has been going to the Costa Brava since before it became fashionable – I think she said when San Feliu was just emerging from being a fishing village in the early 1960s. She remembers Catalonia when the natives were forbidden to speak Catalan, and when food was really poor and scarce, and when women had to wear real bathing suits, and wear headscarves or hats in church. All this slightly beside the point. Lately she has been taking groups to China!

Anyway, she told me how her travel wardrobe for Spain in every season but winter, when no tourists were going, had evolved. It all seemed so sensible that I thought I'd put down what she told me, for whatever use you want to make of it. She would be delighted if you'd mention her name in the credits!

This is the foolproof, travel-proof, season-proof wardrobe devised by Ms. PAMELA CAREWE. She takes:

• Two cotton short-sleeved T-shirts, in neutral colours (not white). She wears these over a turtleneck and under a cardigan in cool weather, or as cool tops with trousers in hot weather.
• One cotton T-shirt, long sleeves, in a bright flattering colour (coral, deep blue, blue-green). Not black as it quickly looks dusty.
• One or two silk roll-neck jerseys (Miles, she means what we call turtlenecks), long sleeves, very thin, in pale colours.
• One pair of thin uncrushable black trousers.
• One pair of crinkled-cotton beige or off-white trousers (drip dry).
• A Japanese yukata (cotton printed dressing gown with tie sash).
• Flipflops.

- Two pairs of comfortable shoes for walking.
- A pair of warm lightweight ankle socks: she says she has slept in them in chilly bedrooms, used them as temporary slippers when stuck with a room without a private bathroom, and even worn them in damp walking shoes to keep her feet dry.
- Four pairs of tights; four bras; four pairs of cotton, not nylon, pants.
- A lambswool long cardigan, two sizes too big, buttoning to neck – two sizes too big so she can wear it over one or two under-layers, button it as high as she wants to, tie a scarf inside the neck, and feel 'dressed'. She has never travelled with wealthy people who dress up for the Avenida Palace or the Ritz in Madrid, therefore doesn't bother with a dress, and advises her clients not to pack one.
- Three silk scarves.
- Short water-repellent lightweight rain jacket.
- Tiny folding umbrella, a Knirps, expensive, and she says she has never lost it or mislaid it because it cost so much! It folds down small enough to put in a handbag.
- Cotton-jersey ankle-length pants. She doesn't wear nightgown or pyjamas, but says she has slept in the jersey pants (bought in India), with a T-shirt, when taking a group around mountain areas in Spain. Also, if it does turn cool, she wears them under her trousers.
- Bikini or Lycra 'body', which can be worn for swimming, or with cotton trousers on a hot day.
- A pair of inexpensive imitation-leather gloves with a thin lining.
- Depending on what the weather is like on departure day, she wears some of these clothes, and rolls – she does not fold – everything else into a very lightweight nylon carry-on bag, with a shoulder strap.
- She also rolls up and stashes in that bag a strong lightweight leather carrier bag into which she will cram the day's necessities: maps, guide books, Kleenex, sunglasses, whatever.

Her theory, like ours, is: travel light, dress in layers,and always take a warm sweater: even in the south of Spain nights can turn cold, and she's been glad of extra warmth in May and June in Catalonia.

She always takes a small selection of medicines for real emergencies, and says that anywhere in Europe she can always get more over the counter in chemists' shops, to add to or replace her emergency supplies. She also takes:

- A packet of 'baby wipes' for cleaning the neck at the end of the day, wiping sticky hands, and as a sort of travelling substitute for a bidet.
- Paracetamol or aspirin.
- Proprietary diarrhoea tablets – packet of 12.
- Eye drops.
- Soothing anaesthetic cream for stings, bites, chafes.
- Self-adhesive bandage strips, half a dozen assorted sizes.
- A little bunch of cotton wool in a plastic bag.
- What she calls 'embrocation cream' for stiff neck, sore arms, shin splints.
- Prescription for reading glasses in case she loses them.
- A small tin of baby powder – invaluable for chafing and prickly heat.
- A plastic bottle of supermarket inexpensive shampoo, which she uses to wash out her smalls as well as to wash her hair.
- And – very important – a small bottle of really expensive cologne, to cheer her up when everything goes wrong!

She packs her underwear and scarves in plastic bags from London supermarkets, which she uses en route a) as laundry bags, b) as picnic bags, c) to put over her head in a downpour, d) to roll up and use as padding for breakables.

I told her Sandy Sanderson's advice about taking a little bottle of cognac . . . She said she always buys a small bottle in the duty-free on the way out. On her last trip with twelve English ladies to China, she consumed it all herself the very first day, in order to stay sane.

Regards,

Martha

Appendix B: *Knavish tricks*

One newspaper recently commented that Barcelona is a 'gold medallist in the snatch-and-grab Olympics'. In fact this lovely city is no worse than any other honeypot for tourists (a travel magazine has listed Salzburg, Verona, St Tropez and Versailles as places to watch your pockets). But Barcelona street thieves seem to have come up with some fairly spectacular ploys for relieving you of your goods and your peace of mind.

For English and American tourists, the most unnerving are gangs of child thieves – some who seem to be not more than 5 years old. No 'proper' Spanish child will ever approach a strange adult in the street, so these little dears are up to no good. While some are patting your arms and pulling your fingers, others are agilely into handbag, wallet and pockets. And even if they're caught, police can hold them for only a very brief time – long before which the swag has passed from young hands into older ones in a doorway or side street.

A plague in Barcelona, as in Rome and Paris, is the helpful-stranger scam: the person who calls your attention to a mess on your coat, eagerly mopping and blotting while an unobtrusive friend has pinched the wallet from your inside pocket.

Recently one Barcelona stroller on the Ramblas was squirted with mustard from a squeeze tube; others have been doused with chocolate sauce or smeared with ice cream. If some such unlikely 'accident' happens to you, do some yelling and pointing and let the stain stay where it is – don't accept 'help'. Immediately protect your valuables with elbows and hands. Better a stained jacket and a dry-cleaner's bill than a ruined holiday.

Look out for the man or woman who approaches with a flapping map and asks you – an obvious foreigner – for directions. Be wary, too, of anyone who sees you looking at a map or guide book and offers to help you out.

Airports and bus stations are prime picking spots for sneak thieves. So are hotel lobbies and reception desks: whatever you put down can be gone in less time than it takes to give your name to the receptionist. Never set luggage – especially hand luggage – on the ground unless you can keep it between your feet, and preferably with one foot on your bag.

Never pack your passport, traveller's cheques, travel tickets and insurance forms all in one place, and certainly never stow them in your luggage: anything really vital should be divided between an inside pocket, zipped compartment in handbag and money belt.

One woman we know swears by a sturdy shiny plastic Sainsbury's carrier bag. She buries her most important travelling stuff at the bottom in a cosmetic bag, and stuffs tissues, scarves, maps, guide books, sunglasses on top. She doesn't carry a camera. She shops in street markets and has been known to cram a loaf of bread on the top. What thief would think she had anything worth pinching?

The best defence is a soft, thin, zip envelope on a loop which can be slid on to your belt and dropped between trousers and skin. Passport, serious money and traveller's cheques fit into it. You may feel like a hick when you haul it out in a bank or restaurant, but you always know where it is. Don't carry in your pockets any more money than you can afford to lose.

For bulkier stuff like tickets and insurance forms, rely on a lightweight airline bag carried with the strap crosswise on the chest, the zip side against the body. Women who carry shoulder bags should wear them the same way. Never let any bag containing any valuables leave your hand while you are dealing with hotel clerks or at airport desks or in bus stations.

Credit cards should be protected by one of the cheap and useful card-care schemes such as Card Safe (071 376 5844), and CPP (071 351 4400). You pay them a fee of about £6 a year, and list all your plastic with them. In case of loss or theft, one phone call from you will cancel everything and get replacement cards on their way to you. From Spain, dial 07, wait for a second dialling tone, then dial 44 and the area code minus the initial zero. If you're cleaned out of money as well as credit cards, ask the telephone operator to put through a reverse-charge call for you.

If you carry traveller's cheques, keep the fiddly little record blank well away from the actual cheques, and don't lose the receipt given you by your bank or American Express when you bought them, as without it you will need more than an honest face to convince them to replace lost or stolen ones.

Keep your PIN (personal identification number) separate from your Visa, Access and Amex cards. And stash your Eurocard away from the book of Eurocheques. These are very easy for thieves to use to get money from Spanish banks, or to splash out in expensive shops, and singularly difficult to cancel: the card protection schemes can't protect you here. Thieves don't mind paying the sometimes exorbitant surcharge for cashing them, and you will greatly mind coming home to find your bank account cleaned out.

If you do travel with Eurocheques, make a note of the phone number of your bank branch at home, and immediately put in a stop-payment order, following it up with a confirming letter the same day.

In the summer of 1991 there was a rash of train robberies – gangs who slipped into sleeping compartments of the night trains moving south through France, deftly removing cameras, jewellery and money without waking the occupants, dropping off the train at the next station. If caught in the act, they'd pull the emergency cord and hop off when the train stopped, disappearing into the night. It's a lucrative business, despite heightened security on the trains, and you can expect it to continue in summers to come. Protect yourself by keeping valuables tucked into your berth with you, out of reach of light fingers.

If you drive a car in Spain, there are other thievish tricks: the best-known one is the car that overtakes you and slows down, hooting, flashing lights and pointing frantically at your tyres. Either ignore it, or if you do decide to pull up and get out, lock all the locks before the 'helpful' fellow motorist gets his mitts on your bags.

In car parks and petrol stations, make sure luggage is hidden under a parcel shelf or seat; don't leave passports, credit cards, money, or car papers in the vehicle even if you're just paying for petrol or popping into the loo.

Having said all this, a few words of reassurance: if you can avoid getting jostled in thick crowds on the Ramblas, and if you can manage not to look like an obvious tourist in the Barri Xinès, Barcelona is a reassuringly safe place to visit. All of its inhabitants and many, many visitors travel around it with ease and safety every hour of the day.

You can shop, stroll, eat, have coffee or a drink or a snack in tranquil confidence in at least 90 per cent of Barcelona's public places. You can prowl the little street markets such as the Pça. del Pi without being more than ordinarily careful of the safety of your possessions.

As Spanish meals begin late – 21:30 or later, ending usually about 23:00 – the streets are well populated and so is public transport. You can travel home on the last Metro without a vestige of fear, in company with a considerable number of very ordinary people all doing what you are doing: going home after a meal out.

In our experience Barcelona taxi-drivers are a good example of honesty: they may be oblivious of the value of human life, but they're scrupulous about taking the most direct route to your destination. We have several times handed over too much money for a fare, and each time the exact balance was politely returned.

Women are safe from molestation on streets and public transport. An American woman we know has lived in the heart of the city for eight years, travels on buses and Metros three or four times a day, and has never been groped, stroked, even had a brushing touch by a stranger. She can eat or drink alone without attracting unwelcome attention, she walks anywhere she pleases (except in areas where it wouldn't help to have an armed guard) and at any time. If she sits alone in a cafeteria booth she may be politely asked to share, but no one will crowd her.

Appendix C:
Day trips and getaways

Montserrat

Montserrat looms above a valley 60 km from Barcelona, and for centuries has drawn pilgrims, worshippers, sightseers, the curious and the faithful from the corners of the earth. It has been called the soul of Catalonia.

The buff sandstone cliffs, 1200 m high, are a source of wonder in themselves, but the lodestone is Our Lady of Guadelupe – the delicately carved 'Black Virgin' who has been the mother-figure of the Hispanic world for nearly a millennium. Carved from wood that has darkened and oxidized over the centuries – from air, from the waxy fumes of candles, from the loving touch of hands and lips before she retreated behind a curved screen of glass – she has none of the pale, ethereal quality of most painted and sculpted Virgins. She charms the faithful and the agnostic alike with what a nineteenth-century writer called 'the beginning of a sweet smile that seems about to light up her face'. She gazes not into eternity but directly into your eyes.

If you believe one legend, she was created by St Luke and carried to Catalonia by St Peter a few years after the Crucifixion. Throughout Roman and Visigothic rule in Catalonia, a dark Virgin, in one incarnation or another, has rested in various places on the mountain, ancestor of the current occupant, a twelfth- or thirteenth-century carving. After the invasion of the Moors she vanished for a hundred years, and then was found once again, by peasants. Claimed by the Bishop of Vic, she demonstrated a very Catalonian stubbornness in refusing to be carried further than a cave on the mountain of Montserrat – the Santa Cava which can be visited today from the plateau of the present monastery and shrine.

Visiting the Sacred Mountain and the shrine of its patroness is an experience which leaves no one untouched. Believers are thrilled and made radiant by the experience. The train and cable-car ride, or the long journey up the switchback roads that snake around the mountain, is a small price to pay.

The agnostic and those of little faith are irritated by the massive tourist coaches and put off by the commercial air of the town. The famous view over the valley from the telefèric and from the ramparts is just a view: it doesn't stop your heart. But once the queue of silent people has moved slowly through the little chapels to the Black Virgin's tiny room, something mysterious happens: the supplicant faces are transformed. The little figure, whose eyes seem to look deep into your soul, is from another world.

The shuffling queue presses behind you and you move on – thirty seconds, a minute at most, to absorb the special quality of the Black Virgin. The impression remains. Then you are out in the air, and the world returns: tourist guides, footsore crowds of visitors, arid nineteenth-century walls of reconstructed hostels and office buildings. An 'Information Booth' which exists only to sell postcards, guide books and T-shirts. The tired and the bored, longing for the next cable-car down and the train out. High up in thin air, Montserrat is exposed to merciless sun and bone-piercing wind.

The ancient monastery and library of Montserrat were wiped out by French troops in 1811: chapels desecrated, relics trampled, black masses held on the high altar. The monks were not to return to Montserrat until the mid-l870s, when they found desolation and ruins. The sixteenth-century Cathedral was restored, its old buildings re-faced with pinkish sandstone as characterless as concrete. After an interview with the Virgin it's anti-climactic: formalized High Renaissance adornment; a soaring roof; echoing, amplified sermon and creed – the only magic is the plangent voices of the children's choir, if you're lucky enough to be there when they sing.

The Shrine of the Black Virgin is open daily from 09:00–10:30, 12:00–13:30, 15:00–18:30. The Museum of the Monastery (250 ptas, students 100 ptas) is open 10:00–14:00. Cathedral opening hours or masses: check on the spot, as we've been unable, in 1991, to obtain precise information.

Practicalities

Trains to the Aëri de Montserrat leave from the FFCC platform at Pça. d'Espanya, Barcelona, in the Metro station where Lines 1 and 3 join. See page 33 about how to find it. Trains run every two hours between 05:10 and 19:10. Return fare: 660 ptas. Automatic ticket machines take cash and credit cards.

Hang on to your ticket for the return trip. You'll also need it to buy your ticket on the cable-car to the monastery. Journey time: 1 hour 16 minutes.

Telefèric: 1 March–30 June, weekdays: every 15 minutes from 10:00–13:45, and 15:00–18:45; Sundays and holidays 10:00–18.45, at (roughly) 5 minute intervals. July–September: 10:00–18:45, every 5 minutes or so. Winter schedule not available at this writing; check with the Tourist Office in Barcelona.

Telefèric tickets: 450 ptas round-trip. You must show your train ticket at the booking window.

Returning: trains from Montserrat Aëri station to Barcelona run every two hours from 11:33 to 19:33, with a last train at 21:38.

Excursions to Montserrrat

Pulmantours
Gran Via 635
Tel: 317 12 97 and 318 02 41

Julià Tours
Ronda Universidad 5
Tel: 317 64 54

Both do half-day – morning or afternoon – trips to the mountain by luxuriously equipped buses with multilingual guides. Morning tours include the singing of the children's choir; afternoon tours throw in a trip up the funicular railway from the plateau of Montserrat to the Santa Cava. No meals, snacks or coffee included. Each excursion costs 3675 ptas.

We advise: wear low-heeled walking shoes for the long steep flight of steps from the telefèric landing up to the monastery plateau. All of Montserrat is stony, and you'll do a lot of unavoidable walking. There are no places to sit except low walls and steps, or in the self-service restaurants.

If you suffer from acrophobia, stand back from the windows of the cable-car, and look out, not down, as it sways across the valley.

If you are claustrophobic, or can't bear being pressed against your fellow beings – warm and damp or with bare arms pebbled with chill – be prepared for the long, silent, slow, crowded shuffle to the shrine of the Virgin. Even off-season it can take 40-60 minutes. None of our researchers has ever done this on a Sunday, a holiday, or in the main tourist season.

Take: sunscreen in hot weather. Sunglasses all year round. A scarf and a thin jacket at almost any time of the year. The wind blows even when the sun is hot. Shuffling in the queue for the Virgin under sunless arches can be very chilly.

There seems to be no place to eat even moderately well here. If you can, take sandwiches, a bottle of mineral water, possibly some fruit or chocolate. Food in the immense self-serveries of Montserrat is best not dwelt upon.

Costa Brava resorts

When you've had enough of the city, you may want to have a look at the string of resorts that cling to the rocky coast – the Costa Brava – on either side of Barcelona. We'd better say, before making a brief run-down on them, that they are almost without exception crowded with tourists – package variety English, French, German, and the Spanish themselves who run away from the city heat – in July and August. If you can manage it you'll do much better to avoid the school-holiday months. All these resorts are cheaper and much more pleasant when the summer crowds have gone home. We have to warn you, too, that if it's constant blazing sun you want, the Costa del Sol in the south is much more dependable. The weather of Catalonia can be moody – glorious in the morning, cloudy at lunch, possibly sunny and clear after your siesta, and after the sun goes down the wind off the sea can be chilly. However, it is a beautiful and dramatic coast, and so far doesn't suffer from the booze-and-broads syndrome of the southern resorts.

Blanes, 75 km from Barcelona, is a pleasant, low-pressure place with a wide beach. The beach is a little more than 3 km long, and the sand shelves rapidly down into the Mediterranean, so be careful with swimming.

Hotels are what you'd expect, and there are many high-rise blocks of flats. *Holiday Which?* magazine, in 1989, recommended some hotels; we have friends who, on the basis of the *Which?* report, have stayed comfortably at the Park (an inexpensive seafront hotel with good views) and the Stella Maris (less modern, and popular with package-tour operators). Contact your travel agent for details.

Lloret de Mar is big, hideous, noisy and we wouldn't stay there if you gave us the place. The beach is clean but very crowded. What saves it is that many boat companies offer trips that take you away to small, still unspoiled, rocky coves nearby – such as Fanals and Canyelles. The only hotel we could possibly recommend is the Santa Marta, which is fairly expensive.

Tossa de Mar is big, too, but the beach along the bay is long, and doesn't get overcrowded in the months between June and September. If you get bored with the main beach, there's another one quite close. The Old Town is very much restored, but still fascinating, and you can climb out of the modern part of Tossa into a network of lanes patterned with nice little restaurants. The best hotel we have heard of is the Neptuno, in the Old Town.

S'Agaró has a fine golden sand beach, and another cut into the red rocks of the coast. The town itself is still quite unspoilt, and we have been told that you can walk along to a beach called Sa Conca (The Shell) which attracts quiet people who like to swim from the rocks. Check out the current rates for the S'Agaró hotels – they are somewhat more expensive than others along the coast or so we are told.

Palamos is very well known, but it's still a fishing town, not over-built, with a good beach, La Fosca, just north of it.

Calella de Palafrugell is a little beauty, the kind of fishing town that looks like a picture postcard. It has resisted the ugly pockmark-ing of high-rise hotels and giant mock-Moorish apartment blocks. We hear good reports of its restaurants and bars, and although it's well known and popular, if you go in June or September you'll enjoy the little beaches cut out of the rocky coast, and the freshly white-painted houses in the winding, climbing streets. *Holiday Which?* magazine, in 1989, mentioned the Hotel Sant Roc, not new but gracious and comfortable. It does package tours, and you may find a good deal for a week here.

The beach at **Tamariú** is said to be lovely, and has one or two very simple hotels – we don't know anyone who has stayed there, but your travel agent might have a recommendation.

Aiguablava – not a town but a line of small coves with beaches – is tranquil, the swimming safe and delightful in translucent water. Try for a booking at one of Spain's famous Paradors (guesthouses run by the State), the Nacional Costa Brava, which looks out over the sea.

There are other resorts as you go north along the coast; the most interesting is **Cadaqués**, out on a headland overlooking the bay where fishing boats bob at anchor. It is most famous for its proximity to Dalí's house at Port Lligat – but for our money, the most interesting thing to see is the eleventh-century monastery of Sant Pere de Roda up in the mountains. Ask your travel agent for a hotel recommendation: the Rocamar, very well known and quite inexpensive, is usually booked up months in advance.

We suggest that you might profitably do a swap through Intervac (see page 83), as many of its members have holiday flats or houses along this coast.

Appendix D: Vocabulary
Getting by in Catalan and Castilian

Don't think of taking a step in Spain without a good Castilian phrasebook – such as the pocket-size Penguin, 1988 edition, £2.99, or the thinner Pan book at the same price. Both give you well-organized words and phrases to cover almost every happening, and the pronunciation guides are highly useful. The dictionary sections are necessarily fairly basic, and you may want to take along something like the *Collins Gem* Spanish/English dictionary, a fat little book well worth £2.50.

Just as vital, in our view, is a Catalan/English dictionary, and luckily for you there is a superb one available in paperback in Barcelona bookshops and department stores: Jordi Colomer's *Diccionari Anglès-Català/Català-Anglès*, published by Editorial Pòrtic, 575 ptas. It's enlivened by English versions of Catalan proverbs (and Catalan versions of English ones) at each alphabetical heading.

Almost every restaurant, shop, hotel and museum uses Castilian in writing and in speech, but the Catalans are a proud race and you will very often find menus and notices in the Catalan language. It is in some ways closer to Provençal French than to classic Castilian, and seems to have fewer words of Arabic derivation.

Until you've equipped yourself with phrasebook and dictionary, here is a beginners' guide to words and phrases you may encounter in Catalan, with their Castilian and English equivalents. Where words are almost identical, or fairly easily grasped – such as chocolate/*xocolata*, café/*café*, soup/*sopa*/*sopa* – you'll have no problems. But when faced with a choice of *pastenagas* or *cigrons*, you may find it useful to know that it's carrots and chick-peas on offer, in Catalan; and what the rest of Spain calls *caracoles* are *cargols* in Catalan, and snails in English.

CATALAN	CASTILIAN	ENGLISH

IN RESTAURANTS...

cullera	cuchara	spoon
forquilla	tenedor	fork
ganivet	cuchillo	knife
plat, planxa	plato	plate
propina, punta	propina	tip
tassa, copa	taza	cup
taula	mesa	table

ON MENUS...

ànec	pato	duck
aigua	agua	water
albercoc	albicoque	apricot
bacallà	bacalao	salt cod
bikini	bikini	toasted ham and cheese sandwich
bolets	setas	mushrooms
callos	tripa	tripe
carbassa	calabaza	pumpkin/squash
cargols	caracoles	snails
carn	carne	meat
carn de bou	carne de vaca	beef
cigrons	garbanzos	chick-peas
cloisses	almejas	clams
copa, got	vaso	glass
fetge amb ceba	higado con cebollas	liver and onions
formatge	queso	cheese
gambes	camarón	shrimp
gel	hielo	ice
gelat	hielado	ice cream
gerdo	frambuesa	raspberry
llagosta	langosta	lobster
llet	leche	milk
madiuxot	fresa	strawberry
mantego	mantequilla	butter
mongetas	judias	beans
musclos	mejillones	mussels
nap	nabo	turnip
ou	huevo	egg
pa	pan	bread

pastanaga	zanahoria	carrot
pebrots farcits	pimientos rellenos	stuffed peppers
peix	pez	fish
peix espasa	pez espada	swordfish
pernil	jamon	ham
pollastre	pollo	chicken
pome	manzana	apple
pésols	guisantes	peas
raim	uva	grape
tonyino	atun	tuna
uves	uvas	grapes

IN HOTELS . . .

llit	cama	bed
	cama matrimonial	double bed
	habitacion cambra	bedroom
	habitacion doble	double room
	habitacion individual	single room
amb dutxa	con ducha	shower
amb bany	con baño	with bath
sense bany	sin baño	without bath

IN EMERGENCIES . . .

Since you want to ask for help or describe a symptom, we've put the 'request' word in English, the 'answer' words in Castilian alone. You won't need Catalan for these.

Report these to the police first, then to your consulate:

My passport has been stolen.	Me han robado mi pasaporte.
My money has been stolen.	Me han robado mi dinero.
thief	lladre
doctor	medico
a blister	un ampolla
sticking plasters	tiretas
a cough	una tos
cough lozenges	pastillas para tos
to have a sore throat	tener dolor de garganta
to catch cold	refriarse, accatarse
to have a stiff neck	tener dolor al cuelo
to have a headache	tener dolor de cabeza
diarrhoea	the same in English, Castilian and Catalan!

THE CALENDAR ...

dilluns	lunes	Monday
dimarts	martes	Tuesday
Dimecres	miercoles	Wednesday
dijous	jueves	Thursday
divendres	viernes	Friday
dissabte	sabado	Saturday
diumenge	domingo	Sunday
gener	enero	January
febrer	febrero	February
marc	marzo	March
abril	abril	April
maig	mayo	May
juny	junio	June
juliol	julio	July
agost	agosto	August
setembre	septiembre	September
octubre	octubre	October
novembre	noviembre	November
decembre	diciembre	December

NECESSARY TO KNOW ...

In Catalan only, as public notices invariably are in that language.

tancat	closed
obert	open
matí	morning
tarde	afternoon
madrugada	early hours of morning
enlaç	junction of Metro and rail lines
senars	odd (numbers)
paralls	even (numbers
enguany	this year
primavera	spring
estiu	summer
tardor	autumn
hivern	winter
c:do	closed Sundays
c:do i fest	closed Sundays and holidays
feiners	weekdays (working days)

ODDS AND ENDS . . .

bossa	bolso, cartera	handbag
maleta	maleta, valija	suitcase
tenda di sabata	zapatería	shoe shop
bizouteria	joyeria	jewellers' shop
perruquer	peluquería	hairdresser, barber
mocador	pañuelo	tissue, handkerchief
papel higienico		toilet paper

Index

ABTA, 17
Access cards, 14
accidents, traffic, 202, 203, 229
accommodation: bed and breakfast, 81–3
  home exchange, 83–4, 243
  hotels, 42–80
  youth hostels, 84–5
addresses, 44–5
Aerobus, 21, 22
agencies: bed and breakfast, 81–2
  home exchange, 83–4
  travel agents, 17–19, 211
Aiguablava, 242
air travel, 11, 17–19, 24, 211
airlines, 24
airports, 20, 22
Ajuntament (city government), 1, 26, 139
Akeora, 187
albergs (youth hostels), 84–5
Alfarràs, Marques d', 157
ambulances, 226
American Express, 14, 15, 67, 215, 216,
  220, 229, 235
American Visitors Bureau, 209
Anarchists, 221
Andreu, 144
Andrews, Colman, 87, 120, 130, 205
Angel Guimara, 157
Angel Jobal, 197
animals, 199
antiques, markets, 192–4
Apolo theatre, 157, 177
appearance, Catalans, 5
Appel, 168
Aragón, Kings of, 139, 159
Arc de Triomf, 154
Archaeological Museum, 155, 156, 166
architecture, 8, 137–8
  early period, 138–40
  guide books, 204, 206
  Moderniste movement, 39, 55, 56, 140–8,
    149, 165, 206
  Noucentiste style, 155

Renaixença, 149–51
Argot Barceloní, 204
Arnau, Eusebi, 55
Ars Studio, 174
art, 137, 151–7
Art Deco, 169
art galleries, 8, 167
  Dau Al Set, 168
  Galeria Alejandro Sales, 170
  Galeria Benet Costa, 168
  Galeria Berini, 169
  Galeria Ciento, 168
  Galeria Eude, 168
  Galeria Maeght, 169
  Galeria Subex, 168
  Galeria Taché Editor, 169
  Galuchat/Barcelona, 169
  Lino Silverstein, 169
  Sala Gaspar, 167
art nouveau, 137
Artespania, 187
Ataulfo, 139
ATOL, 17
aubergines: *escalivada*, 118–19
  samfaina, 130–1
Australian consulate, 230
Auto-Stop, 207
Autòmates del Tibidabo, 165
automatic cash machines, 15, 20, 217
Avui, 217

babysitters, 199
bail bonds, 203
'bait-and-switch', travel agents, 18
Baix Guinardó, 40
Balearics, ferries, 24–5
ballet, 172
Banda Municipal de Barcelona, 173
Banesto, 215–16
banknotes, 214
banks: automatic cash machines, 15, 20, 217
  currency exchange, 14–15, 215–16
  Eurocheques, 14, 236

(banks *continued*)
   opening hours, 209, 216–17
   travel insurance, 211
   traveller's cheques, 14
Barcelona, Counts of, 139, 159
Barcelona (guide book), 204–5
Barcelona: A Thousand Years of the City's Past, 205
Barcelona Carrers i Plànols, 26–7
Barcelona Design Guide, 204
Barcelona Nautical College, 159
Barcelona Zoo, 39
Barceloneta, 37–8, 227
Barcino, 35
Barclays Bank, 215, 216–17
bargains, 182, 193
baroque architecture, 138
barres (bars), 133
Barri del Raval, 178
Barri Gòtic, 26, 35–6, 40
   hotels, 46–52
   restaurants, 93
Barri Xines, 37, 56, 143
bars, 132, 133, 134–6
   lavatories, 213
   telephones, 223–4
Basilica de la Mercè, 36
Basque language, 4
Bastiaans, Christiaan, 169
bathrooms, 45
Batllevell i Arús, 147
BCN Books, 185
BD Ediciones de Diseño, 191
beaches, Costa Brava, 241–3
beans, sausages with, 123
Beardsley (gift shop), 187
Beckett, Samuel, 175
bed and breakfast, 81–3
beggars, 218
Berenguer Counts, 138
Besòs, 193
bills, hotel, 45–6
birds, 199
'Black Virgin', 161–2, 238–9, 241
Blanco y Negro, 217
Blanes, 241–2
Blum, Heiner, 168
Boada i Piera, 148
boats, ferries, 24–5
Bodega Bohemia, 176
bodegas (wine cellars), 114–15, 132
Bofarull, Angel, 168
bolets et all (mushrooms in garlic sauce), 119
books: bookshops, 185–7
   phrasebooks, 244
   see also guide books
Boqueria, 37, 47, 195
Bordeta, 41

Borghoff, Rainer, 167
El Born, 26, 36
   architecture, 140
   art galleries, 168–9
   restaurants, 90–2
botifarra amb mongetes (sausages with white beans), 123
Bourbons, 5, 37, 154, 155, 179
brandy, 198
Braque, Georges, 169
bread, *pa amb tomàquet*, 121–2
breakfast, 89
British consulate, 230
Brossa, Joan, 151
El Brusi, 217
Bulevard Rosa, 183
bullfights, 171
buses, 27–8, 31–2
   Aerobus, 21, 22
   Nitbus, 21, 22, 28, 31–2

Cadaqués, 243
cafés *see* restaurants and cafés
La Caixa de Fang, 187
caixas (banking service centres), 15, 20
cakes, *pastel de natas y crema*, 126–7
Calder, Alexander, 169
Calella de Palafrugell, 242
calendar, words and phrases, 247
Cambio 16, 217
cambios (currency exchange), 216
Camper, 183
Canadian consulate, 230
canaries, 199
Capella de Santa Llúcia, 138–9
Carewe, Pamela, 231–3
Carmel, 41
Carnival, 178–9
cars: accidents, 202, 203
   crime, 236
   documents needed, 202
   driving, 202–3
   hiring, 200–1
   insurance, 202–3
   parking, 202
Casa Amatller, 141
Casa Antoni Salvadó, 147
Casa Antònia Costa, 148
Casa Batlló, 63, 141–2
Casa Calvet, 142, 147
Casa dels Canonges, 36
Casa Comalat, 142–3
Casa Enric Laplana, 148
Casa Esperança Isern, 148
Casa Francesc Cairó, 148
Casa Francesc Pastor, 148
Casa Fuster, 143
Casa Isabel Pomar, 148

Casa Lamadrid, 144
Casa Lleó i Morera, 146
Casa Macaya, 144–5
Casa Milà, 145
Casa Miquel Sayrach, 147
Casa Morera, 141
Casa Mulleras, 141
Casa Museu Gaudí, 156
Casa Padellàs, 158
Casa de les Punxes, 147
Casa Ramon Casas, 142
Casa Terrades, 147
Casa Thomas, 148
Casa Viçens, 40
Casacas Rojas, 210
Casals, Pau, 158
Casas, Ramon, 8, 137, 142, 144, 158, 191
cash, 14
cash-dispensers, 15, 20, 217
Castell de Montjuïc, 155–6, 166
Castell dels Tres Dragons, 154
Castilian language, 4, 7–8
   words and phrases, 244–8
Catalan Cuisine, 205
Catalan language, 2–3, 4, 5, 222
   words and phrases, 244–8
Catalans, character and appearance, 4, 5–6
Catalonia, 4–5
Cathedral, 36, 138, 178, 179, 218
Catholic church, 221, 222
cats, 199
cava (champagne), 133–4
cemeteries, Montjuïc, 156
Ceramica Artistica, 188
ceramics, shopping, 188–90
Cerdà, Ildefons, 38, 39, 145, 149, 152
champagne, 133–4
character, Catalans, 4, 5–6
charcuterias, 196–8
charter airlines, 17
cheese, 196
chemists, 207, 232
cheques: personal, 14, 45, 215
   traveller's, 14, 45, 215–17, 229
child thieves, 234
children, babysitters, 199
Chillida, Eduardo, 151
chocolates, 197
Church of Mare de Déu de la Mercé, 179
churches, 35, 221–2
cigarette smoking, 222
cigars, 222–3
Cinco Dias, 217
cinemas, 170–1
Circus, 177
Citadel, 154–5
The City of Marvels, 205
La Ciutadella, 26, 39–40, 152, 154–5, 157

Ciutat Vella, 35–7
   architecture, 138
   art galleries, 168–9
   hotels, 46–61
   shopping, 181, 182
Civil War, 6
Clavé, Antoni, 167
climate, 9, 241
clinics, emergencies, 227
clothes: laundry, 10, 212
   shopping, 182–5
   sizes, 201
   what to take, 9–10, 231–2
cobla (music), 178
coffee, 89, 132–3
coins, 214
Col·lecció d'Indumentària i Accessoris de
   Bombers, 167
colds, 207
Colmado Pijoan, 197
Columbus, Christopher, 139, 151, 159
Columbus Monument, 151
Comes i Busquets, Josep, 168
Communidad Israelita de Barcelona, 221
Companys, Lluís, 166
confeccionistas (clothes shops), 182
consigna (left luggage lockers), 212
consulates, 230
contact lenses, 10
cookery, recipes, 118–31
Coping with Spain, 206
El Corte Inglés, 182–3
Coses de Casa, 188
Costa Brava, 20, 34, 202, 241–3
Costume Museum, 160–1
Cot i Cot, 148
courgettes, *samfaina*, 130–1
Craccrac, 197
crèches, 199
credit cards, 14–15, 17, 45, 211
   lost, 229
   safety, 235–6
crime, 227–8, 234–7
La Cuina, 175
cultural institutes, 201–2
currency exchange, 215–16
custard, *pastel de natas y crema*, 126–7
customs and excise, 20

Dalí, Salvador, 8, 163, 243
Dama del Paraguia, 157
dance, 171–2, 178
dance halls, 177
Daum, 163
dehydration, 225
department stores, 181–3
   opening hours, 180, 208
   public lavatories, 212–13

desserts, *mel i mató*, 118
Dia del Llibre i de la Rosa, 179
Diada Nacional de Catalunya, 179
Diagonal, 26, 181
dialling codes, 223
El Diari de Barcelona, 217
dictionaries, 244
dinner, 89
disabled travellers, 225
discounts: cinemas, 171
  shopping, 181
districts, 2
  Barceloneta, 37–8
  Ciutadella, 39–40
  Ciutat Vella, 35–7
  Eixample, 38–9
  Gràcia, 40
  Ramblas, 38
dockyards, 37, 140, 159
doctors, 212, 226–7
dogs, 199
Domènech Estapa, 164
Domènech i Montaner, Lluís, 39, 40, 55,
    137, 141, 143, 144, 145–6, 148, 149,
    154, 158, 163, 165
Dos i Una, 188
Drassanes, 35, 37, 140, 159
La Dreta, 39
drinks: coffee, 89, 132–3
  water, 224–5
  wine, 89, 198
driving, 202–3
driving licences, 202
drugs: addicts, 54–5
  what to take, 10, 232–3
Drugstore, 180
dry-cleaning, 10

Editorial Montaner i Simón, 145–6
eggs, *ous romesco* (eggs in Romesco sauce),
    128–9
Església de Santa Anna, 174
Eixample, 26, 38–9, 40
  architecture, 137, 138, 140–1, 206
  art galleries, 167–8
  hospitals, 226
  hotels, 61–71
  restaurants, 99–102
electricity, 203
embassies, 230
emergencies, 13, 226–30
  words and phrases, 246
Els Encants, 192
entrances and exits, 204
escalivada, 118–19
Espai, 13, 162
espinacs a la catalana (Catalan spinach),
    129–30

L'Esquerra, 39
Estació del Nord, 154
Ethnological Museum, 156
etiquette, 181–2, 213–14
Eurocheques, 14, 45, 236
exchange rates, 13, 14
excursions: Costa Brava, 241–3
  Montserrat, 238–41
exits and entrances, 204

fairs, 178
Fargas, 197
farmàcias (chemists), 207
Fascists, 5
Felipe V, King, 37
Ferdinand II, King, 139
ferries, 24–5
Ferrocarrils de la Generalitat (FFCC), 23,
    30, 33–4
Festa i Cavalcade dels Reis d'Orient, 178
Festa Major, 178
Festes del Carmestoltes, 178–9
Festival d'Estiu, 171–2
Festival de Tardor, 172
festivals, 178–9, 208
Festivitat de la Mare de Déu de la Mercé,
    179
Festivitat de Sant Jordi, 179
Festivitat de Sant Ponç, 179
festivitats, 178
Fetting, Reiner, 168
FFCC (Generalitat Rail System), 23, 30,
    33–4
films, 170–1
Financial Times, 217
fines: fare dodgers, 32
  traffic offences, 203
Fire Department Museum, 167
fish, 86, 195
  sarsuela Barceloneta, 120–1
Flamenco gear, 184
flamígero style, 140
flower markets, 194
Font Castellana, 41
Font de la Maja, 36
food, 8, 86–9
  charcuterias, 196–8
  costs, 12
  guide books, 205
  Indian, 105–6
  markets, 194–6
  restaurants, 87–9
  vegetarian, 107–8
food poisoning, 207
Form E111, 210
form letters, hotel reservations, 16
Fossar de les Moreres, 179
Francia station, 34

Franco, General, 5, 151, 166, 222
Francoistas, 5
Franks, 35
French Railways (SNCF), 23
fruit, markets, 195
Fuixarda Stadium, 155
fun fairs, 155
Fundació Miró, 156, 162
Fundació Tàpies, 145–6, 163–4
funeral carriage museum, 166
funiculars, 30–1
furniture, shopping, 191–2

Gaietà Buïgas, 151
Galí, 158
Galician language, 4
galleries *see* art galleries
Galon Glacé, 183
gambes en all (prawns in garlic), 131
game, markets, 195
garlic: prawns in, 131
    mushrooms in, 119
Gaudí, Antoni, 36, 37, 39, 40, 54, 63, 137,
    141–2, 143–4, 145, 147, 150, 154, 156,
    158
Generalitat (Catalan provincial
    government), 1
Generalitat Rail System (FFCC), 23, 30, 33–4
George, Saint, 139
Gerdes, Ludger, 169
gift shops, 187–91
Gimeno, 188
Giro Bank, 216
glasses, 10
Goldoni, Carlo, 175
gospel music, 174
Gothic architecture, 138
Gothic quarter *see* Barri Gòtic
Gràcia, 26, 40, 152
    hotels, 43, 71–3
    restaurants, 102–14
    street fairs, 178
    theatres, 175
Gran Teatre del Liceu, 47, 172
granjas (milk-bars), 132–3
Grec (Festival d'Estiu), 171–2
El Greco, 5
Green Cards, 202–3
Guàrdia Civil, 228
Guàrdia Urbana, 228, 229
Güell family, 143
guesthouses, 45
Guía del Ocio, 217
Guia Urbana de Barcelona, 27
guide books: *Argot Barceloní*, 204
    Barcelona, 204–5
    *Barcelona: A Thousand Years of the City's
        Past*, 205

Barcelona Design Guide, 204
Catalan Cuisine, 205
The City of Marvels, 205
Coping with Spain, 206
Guia Urbana de Barcelona, 27
Homage to Barcelona, 206
Manifestacions Ciutadanes, 179
Nits de Bars, 204
The Quadrat d'Or, 206
The Spaniards: A Portrait of the New Spain,
    206
Guinardó, 40
Guineueta, 41
Gumerá, 175
gypsies, 218

Habsburgs, 4–5
hairdressers, 207, 224
ham, 196
handbags, safety, 235
handshakes, 214
Happy Books, 185
Hartung, 168
hats, shopping, 185
health, 207
Heathrow Airport, 22
herbalists, 188–9
L'Herbolista del Rei, 188–9
herbs, 196
hiring, cars, 200–1
history, 4–5
    guide books, 205, 206
hitch-hiking, 207
Hivernacle, 154, 172
Hockney, David, 168
¡Hola!, 217
Holiday Which magazine, 241–2
holidays, public, 208–9
Homage to Barcelona, 206
home exchange, 83–4, 243
Horn, Rebecca, 169
Horta, 41
Hospital de la Santa Creu de Sant Pau, 37,
    40, 149–50
hospitals: emergencies, 226–7
    medical insurance, 210
hostels, 42, 43, 45
    see also hotels, recommended
hotels, 42–6
    bills, 45–6
    booking in advance, 15–16
    classification, 45
    Costa Brava, 241–3
    credit cards, 45
    lavatories, 213
    prices, 12, 43
    telephone bills, 46

(hotels *continued*)
  theft from, 227–8
  wheelchair access, 225
  words and phrases, 246
hotels, recommended: Abrevadero, 73–4
  Amilcar, 80
  Aneto, 58–9
  Ballestero, 77–8
  Barcelona, 74–5
  Bonavista, 71–2
  California, 46
  Campi, 59–60
  Cartuja, 72
  Ciudad Condal, 61–2
  Condal, 47–8
  Coronado, 75–6
  Dalí, 48
  Din, 62–3
  España, 55
  Fani, 63–4
  Felipe II, 64–5
  Fontanella, 53
  Inglés, 49
  Jardí, 50–1
  Layetana, 51–2
  Llopart, 76–7
  Maria, 66
  Mediterraneo, 66–7
  Neutral, 67–8
  Noya, 60–1
  Oliva, 68–9
  Palacios, 69–70
  Paris, 52
  Peninsula, 56
  El Putxet, 78–9
  Ramos, 57
  Roma, 53–5
  Sans, 79
  Segura, 58
  Travesera, 79–80
  Valls, 73
  Windsor, 70–1
Hunt, Bryan, 153

Ibiza, ferries, 25
Ibsen, Henrik, 174
illness, 207
  emergencies, 226–7
Independent, 45–6, 217
Indian restaurants, 105–6
information sources, 209–10
Inquisition, 139
Insolit, 192
Institut Alemany de Cultura, 201
Institut Britànic, 202
Institut Català de Bibliografia, 185
Institut Francès, 202
Institut Italià di Cultura, 202

insurance: cars, 202–3
  medical, 210
  travel, 18, 210–12
International Driving Licence, 202
International Exposition (1929), 155
International Herald Tribune, 217
International Jazz Festival, 174
International Reply Coupons (IRCs), 16
International Sea Terminal, 24
Intervac, 243
Irish consulate, 230
Isabella, Queen, 139
IVA tax, 46

jamon serrano (ham), 196
Jaume II, King, 139
jazz, 174
Jews, 155, 166, 221
Jocs i Coses, 189
Jutglar, 189

Kelly, Ellsworth, 153
Kleist, Heinrich von, 174

Lalique, René, 163
language: Castilian, 4, 7–8, 244–8
  Catalan, 2–3, 4, 5, 222, 244–8
  entrances and exits, 204
  guide books, 204
  numbers, 219
  postal services, 220
  pronunciation, 220–1
  slang, 222
  words and phrases, 244–8
laundry, 10, 212
lavanderia, 10
lavatories, public, 213
left luggage, 213
lemon, lentil salad with, 124
lenguado a la naranja (sole with orange),
  124–5
lentil salad with lemon, 124
letters, hotel reservations, 16
Lewitt, Sol, 168
Liceu theatre, 47, 172
Lichtenstein, Roy, 153
lifts, 225
lighting, in hotels, 11
llenguado a la nyoka, 125–6
Llibreria Come-in, 186
Llibreria Francesca, 186
Llimona, Josep, 155, 158
Lloret de Mar, 242
lost property, 228
lottery, Onze, 218
luggage: air travel, 22
  insurance, 211
  left luggage, 212

safety, 235, 236
what to take, 9–11, 231–2
Luke, St, 238
lunch, 89
Luy, Wolfgang, 168

Madrid, 4
magazines, 217
Magicus, 189
Mallart, 189
Mallorca, ferries, 25
Manifestacions Ciutadanes, 179
manners, 181–2, 213–14
Mansana de Discòrdia, 141
La Manual Alpargatera, 184
maps, 26–7
  Metro, 28–9
Maragall, Pasqual, 1–2
Maragall gardens, 156
Mari, Ismail Smith, 158
markets: Boqueria, 195
  Centre d'Antiquaris, 194
  Els Encants, 192
  flowers, 194
  food, 194–6
  Mercadillo Sant Adrià, 193
  Mercat Gótic d'Antiguitats, 192–3
  Mercat Sant Antoni, 194
  Pça. Reial, 193
Martorell i Puig, 148
Mauri, 197
measurements, clothes, 201
medical emergencies, 226–7
medical insurance, 210
medicines, 232–3
Mediterranean, 27
  Costa Brava resorts, 241–3
mel i matò, 118
Meller, Raquel, 157
Menkes, 184
Menorca, ferries, 25
menus, 88–9
  words and phrases, 245–6
Mercat de la Concepció, 62, 194
Mercat de les Flors, 172, 176
Mercat Sant Josep, 47
Mercè, 36
  hotels, 53–5
  restaurants, 93–5
Metro, 12, 21, 27–30, 237
  maps, 27
Meyerhoff, Moreno, 170
Mies van der Rohe, Ludwig, 155, 216
Military Museum, 156
milk-bars (*granjas*), 132–3
Millà, 186
mineral water, 224–5
La Mirada Encantada, 184

Miró, Joan, 8, 151, 153, 156, 162
Moderniste architecture, 39, 55, 56, 140–8, 149, 165, 206
Moderniste painting and sculpture, 137, 158, 169
El Molino, 176
monasteries: Montserrat, 239
  Sant Pere de Roda, 243
money: automatic cash machines, 15, 20, 217
  banks, 215–17
  cash, 14
  credit cards, 14–15, 17, 45, 211, 229
  currency exchange, 215–16
  denominations, 214–15
  exchange rates, 13, 14
  how much to take, 11–13
  insurance, 211
  personal cheques, 14, 45, 215
  prices, 3, 5
  safety, 235–6
  traveller's cheques, 14, 45, 215–17, 229
Monorqueña company, 88
Mont Tàber, 35, 138
Montbau, 41
Montjuïc, 27, 37, 40, 155–6, 172
Montjuïc Parc d'Atraccions, 155
Montserrat, 33–4, 202, 238–41
Moors, 35, 86, 238
Mossos d'Esquadra, 228
motorbikes, 202, 218
movies, 170–1
Mudejár architecture, 145
Murria, J., 198
museums, 8
  Autòmates del Tibidabo, 165
  bullfighting, 171
  Col·lecció d'Indumentària i Accessoris de Bombers, 167
  Fundació Miró, 162
  Fundació Tàpies, 163–4
  lavatories, 213
  Museu Arqueològic, 166
  Museu d'Art de Catalunya, 166
  Museu d'Art Modern, 9, 39, 154–5, 157–8
  Museu de les Arts de l'Espectacle, 143–4
  Museu del Calçat Antic (Shoe Museum), 51, 166
  Museu de Carrosses Fúnebres, 166
  Museu de la Ciència, 164
  Museu Etnològic, 167
  Museu Frederic Marés, 35, 161–2
  Museu d'Història de la Ciutat, 35, 139, 158–9
  Museu Marítim, 140, 159
  Museu Militar, 166
  Museu del Monestir de Pedralbes, 167

(museums *continued*)
  Museu de la Música, 146
  Museu del Parfum, 163
  Museu Tèxtil i de la Indumentària,
    160–1
  Museu de Zoologia, 39, 154, 165
  Picasso Museum, 12, 91–2, 160, 213
mushrooms: dried, 196
  in garlic sauce, 119
music, 171–2
  Ars Studio, 174
  Banda Municipal de Barcelona, 173
  buskers, 218
  Església de Santa Anna, 174
  Gran Teatre del Liceu, 172
  International Jazz Festival, 174
  opera, 172, 173
  Palau de la Música Catalana, 172–3
  Teatre de l'Alinça del Poblenou, 173
music halls, 37, 176

National Giro Postcheque scheme, 216
NatWest, 215, 217
Neumann, Max, 169
newspapers, 217
nightlife, 132–6
  bars, 132, 133, 134–6
  guide book, 204
  xampanyerias, 133–4
Nitbus, 21, 22, 28, 31–2
Nits de Bars, 204
noise, 218
Noucentiste architecture, 155
nuisances, 218
numbers, 219

Oficina de Turisme, 209
Oldenburg, Claes, 222
Olimpiada Cultural, 172
olive oil, 198
olives, 195–6
Olympic Games, 1–2
Olympic stadium, 156
Olympic Village, 227
onions, *samfaina*, 130–1
Onze lottery, 218
opening hours, 180, 208–9, 216–17
opera: Gran Teatre del Liceu, 172
  zarzuela, 173
Opus Dei, 221
orange: *lenguado a la naranja* (sole with
    orange), 124–5
  pastel de natas y crema (orange sponge cake
    with rum custard), 126–7
Orquestra Ciutat de Barcelona, 172–3
Our Lady of Guadelupe, 238–9, 241
ous romesco (eggs in Romesco sauce), 128–9

pa amb tomàquet, 121–2
painters, 137
El País, 217
Palamos, 242
Palau Baró de Quadras, 146
Palau del Bisbe, 36
Palau Castanyer, 36
Palau de la Generalitat, 139–40
Palau Güell, 37, 143–4
Palau del Lloctinent, 36, 139
Palau de la Música Catalana, 36, 149
Palau Nacional, 155
Palau Ramon de Montaner, 148
Palau Reial Major, 36, 139, 159
Palau de la Virreina, 171, 209–10
La Paloma (dance hall), 177
Parc d'Atraccions, Montjuïc, 155
parking, 202
parks and gardens, 151–7
  Estació del Nord, 154
  Maragall gardens, 156
  Parc de la Ciutadella, 26, 37, 152, 154–5,
    157, 199
  Parc del Clot, 152, 153
  Parc Crueta del Coll, 151, 152, 153
  Parc d'Espanya Industrial, 152
  Parc Güell, 40, 152, 156
  Parc de Joan Miró, 151, 153, 162
  Parc del Labyrint, 157
  Parc de Montjuïc, 74, 75, 155–6
  Parc de Pedralbes, 153–4
  Parc Pegaso, 153
Parlament de Catalunya, 39, 154–5
Parroise Française, 222
passports, 20, 228, 235
pastel de natas y crema (orange sponge cake
    with rum custard), 126–7
pastries, 197
patatas bunuelos, 127
Patronat de Turisme, 26, 146, 209
Pavelló de les Arts Gràfiques, 155
Pavelló de la Ciutat, 155
Pedralbes, 5, 117
La Pedrera, 145
peix espaza en safrà (swordfish in saffron
    sauce), 128
pensions, 42, 45
  see also hotels, recommended
Pepa Paper, 190
Pepper, Beverly, 154
peppers: *escalivada*, 118–19
  ous romesco (eggs in Romesco sauce),
    128–9
  Romesco sauce, 122–3
  samfaina, 130–1
Pere III, King, 139
Perfume Museum, 163
El Periódico, 217

Perla Gris, 184
perruquerias (hairdressers), 207
personal cheques, 15, 45, 215
Peter, St, 238
Peter the Ceremonious, 159
pharmacies, 207, 232
Philip II, King, 4
phrasebooks, 244
El Pi, 35
Picasso, Pablo, 8, 158, 160
Picasso Museum, 12, 160, 213
  café, 91–2
pickpockets, 48, 234
picnics, 10
pillar-boxes, 219
Pilma, 192
PIN (personal identification number), 236
pine nuts, *mel i matò*, 118
Pitarra (Frederico Soter i Hubert), 95
Pça. d'Espanya, 33
Planelles Donat, 198
Poble Espanyol, 155
Poble Sec, 37, 152
  hotels, 73–7
  restaurants, 115–17
police, 203, 228–9
Policía Nacional, 228–9
pollution, 207, 218
Poor Clares, 167
Port Lligat, 243
Portal de l'Angel, 36
  hotels, 59–61
  restaurants, 95–6
post-Impressionism, 137
post offices, 216, 219
postage, International Reply Coupons, 16
postal services, 219–20
poste restante, 220
potatoes, *patatas bunuelos*, 127
La Poterie, 190
pottery, shopping, 188–90
El Prat airport, 20
prawns, *gambes en all* (prawns in garlic), 131
prices, 3, 5
Primo de Rivera, Miguel, 155
pronunciation, 220–1
Prosperitat, 40
public holidays, 208
public lavatories, 212–13
Puig i Catafalch, Josep, 39, 137, 141, 144,
  146, 147, 158
Pyrenees, 4, 7, 200

Quadrat d'Or, 39, 141
The Quadrat d'Or (guide book), 206
queues, in shops, 181

railways, 17, 20–1, 22, 23, 34, 239–40

rain, 9
raincoats, 10
Rambla de les Flors, 194
Ramblas, 38, 162
  restaurants, 96–9
Ramon Albó, 41
Raval de Ponent, 37
  hotels, 58–9
Raval de Sant Pau, 37
  hotels, 55–8
  restaurants, 96
Raventos i Cadafach, Juanita, 86, 87
reading lights, 11
recipes, 118–31
Red Cross, 226
religion, 221–2
Renaixença architecture, 138, 149–51
RENFE (Spanish Railways), 23, 34
reservations, hotels, 15–16
resorts, Costa Brava, 241–3
restaurants and cafés, 87–9
  lavatories, 213
  menus, 88–9
  tipping, 224
  words and phrases, 245–6
restaurants, recommended:
  Agut, 94–5
  Amaya, 96–7
  Asador de Aranda, 117
  Atzavara, 109
  Batista, 104
  Bilbao, 111
  La Bota de Raco, 117–18
  La Buena Tierra, 107–8
  Ca l'Agusti, 108
  Cal Majó, 110
  Can Culleretes, 93
  Can Margarit, 115
  Can Punyetes, 112–13
  Can Soteras/Restaurante Diagonal, 99
  Cantina Mexicana, 105
  Cardoner, 94
  Cerveceria Lesseps, 102–3
  Costa Brava, 90–1
  Flash-Flash, Truiteria, 103
  Font de l'Estel, 110
  El Glop, 111–12
  El Gran Colmado, 100–1
  Madrid-Barcelona, 99–100
  Minerva, 103–4
  La Morera, 96
  Neyras, 95–6
  Niu Toc, 108–9
  Nou Celler, 90
  El Nou Glop, 112
  Pa i Trago, 116–17
  La Palmera, 98–9
  La Parilla, 93

(restaurants, recommended *continued*)
  Picasso Museum Café, 91–2
  Pitarra, 95
  Rebost de la Plana, 107
  Restaurant del Teatre, 113
  Sa Lletuga, 106
  Saler, 101–2
  Sangita, 105–6
  Senyor Parellada, 92
  El Settrill, 116
  Taberna Marcelino, 104–5
  Taberna Santa Maria, 91
  La Taca d'Oli, 98
  El Tastavins, 114
  Tot Bo, 100
  Tres Xemeneias (Casa Jaime), 115–16
  Vineteria Verdi, 113–14
  Xaloc, 97–8
Revetlla de Sant Joan, 179
La Ribera, 36, 37, 39, 160
  restaurants, 90–2
Ricart, Eric, 158
ricotta, *mel i mató*, 118
Rius y Taulet, 39
Rivora, Antoni, 157
robbery, 227–8
Robbins, Nancy, 192
Roman Catholic church, 221, 222
Romanesque architecture, 138
Romans, 35, 86, 138
Romesco sauce, 122–3
  ous romesco (eggs in Romesco sauce),
    128–9
Romeu, Pere, 158
Roquetes, 41
Rovira i Rabassa, 142
Rovira i Trias, Antoni, 38, 40
Rubió i Bellver, 148
rum, *pastel de natas y crema*, 126–7
rush hours, 27, 218
Rusiñol, Santiago, 8, 137, 144, 158

Sabartés, Jaime, 160
safety: crime, 234–7
  Metro stations, 29
  theft, 48, 227–8
saffron, *peix espaza en safrà* (swordfish in
  saffron sauce), 128
S'Agaró, 242
Sagnier i Vellavecchia, 141, 148
Sagrada Familia, 9, 40, 150
St George's Church, 222
Sala Beckett, 175
salads, lentil with lemon, 124
sales, 181–2
Saló de Cent, 35
Saló del Tinell (Museu d'Història de la
  Ciutat), 35, 159

samfaina, 130–1
Sant Agustí, 36, 57
Sant Antoni, 40
Sant Pau del Camp, 138
Sant Pere, 36
Sant Pere de Roda, 243
Santa Anna, 36
Santa Catarina, 36
Santa Cava, Montserrat, 238, 240
Santa Maria del Mar, 35, 36, 140, 221
Sants Estació (railway station), 14, 20–1, 22,
  23, 34
Sardana, 178
Sarrià, 40
sarsuela Barceloneta, 120–1
sauce, Romesco, 122–3
sausages, 196
sausages with white beans, 123
Sayrach i Carreras, 147
Schiaparelli, Elsa, 163
Schiller, J. C. F. von, 175
Sciascia, Leonardo, 168
Science Museum, 164
scooters, 202
sculpture, 137, 151–7
sea transport, 24–5
seafood, *sarsuela Barceloneta*, 120–1
Sert, Josep Lluis, 162
Servicio Estación, 190
El 7 Peus, 190
Shakespeare, William, 174
shaking hands, 214
shaver points, 44
shellfish, 86
shoes, 10, 232
  museum, 51, 166
  shopping, 183, 184
  sizes, 201
shopping, 180–98
  books, 185–7
  chemists, 207, 232
  clothes, 182–5
  etiquette, 181–2
  flowers, 194
  furniture, 191–2
  gifts, 187–91
  markets, 192–4
  opening hours, 180, 208
  prices, 13
  shopping malls, 183
shoulder bags, safety, 235
siestas, 208
sightseeing, costs, 12–13
Simons and Ko., 186
slang, 222
smoking, 222–3
SNCF (French Railways), 23
socks, shopping, 184

sole: *lenguado a la naranja* (sole with orange), 124–5
  lenguado a la nyoka, 125–6
Sole, E., 184
Soler, Frederic, 165
Sombrereria Obach, 185
Sosa, Antonio, 169
The Spaniards: A Portrait of the New Spain, 206
Spanish Railways (RENFE), 23, 34
Spanish Tourist Office, 42, 43–4
Spectacles Diplomados, 191
spinach, *espinacs a la catalana* (Catalan spinach), 129–30
stamps, postage, 219
stations: Metro, 28, 29
  railway, 34
  Sants Estació, 14, 20–1, 22, 23, 34
stranded travellers, 230
street addresses, 44–5
street fairs and festivals, 178–9
street scenes, 178–9
Strindberg, August, 175
Sunyer, 158
sweets, 197, 198
swordfish, *peix espaza en safrà* (swordfish in saffron sauce), 128

Tabacs, 219
Tamariú, 242
Tango (dance hall), 177
tapas, 88, 128–9, 207
Tàpies, Antoni, 8, 145–6, 164
taxes, IVA, 46
'Taxi Cards', 33
taxis, 12, 21–2, 28, 32–3, 224, 237
Tea Centre of Barcelona, 198
Telefèric, 31, 239, 240
Telefonica, 223
telephones, 223–4
  in hotels, 46
  Sants Estació, 22
  for taxis, 33
  tourist information, 210
theatres, 171–2
  Mercat de les Flors, 176
  Sala Beckett, 175
  Teatre Adrià Gual, 175
  Teatre de l'Alinça del Poblenou, 173
  Teatre Grec, 156, 172
  Teatre, Lliure, 113, 175
  Teatre Malic, 175
  Teatre Romea, 174
  Teatre Victoria, 173
theft, 227–8, 234–6
Tibidabo, 12, 27, 40, 152
  Autòmates del Tibidabo, 165
  restaurants, 117

tickets: buses, 32
  Ferrocarrils de la Generalitat (FFCC), 30, 34
  Metro, 21, 28
  trains, 22, 34
Tiffany, Louis Comfort, 163
time, 3, 224
Time Out, 18
tipping, 22, 224
tobacco, 222–3
tobacco shops, 219
Toll, 191
tomatoes: *pa amb tomàquet*, 121–2
  Romesco sauce, 122–3
  samfaina, 130–1
Torre Baró, 41
Tossa de Mar, 242
Totem, 187
tourist information, 209–10
tourist offices, 20, 26, 42
toys, 189
traffic, 224
  accidents, 229
  noise, 218
  traffic offences, 203
train robberies, 236
trains, 17, 20–1, 22, 23, 34, 239–40
Tramvia Blau, 30
Transbordador Aëri, 31
El Transwaal, 185
travel agents, 17–19, 211
travel insurance, 210–12
traveller's cheques, 14, 45, 215–17
  lost, 229
  safety, 235
travelling: air travel, 17–19, 24
  buses, 21, 22, 27–8, 31–2
  costs, 11, 12
  Ferrocarrils de la Generalitat (FFCC), 23, 30, 33–4
  funiculars, 30–1
  hitch-hiking, 207
  insurance, 18, 211
  Metro, 21, 27–30, 237
  railways, 17
  by sea, 24–5
  taxis, 21–2, 28, 32–3, 237
  Telefèric, 31, 239, 240
  trains, 20–1, 22, 23, 34
  Tramvia Blau, 30
  Transbordador Aëri, 31
Trinitat Nova, 40
trolleys, 30
Turisme Atenció, 229
Turó de la Peira, 40–1
turrón (sweets), 198
Tuvaché, 163

Umbracle, 154
umbrellas, 10
underground, Metro, 21, 27–30
United States consulate, 230
Universal Exhibition (1888), 39, 151, 154, 165

Valeri i Pupurull, 143
Vall d'Hebron, 40
Vallbona, 40
La Vanguardia, 217
vegetables, markets, 195
vegetarian restaurants, 107–8
vehicle registration papers, 202
Velasquez, Diego, 160
Velòdrom d'Horta, 151, 157, 172
Vespas, 202
Vespucci, Amerigo, 159
Vinçon, 191
Virgin Mary, 238–9, 241
Visa cards, 14

Visigoths, 35, 139
Vivir en Barcelona, 217

War of Spanish Succession, 37
washing clothes, 10, 212
water, 44, 224–5
weather, 9, 241
wheelchairs, 225
Which? magazine, 210, 211, 241–2
wine, 89, 198
   bodegas, 114–15, 132
women, safety, 237
words and phrases, 244–8

xampanyerias, 133

youth hostels, 84–5

zarzuela (light opera), 173
zoo, 155, 199
Zoological Museum, 39, 154, 165

All Pan books are available at your local bookshop or newsagent, or can be ordered direct from the publisher. Indicate the number of copies required and fill in the form below.

Send to: **CS Department, Pan Books Ltd., P.O. Box 40,
            Basingstoke, Hants.   RG21 2YT.**

or phone: 0256 469551 (Ansaphone), quoting title, author
             and Credit Card number.

Please enclose a remittance* to the value of the cover price plus: 60p for the first book plus 30p per copy for each additional book ordered to a maximum charge of £2.40 to cover postage and packing.

*Payment may be made in sterling by UK personal cheque, postal order, sterling draft or international money order, made payable to Pan Books Ltd.

Alternatively by Barclaycard/Access:

Card No. | | | | | | | | | | | | | | | | | | |

Signature:

Applicable only in the UK and Republic of Ireland.

While every effort is made to keep prices low, it is sometimes necessary to increase prices at short notice. Pan Books reserve the right to show on covers and charge new retail prices which may differ from those advertised in the text or elsewhere.

NAME AND ADDRESS IN BLOCK LETTERS PLEASE:

....

Name————————————————————————

Address————————————————————————

————————————————————————

————————————————————————

————————————————————————

3/87